UNIVERSITY *of* LIMERICK

TELEPHONE: 061 202158 / 202172 / 202163

Items can be renewed from BORROWER INFO on the Library Catalogue
www.ul.ie/~library

PLEASE NOTE: This item is subject to recall after two weeks if required by another reader.

LISH

MARTIN KIERAN   **GILL & MACMILLAN**

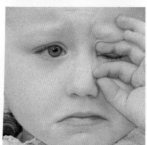

Gill & Macmillan Ltd
Hume Avenue
Park West
Dublin 12
with associated companies throughout the world
www.gillmacmillan.ie

© Martin Kieran 2004
0 7171 3715 5
Print origination in Ireland by Graham Thew
Colour Repro by Typeform Repro Ltd

The paper used in this book is made from the wood
pulp of managed forests. For every tree felled, at
least one tree is planted, thereby renewing natural
resources.

INTRODUCTION

Examstart is aimed at the needs of Second and Third Year students preparing for Junior Certificate English (Higher Level).

The book is full of information, exercises and advice to help you achieve the best results in your examination. It has been designed to make preparation as active and effective as possible. Closely modelled on the latest State Examinations Commission examination papers, it is directly geared to successfully answering questions in all seven sections of the exam.

Examstart includes units on the following:

1 Reading
2 Personal Writing
3 Functional Writing
4 Media Studies
5 Drama
6 Poetry
7 Fiction
8 Revision

These units relate to the different skills you have to practise in English and will be a very useful companion to the literary texts you have already chosen to study. The book will help you build on this essential work by focusing on practice questions and sharpening exam technique. You will find that the standard ranges from accessible, straightforward pieces to more challenging material. As always, teachers can make their own professional judgments in deciding when to use particular units and which exercises will work best with their own students.

A selection of **sample answers** (followed by helpful examiner's comments) are provided. These answers are all based on the actual work of Third year (higher level) students. Some minor editing has been done and spellings have been corrected to avoid re-enforcing errors. The purpose of these exemplars is to increase your awareness of the accepted standard so that you can understand how examiners assess answers when awarding marks.

Of course, the inclusion of model answers does not mean that students should not attempt all the actual questions for themselves during their own schoolwork. The more practice you do, the better your answers will become. There are always new ways of expressing the same basic points, and fresh ideas of your own can be added.

Examstart offers worthwhile advice on study skills and revision, ensuring valuable support right up to exam time. The book contains a great deal of lively material to help students enjoy their English classes while confidently developing their language skills. As a practical guide, it will provide invaluable exam practice and guarantee successful grades in Junior Cert (Higher Level) English.

CONTENTS

UNIT 1 Reading

OVERVIEW

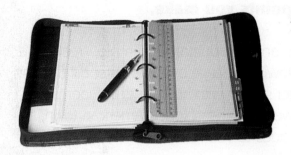

*To be successful in this section of the exam, you will be expected to show that you can read and understand different kinds of writing. Examiners will be interested in seeing your ability to respond to and **interpret a variety of texts**. These are usually non-fiction passages, such as travel writing, newspaper and magazine articles, diaries, letters, information leaflets, autobiography/biography, etc.*

APART FROM QUESTIONS about the actual content and meaning of a passage, candidates are sometimes asked to give a **personal response** to a particular subject or point of view. Regular practice will help you develop critical reading skills so that you can analyse and explain how language is being used for a specific purpose. This involves showing that you understand the various techniques used by writers.

Use common sense when answering. Your study of past papers will help you **plan your time carefully**. If you have to read a passage and answer four ten-mark questions in thirty minutes, you will probably allow about six minutes for reading, followed by six minutes for writing each of the four answers. Obviously, if there are two ten-mark questions and one twenty-mark question, it makes sense to allow about twelve minutes for the twenty-mark question.

Successful answers in the Reading section depend on knowing:
- **What** the passage is about.
- **Why** it was written.
- **How** the writer uses language.

RESPONDING TO READING QUESTIONS

- After reading the passage closely **at least twice**, carefully study the wording of the questions so that you know exactly what the examiners are expecting in the answers.
- **Think out points clearly before writing them down.**

- **Use relevant references or quotations to support main points.**
- **Where possible, develop your answer by commenting on the points you make.**

As an introductory example, read the following passage by travel writer Bill Bryson. After staying with his brother in Bloomsburg, a wealthy old-fashioned American town, he decides to visit New York.

On the Bus

It was ten minutes to seven in the morning and it was cold. Standing outside the Bloomsburg bus station, I could see my breath. The few cars out this early trailed clouds of vapour. I was hung over and in a few minutes I was going to climb onto a bus for a five-hour ride into New York. I would sooner have eaten cat food.

My brother had suggested that I take the bus because it would save having to find a place to park in Manhattan. I could leave the car with him and come back for it in a day or two. At two in the morning, after many beers, this had seemed a good plan. But now, standing in the early morning chill, I realised I was making a serious mistake. You only go on a long-distance bus in the United States either because you cannot afford to fly or – and this is really licking the bottom of the barrel in America – you cannot afford a car. Being unable to afford a car in America is the last step before living out of a plastic sack.

So when the bus pulled up before me, heaving a pneumatic sigh, and its door flapped open, I boarded it with some misgivings. The driver

himself didn't appear any too stable. He had the sort of hair that made him look as if he'd been playing with live wires. There were about half a dozen other passengers, though only two of them looked seriously insane and just one was talking to himself. I took a seat near the back and settled down to get some sleep. I had drunk far too many beers with my brother the night before, and the hot spices from my sandwich were now expanding ominously inside my abdomen and drifting around like the stuff they put in lava lamps. Soon, from one end or the other, it would begin to seep out.

I felt a hand on my shoulder from behind. Through the gap in the seat I could see it was an Indian man – by that I mean a man from India, not an American Indian. 'Can I smoke on this bus?' he asked me.

'I don't know,' I said. 'I don't smoke anymore, so I don't pay much attention to these things.'

'But do you *think* I can smoke on this bus?'

'I really don't know.'

He was quiet again for a few minutes, then his hand was on my shoulder again, not tapping but resting there. 'I can't find an ashtray,' he said.

'No fooling,' I responded wittily, without opening my eyes.

'Do you think that means we're not allowed to smoke?'

'I don't know. I don't care.'

'But do you *think* it means we're not allowed to smoke?'

'If you don't take your hand off my shoulder, I am going to dribble vomit on it,' I said.

He removed his hand quickly and was silent for perhaps a minute. Then he said, 'Would you help me look for an ashtray?'

It was seven in the morning and I was deeply unwell. 'WILL YOU PLEASE JUST LEAVE ME ALONE!' I snapped at him, just a trifle wildly. It was going to be a long day.

 ADAPTED FROM *THE LOST CONTINENT* BY BILL BRYSON

COMMENTARY

This is a typical example of modern travel writing. The language is simple and the style is light and humorous. Travel writing often works on contrasts between places or people. In this extract, the writer is feeling uncomfortable and antisocial while the other passenger clearly wants to talk.

If you had thirty minutes to study this passage and answer the two twenty-mark questions below, you should allow about eight minutes for reading, followed by eleven minutes for writing each of the answers.

Q1 How does the writer let us know that he regrets his decision to travel by bus?

A successful answer should refer to at least three of these key points:

- The early morning weather.
- How he decided to travel by bus.
- The embarrassment of bus travel.
- The other people on the bus.
- Bryson's sickness.
- His increasing anger with the passenger behind him.

 SAMPLE ANSWER

It is clear from the start that Bill Bryson feels he has made the wrong decision by taking a bus to New York. After drinking too much the night before, he is feeling so hung over and unwell in the cold morning air that he openly admits 'I was making a serious mistake'.

The minute he gets on the bus, the look of his fellow travellers adds to his 'misgivings'. He feels very uneasy about the other passengers, who all seem a little bit weird. Even the bus driver 'didn't appear too stable'.

The journey gets off to a bad start when Bryson is soon bothered by irritating questions, e.g. 'Can I smoke on this bus?', from the man sitting behind him. We can sense his growing annoyance as he struggles to be left alone. The passage finishes on a tone of regret and self-pity with the writer saying, 'It was going to be a long day'.

This is a good grade A answer that addresses the question directly and includes a number of clear points to show the writer's regret. Although it is short, the ideas are well expressed and are supported by apt references and quotations. Because of the limited time available, answers must be brief and to the point.

Q2 What methods does the writer use to make the passage humorous? Illustrate your answer by appropriate reference to the text.

To achieve a top grade, you should write about three of these main points:
- The contrast between the night before and the morning.
- Bryson's comments on American snobbery.
- Bryson's use of exaggeration.
- The description of the people on the bus.
- Sarcastic phrases that show Bryson's sense of humour.
- The way the writer builds up his anger with the annoying passenger.

SAMPLE ANSWER

The writer's attitude to his five-hour bus journey is emphasised by a reference to eating. He tells us: 'I would rather have eaten cat food'. This is typical of his overstatement and the humorous tone used throughout the passage. Bryson is feeling sorry for himself and he likes to exaggerate his problems, e.g. he sees most of the other travellers as insane.

The comic description of his hangover is also meant to show Bryson as a figure of fun who is battling against the whole world. He forces us to imagine the rumblings inside his stomach. His language is down to earth and amusing as he compares the hot spices to 'the stuff they put in lava lamps'. We can picture the awful blobs wobbling up and down to make patterns inside his abdomen as he tries hard to keep his food down.

The conflict with the Indian passenger is another method of creating humour. As if things weren't bad enough, the writer meets this annoying character, who is likely to pester him for the full five-hour trip. Readers can easily imagine the situation as Bryson tries to keep calm throughout all the interruptions. His rising anger and frustration are gradually built up and this makes the scene amusing.

Again, the points here are relevant, concise and well organised into three short paragraphs. The focus is on the methods used by the writer to let readers see the funny side of the situation. Textual support is strong and points are very well developed. The expression is fluent and sentences are varied, all of which adds to the high grade A standard.

ANSWERING QUESTIONS

- Always study the actual wording of every question.
- Think about what the examiners are expecting in your answer.
- It is vital to understand the key **command words** used in the question. This applies to all sections of the Junior Cert English paper.

The most common **key words** are as follows:

- **Analyse:** Investigate, break up into parts.
- **Account for:** Explain, show you can interpret a subject.
- **Compare:** Show similarities, but also point out main differences.
- **Contrast:** Show differences.
- **Criticise:** Analyse and judge.
- **Define:** Give a short, concise statement of what something means.
- **Describe:** Give a clear and detailed account of the subject.
- **Discuss:** Consider a subject, comparing strengths and weaknesses.

- **Evaluate:** Give your opinion of a subject, stating points for and against.
- **Examine:** Look closely into.
- **Explain:** How does it work? What is the point? What are the reasons?
- **Explore:** Closely examine from a variety of viewpoints.
- **Illustrate:** Give clear examples.
- **Interpret:** Explain and give your opinion.
- **Justify:** Give good reasons for your views.
- **Outline:** Summarise, giving an overview.
- **Prove:** Support with references.
- **State:** Present clearly and briefly.
- **Summarise:** Give a brief account of the main points.
- **Trace:** Describe the order in which things happen from start to finish.

Although some of the key command words used in examination questions have similar meanings, it is still useful to underline and ask yourself why a particular word has been chosen. Remember that you will be assessed on how your answer responds to that key term. To simply *summarise* what a character does is altogether different from *explaining* why the character behaves in a certain way.

STYLE AND TECHNIQUE

A great many Reading section questions will involve some discussion about style, either directly or indirectly. A writer's style is simply the way the writer uses language. No two writers have exactly the same style.

Once you start reading a passage, you will soon notice whatever is special about how a writer expresses his or her ideas. A pattern may emerge where the writer repeatedly uses a particular technique. For example, in writing about his bus journey, Bill Bryson's style is personal and humorous. This is achieved in part through his use of witty dialogue.

Anything you notice about how writers use words will help you understand their style or technique. Style can be formal, informal, objective, biased, persuasive, etc. The following are other popular examples of style:

- Descriptive (using detail).
- Factual (using facts and figures).
- Poetic (using comparisons, interesting images, etc.).
- Personal (using a tone that moves the reader).

When you're reading, look out for other aspects of a writer's style, such as:

exaggeration

strong adjectives, verbs, etc.

direct speech

contrasts

questions

quotations

lessons (morals)

drama

references to history, geography, etc.

anecdotes (stories)

varied sentence length

irony

humour

slang

In *Driving Hints*, questions two and three ask you to examine aspects of **style** even though the term itself is not actually mentioned. For example, the colourful imagery used by PJ O'Rourke makes his experience come to life for the reader. This is an engaging part of the writer's style. O'Rourke's comic technique is another distinctive feature of his lively style. Most answers to question 1 are also likely to link the writer's humorous style to his character.

Carefully read the following article and then answer the questions that follow.

In this extract, PJ O'Rourke shows that just going out on the roads in parts of the developing world can provide unexpected thrills and spills for the unprepared visitor behind the wheel.

Driving Hints

Road Hazards

What would be a road hazard anywhere else, in the Third World is probably the road. There are two techniques for coping with this. One is to drive very fast so your wheels 'get on top' of the ruts and your car sails over the ditches. Predictably, this will result in disaster. The other technique is to drive very slowly. This will also result in disaster. No matter how slowly you drive into a ten-foot hole, you're still going to get hurt. You'll find the locals themselves can't make up their minds. Either they drive at 2 mph – which they do every time there's absolutely no way to get around them, or else they drive at 100 mph – which they do coming right at you when you finally get a chance to pass the guy going 2 mph.

Basic Information

It's important to have your facts straight before you begin piloting a car around an underdeveloped country. For instance, which side of the road do they drive on? This is easy. They drive on your side. That is, you can depend on it that any oncoming traffic will be on your side of the road. Also, how do you translate kilometres into miles? Most people don't know this, but one kilometre = ten miles, exactly. True, a kilometre is only sixty-two per cent of a mile, but if something is one hundred kilometres away, read that as one thousand miles because the roads are 620 per cent worse than anything you've ever seen. And when you see a 50 mph speed limit, you might as well figure that means 500 mph because nobody cares.

Traffic Signs and Signals

Most developing nations use international traffic symbols. Americans may find themselves perplexed by road signs that look like Boy Scout merit badges and by such things as an iguana silhouette with a red diagonal bar across it. Don't worry, the locals don't know what they mean, either. The locals do, however, have an elaborate set of signals used to convey information to the traffic around them. For example, if you're trying to pass someone and he blinks his left signal, it means go ahead. Either that or it means a large truck is coming round the bend, and you'll get killed if you try. You'll find out in a moment.

Signalling is further complicated by festive decorations found on many vehicles. It can be hard to tell a hazard flasher from a string of Christmas tree lights wrapped around the bumper, and brake lights can be confused with the dozen red Jesus statuettes and the ten stuffed animals with blinking eyes on the package shelf.

Dangerous Curves

Dangerous curves are marked, at least in Christian lands, by white wooden crosses positioned to make the curves even more dangerous. These crosses are memorials to people who've died in traffic accidents, and they give a rough statistical indication of how much trouble you're likely to have at that spot on the road. Thus, when you come through a curve in a full-power slide and are suddenly confronted with a veritable forest of crucifixes, you know you're dead.

Learning to Drive like a Local

It's important to understand that in the Third World most driving is done with the horn, or 'Egyptian Brake Pedal', as it is known. There is a precise and complicated etiquette of horn use. Honk your horn only under the following circumstances:

1 When anything blocks the road.
2 When anything doesn't.
3 When anything might.
4 At red lights.
5 At green lights.
6 All other times.

 FROM *HOLIDAYS IN HELL* BY PJ O'ROURKE

Answer **all** the questions that follow.

1 What does this piece of writing tell you about the writer himself as a person? Use appropriate references to support your answer. (10)

2 How does the writer make his experience vivid for the reader? (10)

3 Using close reference to the text, comment on **two** methods used by the writer to make the passage humorous. (20)

 SAMPLE ANSWER (Q3)

The writer's use of exaggeration shows that he wishes this passage to be humorous. This is evident from the very first sentence – 'What would be a hazard anywhere else, in the Third World is probably the road'. I was expecting a serious point on this serious subject, but PJ O'Rourke isn't really treating the subject too seriously. This is also clear from the sentence 'They drive at 2 mph or at

100 mph.' Extreme statements, such as 'nobody cares' and 'you know you are dead' are so general that we do not take them seriously.

There is also a half-serious tone used, which is also funny. It almost appears that the whole passage is like something from a real travel guide. 'Learning to drive just like a local' is clearly sarcastic. I can imagine him pretending to instruct people in a very serious voice. The writer also uses sub-headings, questions and a list at the end. These are usually found in serious guidebooks for tourists, but in this case they just add to the humour.

This answer contains several good points that clearly address the question. While the quotes are a little careless, they do support the points being made about humour in the passage. Although quite short, the answer is sufficiently focused to achieve a grade B.

Carefully read the following passage and then answer the questions that follow.

Holding Court

She's there again. That Woman. I grasp the edge of the counter with the tips of my fingers and lift myself high enough to see her.

'Hello love!'

I drop back down again in *my confusion at being spotlighted*. That Woman would surely speak to me again so I hide myself in the space under the counter hoping that she'll forget about me and start talking. She's a great talker.

'Givus a Woodbine, Ka, and put it on the book.'

My Auntie Kathleen gropes under the counter for the open packet of Woodbines. I push it into her hand. She flicks the top open and withdraws a single cigarette. I know the ritual so well. I hand the matches to her – she snaps one into flame and leans over the counter. I hear That Woman draw in a deep breath, exhale with mighty satisfaction, cough a great chesty rattle and then she begins to tell one of her stories. I watch the grey-blue column of smoke rise above the counter up into the air, it swirls magically and I think of a genie. The sulphur of the match added to the smoky smell means that she can stay a long time telling the latest episode of her eventful life.

I'll never forget that. I'll never forget That Woman. She trots out all sorts of tales while she enjoys the Woodbine right down to the smallest bit. So closely does she smoke the cigarette that her upper lip is permanently brown – as iodine coloured as her index finger and thumb.

Sometimes I sneak along to the other end of the counter to observe her undetected. In my six-year-old eyes, she's a large lady with a moon-shaped face that has threads of broken veins purpling it. Her tweed coat is shorter than the skirt, which hangs lankly some inches below it. The buttons are strained over her broad chest, giving her a slightly humped appearance. A woollen headscarf holds the pepper and salt hair in check.

Other customers come into the little shop. They buy their few groceries – bread, milk, butter, sugar and tea – and go off on their business. That Woman remains and continues her conversation with my Auntie Kathleen, entertaining those who care to listen. I think That Woman is the most interesting person alive. She has time to tell yarns to 'beat the band', as Auntie Kathleen says to me and to me she's a story-teller to the power of brilliant. When my mother comes to collect me, I'm reluctant to leave.

Occasionally I'm sent down to That Woman's house in the Lane with a box of leftover vegetables or bread. I think her family has a wonderful time. They don't have to wash and they have a house that doesn't ever have to be cleaned or anything. There's plaster, like chalk, crumbling off the walls and you can pick it off to draw pictures on the path. The bottom of the front door has been *gnawed into a jagged edge* like a lace border. There's a combination of smells, smoke and dampness, that is acceptable to me because it's part and parcel of That Woman.

Now the world knows her as Angela, she of The Ashes. But she'll never be anything but Mrs McCourt to me.

 MAE LEONARD

Answer **all** the questions that follow. Each question is worth ten marks.

1 How does the writer create a sense of the early 1950s in this passage?

2 This text was specially written for radio. What do you think makes it particularly suitable as a radio broadcast?

3 Explain the two phrases italicised in the passage.

4 What indications are there throughout the passage that might suggest to you that Mae Leonard would grow up to become a writer?

SAMPLE ANSWER (Q4)

Mae Leonard is a bit dramatic and she introduces Mrs McCourt as if she is presenting somebody important onto a stage. We can imagine the child's excitement as she hides below the counter and watches all that's going on. Mae was fascinated by Mrs McCourt and examined every detail about her. This is typical of these writers who are always looking for things to write about. She noticed little things – such as the colours of the smoke from the cigarette and the old house the family had. Sometimes she would sneak after Mrs McCourt. The other thing that makes you expect to see Mae Leonard becoming a writer is that she loved stories and people who told stories.

This answer has two good points based on evidence from the passage. However, both of these could be more clearly stated and developed. Better use could also be made of references and quotations. Greater care would help improve this grade C standard.

THE WRITER'S PURPOSE

Writers have always had a strong social or political purpose. Like human interest documentaries on television, some writers report on issues going on in society. The aims of such writing are to:

- Investigate and expose situations, such as homelessness.
- Inform and educate the public.
- Bring about changes and reforms.

In the following extract, George Orwell describes his experiences with a homeless person he once knew.

Carefully read the following passage and then answer the questions that follow.

Down and Out

Paddy was my mate for about the next fortnight, and, as he was the first tramp I had known at all well, I want to give an account of him. I believe that he was a typical tramp and there are tens of thousands in England like him.

He was a tallish man, aged about thirty-five, with fair hair going grizzled and watery blue eyes. His features were good, but his cheeks had grown thin and had that greyish, dirty-in-the-grain look that comes of a bread and margarine diet. He was dressed rather better than most tramps, in a tweed shooting jacket and a pair of old evening trousers, with the braid still on them. Evidently the braid figured in his mind as a lingering scrap of respectability, and he took care to sew it on again when it came loose. He was careful of his appearance altogether, and carried a razor and toothbrush that he would not sell, though he had sold his 'papers' and even his pocket-knife long since. Nevertheless, one would have known him for a tramp a hundred yards away; there was something in his drifting style of walk, and the way he had of hunching his shoulders forward, essentially abject. Seeing him walk, you felt instinctively that he would sooner take a blow than give one.

He had been brought up in Ireland, served two years in the war, and then worked in a metal polish factory, where he had lost his job two years earlier. He was horribly ashamed of being a tramp, but he had picked up all a tramp's ways. He browsed the pavements unceasingly, never missing a cigarette end, or even an empty cigarette packet, as he used the tissue paper for rolling cigarettes. On our way into Edbury he saw a newspaper parcel on the pavement, pounced on it, and found that it contained two mutton sandwiches, rather frayed at the edges; these he insisted on my sharing. He never passed an automatic machine without giving a tug at the handle, for he said that sometimes they are out of order and will eject pennies if you tug at them. He had no stomach for crime, however. When we were in the outskirts of Romton, Paddy noticed a bottle of milk on a doorstep, evidently left there by mistake. He stopped, eyeing the bottle hungrily.

'Christ!' he said, 'dere's good food goin' to waste. Somebody could knock dat bottle off, eh? Knock it off easy.'

I saw that he was thinking of 'knocking it off' himself. He looked up and down the street; it was a quiet residential street and there was nobody in sight. Paddy's sickly, chap-fallen face yearned over the milk. Then he turned away, saying gloomily:

'Best leave it. It don't do a man no good to steal. T'ank God, I ain't never stole nothin' yet.'

It was fear, bred of hunger, that kept him virtuous. With only two or three sound meals in his belly, he would have found courage to steal the milk.

He had two subjects of conversation, the shame and come-down of being a tramp, and the best way of getting a free meal. As we drifted through the streets he would keep up a monologue in this style, in a whimpering, self-pitying Irish voice:

'It's hell bein' on de road, eh? It breaks yer heart goin' into dem bloody spikes. But what's a man to do else, eh? I ain't had a good meal for about two months, an' me boots is gettin' bad, an – Christ! How'd it be if we was to try for a cup o' tay at one o' dem convents on de way to Edbury? Most times dey're good for a cup o' tay. Ah, what'd a man do widout religion, eh? I've took cups o' tay from de convents, an' de Baptists, an' de Church of England, an' all sorts. I'm a Catholic meself. Dat's to say, I ain't been to confession for about seventeen year, but still I got me religious feelin's, y'understand. An' dem convents is always good for a cup o' tay...'

FROM *DOWN AND OUT IN PARIS AND LONDON* BY GEORGE ORWELL

Many of the **techniques** used here by Orwell are exactly the same as those used by novelists and short story writers to create their effects.
- The topic is clearly a factual account describing the writer's experiences.
- A good deal of factual information is included.
- Paddy is described almost as a 'character'.
- Orwell uses vivid description at times.
- Direct speech is used to add a sense of drama.
- The sentences are varied to heighten mood.

Answer **all** of the following questions.
1 How does George Orwell convey an impression of Paddy to the reader? (10)
2 What evidence can you find in the passage to show that the writer has a strong social conscience? (10)
3 Pick two features of the writer's style that impressed you. Explain your choice in each case. (20)

I liked the way the writer made it easy to picture Paddy. He gave a lot of details about the way Paddy looked and acted. Paragraph two is full of details about the tramp's clothes. We are being told that he once had a better life and this makes him a character who is more interesting. There are also good details about not stealing the milk.

Paddy's own voice is used to show the kind of person he really is. I can imagine him much more clearly as an Irishman who has been living in England for years and has now picked up an English accent. When Paddy says 'It's hell bein' on the road', I can feel sympathy for him. If the writer didn't include what he actually says, it would have been a lot more boring to read.

This answer makes two good points about style. The quotation of actual examples of Orwell's detailed writing would have bridged the gap between making the point and developing it with comments about the effectiveness of the writing. The point about Orwell's use of direct speech to reveal character is supported and is much stronger. Grade C.

TRAVELLERS' TALES

Reading about people's travels is similar to reading an autobiography. Travel writing can also have some of the intimacy of a personal journal and is sometimes written in diary or letter form.

When you are reading a travel piece, think about why it was written. Some writers produce favourable accounts, others set out to ridicule a particular place. In looking closely at travel writing, facts, opinions and the writer's use of language are important when examining the text.

Good travel writing can do the following:

- Convey the experience of a journey or new place.
- Allow the reader to look at the world in a fresh way.
- Allow the reader to appreciate the effect of a new experience on the writer.

Carefully read the following article (in edited form) and then answer the questions that follow.

Paul Theroux describes a journey along the Pacific isles of Melanesia. Years ago, when a remote island was visited by a plane or a ship, the natives would sometimes mistake the travellers for gods – especially when the strangers brought 'magical' gifts (such as glass beads or mirrors). After the travellers left, the islanders would forget what actually happened and the whole episode would pass into legend. Some dreamed that the 'gods' would return with more cargo. They would have created a cargo cult.

Cannibalism and Cargo Cults

I had found circumstantial evidence for cannibalism – the liking in Vanuatu (and it had been the case in the Solomons too) for Spam. It was a theory of mine that former cannibals of Oceania now feasted on Spam because Spam came the nearest to approximating the porky taste of human flesh. 'Long pig', as they called a cooked human being in much of Melanesia. It was a fact that the people-eaters of the Pacific had all evolved, or perhaps degenerated, into Spam-eaters. And in the absence of Spam they settled for corned beef, which also had a corpsy flavor.

But cannibalism was less interesting to me than cargo cults. Most of all I wanted to visit Tanna because I had heard that a cargo cult, the Jon Frum Movement, flourished on the island. The villagers in this movement worshipped an obscure, perhaps mythical, American named Jon Frum who was supposed to have come to Tanna in the 1930s. He appeared from nowhere and promised the people an earthly paradise. All they had to do was reject Christian missionaries and go back to their old ways. This they did with enthusiasm – booting out the Presbyterians. Jon Frum had not so far returned. The Jon Frum villages displayed a wooden red cross, trying to lure him – and his cargo of free goods – to the island. This iconography of the cross was not Christian, but rather derived from the war, the era of free food and Red Cross vehicles.

Chief Tom Namake had returned from his trip to the bush. He had a fat sweaty face and a big belly. He spoke quickly – so quickly he sounded as though he was being evasive. Wiping his hands on his *Holy Commando* shirt, he began.

'It was just down the road here, near Imanaka village, about a hundred years ago. A certain European trader came in a ship looking for – what? Some things – food, water, what-not.

'The Tanna people saw him at the beach. They listened to him and said they could help him. They tell him to follow them and still talk to him in a friendly way, and when they get down into the bush they take out bush knives and kill him, then stab him with spears. He is dead.

'They carry him to their village and prepare the fire and the stones for the oven to cook him. And then they take his clothes off. One man feels the arm and says, "I like this – I eat this!" And another says, "I want this leg."

'And another and another, and so on, until they have the whole body divided, except the feet.

'The last man says, "I want these" – meaning the feet.'

Chief Tom smiled and smacked his lips and poked his thick black forefinger into my chest.

'The dead man is wearing canvas shoes!' he cried 'They never seen canvas shoes before! They take the shoes off and say, "Hey, hey! This must be the best part!" So they throw away the body and keep the shoes.

'They never see such things before,' Chief Tom said. 'That is why they boil them. After they take them out of the pot they chew and chew. Cannot even bite the canvas shoes. They try to tear them with their teeth. No good.

'So they dig a big hole and throw in the canvas shoes and cover them. Then they plant a coconut tree on top of it. I can show you the tree tomorrow.'

Looking for the cannibal palm and the burial place of the canvas shoes late on one hot afternoon, I discovered a wonderful thing: Imanaka was a Jon Frum village – there was the red cross, in wood, at the centre of the lopsided woven huts. A cargo cult flourished within.

Imanaka, wreathed in smoke from cooking fires, was in the woods, on a stony hillside, behind a broken fence, at the end of a muddy track. It was easy to see how such a hard-up village would take to the idea of deliverance and develop faith in the idea that one day an immense amount of material goods would come their way, courtesy of Jon Frum, only if they believed in him and danced and sang his praises. But it was also an article of faith that Jon Frum villages had to neglect their gardens and throw their money away: when Jon Frum returned he would provide everything.

The chief, whose name was Yobas, was old and feeble, carrying a stick that was smooth where his hand gripped it. I greeted him with an insincere speech saying what a delightful village it was and how happy I was to be in it, and hoped that this would put all thoughts of killing me out of their minds.

'So this is a Jon Frum village?'

'Yiss. All dis Jon Frum.' And he motioned with his stick.

'The village dances for Jon Frum?'

'We dance here – also sing-sing. For Jon Frum.'

'Please. Sing-sing for me.'

The old chief considered this, and then hitched himself forward and in a whispering voice that rustled and hissed like tissue paper he began to sing.

Jon Frum
He mus come
Look at old fellas
Give us some big presents

Was Jon Frum a friendly American pilot who had brought supplies here and shared them around? And perhaps he had said, I am John from America. And then had the war convinced the villagers on Tanna how wealthy America was?

It hardly mattered now. The dogma of the movement seemed to suggest that Jon Frum was a sort of John the Baptist, preceding the saviour, who was a redeemer in the form of cargo – every nice and useful object imaginable. And the important aspect was that it had come to the island directly, without the help of missionaries or interpreters. No money was involved, no Ten Commandments, no Heaven or Hell. No priests, nor any imperialism. It was a Second Coming, but it enabled the villagers to rid themselves of missionaries and live their lives as they had before. It seemed to me a wonderfully foxy way of doing exactly as they pleased.

 FROM *THE HAPPY ISLES OF OCEANIA* BY PAUL THEROUX

Answer **all** the following questions.
Each question is worth ten marks.

1 What is the writer's attitude to Chief Tom Namake? Refer to the text in support of your answer.
2 Does he have a different attitude to the Chief of Imanaka? How do you know?
3 Did Chief Tom Namake think the Tanna cannibals were wicked or foolish? Explain your answer.
4 Does the author hold your interest throughout this extract? Give reasons for your answer.

 SAMPLE ANSWER (Q3)

Chief Tom Namake is more concerned with the amazing canvas shoes found on the European trader than with anything else. He has a matter-of-fact attitude to the killing of the man. To the Tanna, it is just another form of hunting – 'They carry him to their village and prepare the fire and the stones for the oven to cook him'. Cannibalism was normal for them and the chief's tone shows no sign at all that he thinks they are evil.

If anything, Chief Namake thinks the Tanna were ridiculous for wasting their time with the man's shoes. They did not understand that canvas shoes could not be cooked and eaten. The chief's tone lets the reader know that he almost seems to be sneering at them when he says, 'After they take them out of the pot they chew and chew'. In the chief's opinion, eating a person wasn't wrong but trying to eat shoes was very foolish.

This is a good, confident answer with clearly expressed points well supported by suitable references. There is a very effective emphasis on tone as a means of understanding Chief Tom Namake's attitudes. Grade A.

FACT FINDING

Very little writing is completely factual. Writers find it hard to keep their opinions and judgments out of what they write – this is particularly the case with advertising. **Facts** are statements that can be proven to be true, whereas **opinions** express a viewpoint.

- Football is a sport – **fact**.
- Buskers perform in public places – **fact**.
- Football is the greatest sport in the world – **opinion**.
- Buskers are a nuisance – **opinion**.

Some statements can be partially true, such as 'busking is an enjoyable aspect of city life'. It may well be that some shoppers and tourists enjoy street performance, but other people might be irritated by buskers.

When you are reading an extract, try to distinguish between fact and opinion. Writers often choose certain words and phrases to influence your feelings. Such **emotive language** is designed to play on readers' feelings.

In the Reading section of the examination, some questions will require an answer based directly on the information in the passage. Others will require a more personal or imaginative response.

While researching the assassination of President Kennedy, William Manchester collected all the eyewitness accounts he could find and used information from many of them. As you read through his account, ask yourself what he learned from the various people who were present at the time.

Carefully read the following extract and then answer the questions that follow.

The Assassination of President Kennedy

On Main Street Ted Clifton said, 'That's crazy, firing a salute here.' Godfrey McHugh said, 'It *is* silly.'

In the VIP bus Dr Burkley was staring out absently at store windows. The President's physician had heard nothing. He was too far back.

The President was wounded, but not fatally. A 6.5 millimetre bullet had entered the back of his neck, bruised his right lung, ripped his windpipe, and exited at his throat, nicking the knot of his tie. Continuing its flight, it had passed through Governor Connally's back, chest, right wrist, and left thigh, although the Governor, suffering a delayed reaction, was not yet aware of it. At the moment, in fact, Connally was glancing over his right shoulder in the direction of what he had recognised as a rifle shot.

As the Lincoln emerged from behind the freeway sign, it reappeared in Abe Zapruder's line of vision. Abe saw the stifled look on the President's face and was stunned. Continuing to train his camera on the car, he wondered whether Kennedy could be pretending. It was as though he were saying, 'Oh, they got me.'

Nellie Connally twisted in her seat and looked sharply at Kennedy. His hands were at his throat, but he wasn't grimacing. He had slumped a little.

Roy Kellerman thought he had heard the President call in his inimitable accent, 'My God, I'm hit!' Roy looked over his left shoulder – Greer, beside him, was looking over his right shoulder; the car, wobbling from side to side, slowly veered out of line – and they saw that Kennedy *was* hit.

At this instant the impact of John Connally's wound hit him. It was as though someone had jabbed him in the back with a gigantic fist. He pitched forward, saw that his lap was covered with blood, and toppled to the left, towards his wife. Both John and Nellie were aware that the Lincoln was slowing down. Huddled together, they glanced up and saw the astounded faces of Kellerman and Greer, inches from their own.

Suddenly the Governor felt doomed. He panicked.

'No, no, no, no!' he shrieked. 'They're going to kill us both!'

Jacqueline Kennedy heard him. In a daze she wondered, *Why is he screaming?*

Already she had started to turn anxiously to her husband.

Greer turned back to the wheel. Kellerman, hesitant, glanced over his shoulder again. Neither had yet reacted to the crisis.

And now it was too late. Howard Brennan, open-mouthed, saw Oswald take deliberate aim for his final shot. There was an unexpected, last-moment distraction overhead. The first shot had alarmed the birds. As the sound ricocheted in the amphitheatre below, the band-tailed pigeons had begun to depart, first in twos and threes, then in swarms, until now there were a thousand wings flapping overhead, rising higher and higher until they had formed a great ragged fluttering fan overhead, a deep blue V blending into the gentler blue of the overarching sky.

Oswald squeezed the trigger.

The First Lady, in her last act as First Lady, leaned solicitously towards the President. His face was quizzical. She had seen that expression so often when he was puzzling over a difficult press conference question. Now, in a gesture of infinite grace, he raised his right hand, as though to brush back his tousled chestnut hair. But the motion faltered. The hand fell back limply. He had been reaching for the top of his head. But it wasn't there any more.

 FROM *THE DEATH OF A PRESIDENT* BY WILLIAM MANCHESTER

Answer **all** the questions which follow. Each question is worth ten marks.

1 Do you find this account factual and convincing? Support your answer with reference to the text.

2 How does the writer manage to create an atmosphere of unreality in his description of the assassination? Refer to the extract in your answer.

3 Why do you think the writer decided to include so many quotes from eyewitnesses?

4 Do you think the final sentence provides an effective conclusion to this piece of writing? Give reasons for your answer.

 SAMPLE ANSWER (Q4)

I think this last sentence is quite shocking to read. Some people would probably find it disturbing. I myself think it is a good ending because everything has been leading up to this. The reality is that the president's head was shot to pieces by the bullets. It is the climax to what really happened. There was nothing left of him.

There was a lot of confusion about what was happening to the president. There was panic and screaming coming from Governor Connally. Jacqueline Kennedy was also in a daze. There was all this drama taking place in the time before the last sentence. The sentences are very short and tense just before this high point. Although the writer does not go into all the gory details, I can understand the horror that has taken place.

This is a very good answer that focuses on the rising tension leading up to the final sentence. This idea is also developed so that the last sentence is clearly seen as the climax of the passage. The final point is a very strong one and shows a close awareness of the way William Manchester conveys the brutal reality without becoming sensational. While there are some language weaknesses (e.g. the repetition of 'There was…'), the answer would achieve a grade A.

ORDINARY LIVES

Some of the Reading section pieces in this unit will give you ideas for writing your own personal essays. When you come to do personal writing assignments (Unit 2), it makes sense to write about **what you know**. Your family life, your friends and neighbours, your experiences in and out of school, your hopes and fears, your opinions and feelings will all help you produce interesting work. You might not always think so, but *your ordinary life is interesting*. Why are television reality shows and fly-on-the-wall documentaries so popular? Because most of us are fascinated by what other people get up to. The 'Fast Workers' extract gives us a glimpse of one young girl's working life in the American fast food industry.

Carefully read the following extract and then answer the questions that follow.

Fast Workers

Every Saturday Elisa Zamot gets up at 5:15 in the morning. It's a struggle, and her head feels groggy as she steps into the shower. Her little sisters, Cookie and Sabrina, are fast asleep in their beds. By 5:30, Elisa's showered, done her hair, and put on her McDonald's uniform. She's sixteen, bright-eyed and olive-skinned, pretty and petite, ready for another day of work. Elisa's mother usually drives her the half-mile or so to the restaurant, but sometimes Elisa walks, leaving home before the sun rises. Her family's modest townhouse sits beside a busy highway on the south side of Colorado Springs, in a largely poor

and working-class neighbourhood. Throughout the day, sounds of traffic fill the house, the steady whoosh of passing cars. But when Elisa heads for work, the streets are quiet, the sky's still dark, and the lights are out in the small houses and rental apartments along the road.

When Elisa arrives at McDonald's, the manager unlocks the door and lets her in. Sometimes the husband-and-wife cleaning crew are just finishing up. More often, it's just Elisa and the manager in the restaurant, surrounded by an empty parking lot. For the next hour or so, the two of them get everything ready. They turn on the ovens and grills. They go downstairs into the basement and get food and supplies for the morning shift. They get the paper cups, wrappers, cardboard containers, and packets of condiments. They step into the big freezer and get the frozen bacon, the frozen pancakes, and the frozen cinnamon rolls. They get the frozen hash browns, the frozen biscuits, the frozen McMuffins. They get the cartons of scrambled egg mix and orange juice mix. They bring the food upstairs and start preparing it before any customers appear, thawing some things in the microwave and cooking other things on the grill. They put the cooked food in special cabinets to keep it warm.

The restaurant opens for business at seven o'clock, and for the next hour or so, Elisa and the manager hold down the fort, handling all the orders. As the place starts to get busy, other employees arrive. Elisa works behind the counter. She takes orders and hands food to customers from breakfast through lunch. When she finally walks home, after seven hours of standing at a cash register, her feet hurt. She's wiped out. She comes through the front door, flops onto the living room couch, and turns on the TV. And the next morning she gets up at 5:15 again and starts the same routine.

Up and down Academy Boulevard, along South Nevada, Circle Drive, and Woodman Road, teenagers like Elisa run the fast food restaurants of Colorado Springs. Fast food kitchens often seem like a scene from *Bugsy Malone*, a film in which all the actors are children pretending to be adults. No other industry in the United States has a workforce so dominated by adolescents. About two-thirds of the nation's fast food workers are under the age of twenty. Teenagers open the fast food outlets in the morning, close them at night, and keep them going at all hours in between. Even the managers and assistant managers are sometimes in their late teens. Unlike Olympic gymnastics – an activity in which teenagers consistently perform at a higher level than adults – there's nothing about the work in a fast food kitchen that requires young employees. Instead of relying upon a small, stable, well-paid, and well-trained workforce, the fast food industry seeks out part-time, unskilled workers who are willing to accept low pay. Teenagers have been the perfect candidates for these jobs, not only because they are less expensive to hire than adults, but also because their youthful inexperience makes them easier to control.

 FROM *FAST FOOD NATION* BY ERIC SCHLOSSER

Answer **all** the following questions. Each question is worth ten marks.

1 Using reference to the passage, sum up your own feelings towards Elisa and the life she leads.

2 What do you think Eric Schlosser's attitude to America's fast food industry is? Support the points you make with close reference to the text.

3 Read the opening paragraph again and comment on the writer's talent for description.

4 What are your own views about the treatment of workers in the fast food industry?

 SAMPLE ANSWER (Q3)

The descriptive writing in the first paragraph is clear and to the point. Elisa is described in some detail – 'She's sixteen, bright-eyed', etc. The opening sentences are short and informative, giving details of Elisa's daily routine. The writer tells us that she always does things in order and seems to act like a machine – 'Elisa's showered, done her hair, and put on her McDonald's uniform'. There is a strong visual feeling to the way we see her preparing for work – it is almost as if we are seeing her on film.

The writer also uses contrast to show how quiet the streets are as Elisa sets off to work in the dark. It will be very different later on when most workers are out and there will be 'the steady whoosh of passing cars'. This is an effective way of helping us to picture the young girl being described in the extract.

This is a very well-written response which addresses the question directly and reflects a close understanding of the descriptive techniques used in the opening paragraph. The point about the effective visual style is excellent. There is also strong textual support throughout. Grade A standard.

CONVERSATIONAL LANGUAGE

Some non-fiction writing styles are so simple and personal that the writer appears to be talking directly to us. Writers who use a friendly, **conversational style** usually seem sincere. They use ordinary, everyday expressions, slang phrases and jokes to engage our interest. This is sometimes called a **colloquial style**. This is the case in the piece that follows in which Patrick Kielty, comedian and devoted Down Gaelic football fan, takes a sideways look at the GAA.

Carefully read the following article (in edited form) and then answer the questions that follow.

Homon Down!

The whole notion of identification with the nationalist community bores me: Catholics play Gaelic football, what's the problem? It's like people saying to me that my comedy is from both sides, as if I'm steering some scrupulous balance. No, I just tell the truth; it just so happens that it hits both sides.

That said, the GAA does have a problem with its dynamics. It's seen as *a very conservative organisation* – Catholic conservatism at its worst. Part of the problem is that young people do not want to become involved in the structure of the organisation because they know they'd be banging their heads off a brick wall. The Pioneer Pins and the Pipes are in the ascendant and resist change.

The response from young people I know is to forget about the politics of it and just play the game. There is a faint hope that maybe in time the walls between the communities will come tumbling down, though knowing the GAA, they'd probably get a grant from the EU to rebuild them.

My father used to book bands, and the manager of a well-known showband told him that they were playing for a GAA club down the country once. They had hired a big marquee and put it up in the field. After the dance, the parish priest came wandering over with a super-cilious grin on his face – an ominous sign.

The ould PP started out saying how well the band played and how well the crowd liked them. All the time he was tap-tapping a wad of notes on the manager's shoulder. Then the face tightened as he relayed how another GAA club down the road had also hired a big marquee and had pulled a bigger crowd, even taking away some of his *potential audience*.

'I'm very, very unhappy,' said the priest, putting on the poor mouth. 'We didn't do as well as we had hoped, now that's the truth.' With that, the manager grabbed the wad of notes, put them in his breast pocket and said, 'Well, Father, there's not much point in the two of us being unhappy.'

There's something special about Gaelic football, particularly if you're a Down fan, because we're better than anyone else. And they hate us with a passion; it doesn't matter where we go: the Dubs hate us, Tyrone men hate us. In fact I love going to a GAA match just to watch some of the fans. They live for the Championship, the whole notion of heading to Clones and getting the sandwiches and cups of tea in. Once they have that into them, they're straight into the pub, fourteen pints and plant themselves in the middle of Tyrone boys shouting, 'How many All-Irelands have you, then?'

It's that Down cry, those culchies with their little paper hats with 'Up Down' scrawled on them, roaring 'Homon Down! Homon Down!' If you sit beside them, you soon realise their knowledge of the game is very little; they don't even know whether the ball is stuffed or blown up.

All those little side-shows are part of the day out, and give it that particular flavour. I suppose you have to count yourself lucky you're from Down. If you're from Antrim or Fermanagh, you can safely book your holidays for the Twelfth fortnight as there's little chance of being at Clones.

There's nothing to beat an All-Ireland weekend, and the day afterwards if you win (or, in Donegal's case, the month afterwards). The atmosphere pervades Dublin in a way that's very special. I have been to big soccer matches but the atmosphere on All-Ireland days is out on its own.

Gaelic also carries a load of baggage that's holding it down. I think it's at its best when it's seen in full flight: a fast-moving, skilful ball game that can take its place among the others.

In fact I know people in Belfast who play all three: Gaelic, soccer and rugby. Granted they are playing with liberal clubs like Carryduff, Malone and Queen's. The days when someone will be able to play their soccer for Newry Town, their rugby for Armagh City and their Gaelic for Crossmaglen Rangers are still a long way off.

Speaking of Crossmaglen, I did a gig there one night and I asked what was the big club there. Immediately, about fourteen fellas shouted in unison: 'Rangers'.

'OK, lads,' I said, 'all together now... "It was old but it was beautiful..." '. I lasted five minutes.

 FROM *TALKING GAELIC* BY PATRICK KIELTY

Answer **all** the questions that follow. Each question is worth ten marks.

1 In your opinion, what is the main serious point the writer is making about the GAA?

2 Comment on the use of exaggeration in this extract, and briefly explain why you think the writer uses exaggeration so much.

3 Explain the two phrases italicised in the passage.

4 Patrick Kielty studied psychology at college. What evidence can you find in the passage to show that he takes great delight in observing people's behaviour?

 SAMPLE ANSWERS (Q4)

(i) I get the impression that Patrick Kielty enjoys the strange things people do. I've seen him on TV and he's always telling jokes and then shaking his head as if he can't believe how mad people are. You only have to look at Temple Bar. Also, he thinks it's funny the way the Down fans speak. It's the same with the priest who didn't want to pay his bills. He tried everything not to hand over the money he owed, but it didn't work. Kielty has a laugh at this kind of mad behaviour, especially from a priest. Also, he loves All-Irelands because there's so many people to watch. People are all completely mental to him.

This lively answer touches on some interesting points, but in a somewhat disorganised way. Illustrations of strange behaviour are mentioned, yet there is little depth or relevant development and the answer strays away from the question at times. The use of slang and awkward expressions also contribute to the average grade D standard.

(ii) From the evidence of this passage, it is evident that the writer, Patrick Kielty, is a student of psychology just as ordinary Irish people show it. Ideas don't seem to interest him half as much as people's behaviour. His comment 'I love going to a GAA match just to watch some of the fans' sums up his great sense of curiosity.

The writer observes people very closely. The anecdote about his father and the parish priest is told in a really dramatic way, especially when he mocks the priest who is busy 'putting on the poor mouth'. He tells other stories throughout the passage – for instance, about annoying Gaelic fans in Crossmaglen – and these are all evidence of his interest in finding out what people are like – particularly when they are under pressure.

Kielty has spent years watching the Co. Down team and its fanatical supporters. He has observed their unusual little paper hats with 'Up Down' slogans. These fans are so caught up in their team that they don't care about the slogan not making much sense. Even the unusual way they pronounce 'Homon Down' seems to fascinate and amuse Kielty. Overall, it's no surprise to learn that he once studied psychology.

This detailed answer shows a clear understanding of the writer's interest in people-watching. Excellent use is made of relevant quotation throughout and points are perceptive and well developed. The references range widely and the style (except for the clumsy opening sentence) is well controlled. Grade A standard.

READING NON-FICTION TEXTS

While prose texts can take many different forms, there are often similarities with fiction writing. For example, non-fiction may be about characters – real people, such as the writers themselves or people they know well. Similarly, non-fiction writers often describe scenes and settings, create moods and atmospheres, and their texts will probably contain themes, ideas or messages that they wish to convey to the reader. Remember that the writing techniques used in a non-fiction text may be similar to those in a play, novel or poem.

Some texts also combine factual information with products from the writer's own imagination. When studying Reading texts, think about these key questions:

- What is the text about?
- How has the author written about it?
- Why has the text been written?

Carefully read the following extract from *David Blaine: Mysterious Stranger.*

In May 2002, the American illusionist performed his 'Vertigo' stunt, a death-defying act, standing on top of a ten-storey high pillar in New York for two days and nights, and then jumping off with little to break his fall.

Vertigo

Ultimately, what I'll remember most about the whole experience was just observing the sun and the moon going through their cycles – the cycles of life. It was the most amazing experience – to have nothing to do, no worries about bills or cleaning the apartment, or any of *the mundane, trivial details of life*. I had to worry about survival, but other than that I was free to watch the sun go up and go down. I really hope that everyone gets the chance, at least one time in their lives, to witness the same thing. It was absolutely spectacular to watch the sunset and see the way the light glimmered off the surrounding skyscrapers. Around four p.m. that first day I saw the moon come up. I tracked it as it went across the horizon and the sky began to blacken. The sun finally receded, and the moon climbed to its apex. Then at about four a.m., I saw a little glint of light blue barely there on the horizon. At five a.m. it was a tiny bit brighter, and time seemed to expand.

The night was finally ending. I knew the day would give me a renewed feeling of energy. Finally the sun itself peeked out, and I saw the birds react, and everything seemed to get lighter and happier. Even though the sun was out, I was still in the shadows, so I was freezing. I counted the minutes until the sun would make its way across the concrete-and-steel canyon formed by the buildings that surrounded me. At last, the sun burst through a slit and hit me right in the face. I had never appreciated the sun like that before. Its warmth washed over me, and I felt like I had been blessed by God.

Now I started tracking the sun. I knew that the next time it went all the way around and turned black again, I would be done. I just waited and waited, but I wanted so badly to jump. My legs had pretty much stopped working and it felt like I was standing on two sticks, but I knew I had enough energy left in me to do this one jump. I was pretty confident, but about four hours before we were to go live on the air, my team on the ground started having a major concern. I didn't know this at the time, but they began to consider closing the whole stunt down because I had started hallucinating.

From the sleep deprivation, the dehydration, and the general fatigue of standing in one place for over thirty hours, my mind had begun to play tricks on me. I started seeing people in the trees surrounding me. Then I turned around for the first time, and I thought I saw a lion's head in the contours of the building behind me. I recounted these observations to my crew and, even though they didn't react, they began to make preparations that I had never authorized. A new layer of boxes was added. The handles on the pillar were raised to their maximum height – thirty-six inches – against my wishes. It upset me at the time, but in retrospect I can see that they were only trying to take measures that would help ensure my safety. The reality was, the doctors later told me, that I was so severely dehydrated I didn't really have total control over my mind.

The last few hours stretched out to what seemed like an eternity. Finally it was ten o'clock, and we went on the air live. By now the entire area was jam-packed with over fifty thousand people, filling the park and overflowing in all directions into the surrounding streets. This stunt was everything that I had dreamed it would be, and I was going to live up to the challenge.

It was time. It's hard to explain what it feels like to be ninety feet in the air, staring down at cardboard boxes like the ones you might store your off-season clothing in, knowing they're all that stands between you and certain death. I had to trick my mind into believing I was going to jump onto an airbag, or else I never would have been able to make that jump. I don't care how organized the boxes looked, anyone's *innate survival mechanism* would stop them from taking that leap. So I fooled myself – I had to. I had no choice. I just listened to the countdown, and then I jumped.

Answer all the following questions. Each question is worth 10 marks.

1 How important was the beauty of nature in helping David Blaine survive this stunt?

2 How would you describe the author's state of mind in the final hours before he jumped?

3 Explain the following phrases italicised in the passage:
   (a) 'the mundane trivial details of life'
   (b) 'innate survival mechanism'

4 Is this a convincing piece of writing? Give reasons for your answer.

 SAMPLE ANSWERS (Q4)

(i) I already knew he had done this trick as I had watched a programme about it on TV. I think it was last year on Channel 4. He gives us the inside story on the trick and that's convincing, at least I think so. It was good to see how he started seeing things. He's a weirdo anyway, but a very good performer compared to the dumb ones you normally see on TV. I was convinced when he explained that he saw people on the trees and a lion looking at him. This means he was losing it completely and I find this very true to life for someone who has been stood up on a tower for as long as him. Also, he seems very afraid at the finish and he thinks about being killed if he falls off the big pillar he's on top of.

This basic Grade D answer drifts off the point at times. Despite the careless expression, however, there are two reasonably good points made about David Blaine's hallucination and fear. More control and less slang would improve the grade.

(ii) I find David Blaine's account of his 'Vertigo' stunt very convincing. The writer gives the readers a real sense of being completely isolated high in the air. All the images are of

the sun and the sky. David Blaine seems very close to the sun – 'Finally the sun peeked out and I saw the birds react'.

I also get a great sense of time dragging by very slowly. He keeps mentioning the time. For example, 'The last few hours stretched out to what seemed like an eternity'. This shows his awareness of every minute and how slow it seems to him.

He also describes the crew of helpers looking up. They are worried about him falling and this adds a very tense feeling. It would seem realistic that the team on the ground is anxious in case he falls to his death. The writing is very credible all the way through and builds to a climax at the end.

A very well-organised response, using paragraphs to make clear and relevant points. Back-up quotes are used effectively and there is an overall control throughout. A well-deserved Grade A answer.

PARODIES

The piece that follows comes from the satirical magazine *Private Eye*, which ridicules and exposes the rich, the powerful and the famous. The magazine regularly includes a diary feature making fun of someone who is in the news. This is a fictionalised, made-up diary written by Craig Brown and is a parody of the real thing. A **parody** mimics someone's style in a humorous or satirical way.

Carefully read the following passage and then answer the questions that follow.

Diary

VICTORIA BECKHAM

There's a big difference between Posh Spice and Victoria Beckham. Posh Spice is part of Victoria Beckham and always will be, but only part. It's hard to say which part exactly, but I'd guestimate it was somewhere roughly near the middle, between the Victoria and the Beckham.

I never follow fashion. I believe in being myself and not being ruled by top designers. Like, when I'm just slouching round the house, I might not feel like wearing my Manola Blahnik high heels with my Versace black leather dress all the time. I prefer to relax and do my own thing and bring out my Victoria Beckham side, maybe wearing some Gucci snakeskin boots with a Vivienne Westwood basque.

Honest, it doesn't make any difference to us that we're rich. There's only so much you can do with money, like spend it. The mistake people are always making is thinking you need money to dress like me. Puh-leeeasse. When I go into Prada or Versace, they always let me have everything for free. Like a lot of celebrities, they're really down-to-earth and they've become really good friends to me and David, letting us have so many presents for nothing.

As a Spice Girl, I've travelled all over the world, including abroad. Paris – full of French and tray elegant. Rome – very old but great if you like pasta. America – as big as they say it is. Japan – much more Japanese than you'd imagine. Madrid – the fashion centre of Italy.

But me and David are very grounded, very down to earth. We'd never want to live anywhere but England except for really good tax reasons. At our home in the English countryside, we live very normal English lives. Good old fish 'n' chips is our absolutely fave meal, and we really appreciate it when Marco Pierre agrees to drop round to cook it for us. Afterwards we make sure of keeping our feet firmly on the ground by popping down to the pub we built in the basement to mix with the ordinary people we've hired specially. They're used to behaving towards me and David not as so-called 'international superstars' but as totally down-to-earth human beings who don't want to be treated any differently from any other employers.

Sometimes it worries me that Geri Halliwell has found the whole fame thing too much. But at least it won't last much longer for her, thank God. On the other hand, I'd hate to see her vanish into obscurity, just when she's beginning to establish herself as someone who really wants to be a star just so long as she can show the hard work, determination and self-belief to conquer those looks of hers.

But I don't just want to be the world's greatest singer-songwriter of all time, you'll also catch me down in the gym every morning training to be our leading classical actress, like the second Liz Hurley. And believe me I hope Geri succeeds with her ambitions to be an actress, because it's sad she hasn't got a husband. If she sticks at it, with her looks she could easily be the next Dot Cotton, but only if she does something about her thighs, bless her.

Girl Power!

Answer **all** the questions that follow.
1 According to the diary, the Beckhams claim to be ordinary, down-to-earth people. Is this true? Give two reasons for your answer. (10)
2 Pick out two examples where Victoria's way of speaking is mocked in the diary. What do you learn about her character from the way she uses language in this extract? (10)
3 How does the writer manage to make this diary funny? Consider the use of exaggeration, repetition, contrast, etc. (20)

SAMPLE ANSWER (Q3)

Posh Spice comes across as a complete airhead who has more money than sense. The writer uses a lot of exaggeration to show how silly and hypocritical Posh is. She says she never follows fashion but then she goes and contradicts herself by listing all the Gucci and other famous designer labels she wears. Also, everything is exaggerated. How could anyone 'slouch around the house' dressed up to the nines like Posh?

A lot of repetition is also a big part of the humour. She keeps going on about them being down to earth. Again, this just makes it worse for her. She is anything but down to earth since her lifestyle is the exact opposite. In the last paragraph, she pretends to be nice to Geri, but ends up insulting her about her figure. By saying the exact opposite, it is funny, e.g. that Geri is good looking and has a future as the next Dot Cotton who is just a wrinkled-up soap opera character. This is some compliment.

This is a reasonably successful attempt to give examples of exaggeration and repetition that contribute to the humour in the text. The expression is awkward in places, such as the start of the second paragraph. The slang used at the beginning and end of the answer is also a weakness. The answer is short (for a twenty-mark question) and the points would need to be developed much more. The overall standard is a basic grade C.

LITERARY NON-FICTION

Texts in the Reading section have one or more of the following purposes:
- To inform.
- To describe.
- To entertain.
- To advise.

Many texts are a mixture of different genres (types) of writing. Literary non-fiction is a genre where literary techniques are applied to factual topics. Such techniques include the creation and development of characters, the use of dialogue and building up particular atmospheres. All writers – including those who produce autobiography and travel writing – want to keep readers interested, so they add drama and exaggerate at times.

An example of this kind of writing is the book *Bury My Heart at Wounded Knee* by Dee Brown. As you read this extract, think about the ways in which the writer combines the features of literary writing with those of non-fiction.

Carefully read the following extract (in edited form) and answer the questions that follow.

Wounded Knee

After issuing hardtack for breakfast rations, Colonel Forsyth informed the Indians that they were now to be disarmed. 'They called for guns and arms,' White Lance said, 'so all of us gave the guns and they were stacked up in the centre.' The soldier chiefs were not satisfied with the number of weapons surrendered, and so they sent details of troopers to search the tepees. 'They would go right into the tents and come out with bundles and tear them open,' Dog Chief said. 'They brought our axes, knives and tent stakes and piled them near the guns.'

Still not satisfied, the soldier chiefs ordered the warriors to remove their blankets and submit to searches for weapons. The Indians' faces showed their anger, but only the medicine man, Yellow Bird, made any *overt protest*. He danced a few Ghost Dance steps, and chanted one of the holy songs, assuring the warriors that the soldiers' bullets could not penetrate their sacred garments. 'The bullets will not go toward you,' he chanted in Sioux. 'The prairie is large and the bullets will not go toward you.'

The troopers found only two rifles, one of them a new Winchester belonging to a young Minneconjou named Black Coyote. Black Coyote raised the Winchester above his head, shouting that he paid much money for the rifle and that it belonged to him. Some years afterward Dewey Beard recalled that Black Coyote was deaf. 'If they had left him alone he was going to put his gun down where he should. They grabbed him and spun him in the east direction. He was still unconcerned even then. He hadn't his gun pointed at anyone. His intention was to put that gun down. They came on and grabbed the gun that he was going to put down. Right after they spun him around there was the report of a gun. I couldn't say that anybody was shot, but following that was a crash.'

'It sounded much like the sound of tearing canvas, that was the crash,' Rough Feather said. Afraid-of-the-Enemy described it as a 'lightning crash'.

Turning Hawk said that Black Coyote 'was a crazy man, a young man of very bad influence and in fact a nobody.' He said that Black Coyote fired his gun and that 'immediately the soldiers returned fire and indiscriminate killing followed.'

In the first seconds of violence, the firing of carbines was deafening, filling the air with powder smoke. Among the dying who lay sprawled on the frozen ground was Big Foot. Then there was a brief lull in the rattle of arms, with small groups of Indians and soldiers grappling at close quarters, using knives, clubs and pistols. As few of the Indians had arms, they soon had to flee, and then the big Hotchkiss guns on the hill opened up on them, firing almost a shell a second, raking the Indians' camp, shredding the tepees with flying shrapnel, killing men, women and children.

'We tried to run,' Louise Weasel Bear said, 'but they shot us like we were a buffalo. I know there are some good white people, but the soldiers must be mean to shoot children and women. Indian soldiers would not do that to white children.'

'I was running away from the place and followed those who were running away,' said Hakiktawin, another of the young women. 'My grand-father and grandmother and brother were killed as we crossed the ravine, and then I was shot on the right hip clear through and on my right wrist. I did not go any further as I was not able to walk.'

When the madness ended, Big Foot and more than half of his people were dead or seriously wounded; 153 were known dead but many of the wounded crawled away to die afterward. One estimate placed the final total of dead at very nearly 300 of the original 350 men, women and children. The soldiers lost twenty-five dead and thirty-nine wounded, most of them struck by their own bullets or shrapnel.

After the wounded cavalrymen were started for the agency at Pine Ridge, a detail of soldiers went over the Wounded Knee battlefield, gathering up Indians who were still alive and loading them into wagons. As it was apparent by the end of the day that a blizzard was approaching, the dead Indians were left lying where they had fallen. (After the blizzard, when a burial party returned to Wounded Knee, they found the bodies, including Big Foot's, *frozen into grotesque shapes.*)

The wagonloads of wounded Sioux (four men and forty-seven women and children) reached Pine Ridge after dark. Because all available barracks were filled with soldiers, they were left lying in the open wagons in the bitter cold while an inept army officer searched for shelter. Finally the Episcopal mission was opened, the benches taken out, and hay scattered over the rough flooring.

It was the fourth day after Christmas in the Year of Our Lord 1890. When the first torn and bleeding bodies were carried into the candlelit church, those who were conscious could see Christmas greenery hanging from the open rafters. Across the chancel front above the pulpit was strung a crudely lettered banner: PEACE ON EARTH, GOOD WILL TO MEN.

 FROM *BURY MY HEART AT WOUNDED KNEE* BY DEE BROWN

Answer **all** the questions that follow. Each question is worth ten marks.

1 From your reading of this passage, how would you describe the writer's attitude to the soldiers? Give reasons for your answer.

2 Rewrite the two italicised phrases in your own words.

3 How would you describe the tone of the final paragraph? Use references to explain your answer.

4 From the evidence of the passage above, do you think Dee Brown is a good writer? Give reasons for your answer.

SAMPLE ANSWER (Q2)

(i) clear complaint
(ii) the bodies were deformed by the cold.
Grade A standard.

CHARACTER STUDY

You are likely to be asked about characters described in passages in the Reading section. Details about physical appearance, clothes, speech and gestures are worth noting, especially for what these suggest about inner character, but nature and personality are much more interesting. Look for any details that give you a deeper understanding of a character.

There have also been questions about how you view the author of a particular piece of writing. When reading through an extract, imagine the person behind the voice you are hearing. What impressions do you get from the expressions and tone used by the writer? How much factual information was given? What are the writer's true feelings? How does the writer see himself/herself? Does this contrast with how others see the writer? Try to build up your own picture of the writer's age, background and attitudes. The use of key evidence will bring the author's character to life.

Carefully read the following article (in edited form) and then answer the questions that follow.

Brian Patten left school at fifteen. He has written numerous collections of poetry for both adults and children. Here he recalls how his childhood in a bookless and often violent house in the back streets of Liverpool shaped his life.

The Life of Brian

I didn't know my father, but everyone knew of the Pattens because they were infamous criminals in Liverpool. I was raised by my mother and my grandparents, and the four of us lived in a small terraced house by the gasworks. My mother was a little, helpless soul under my grandmother's control – that's all I can say about her, really. Any love I got came from an old lady who slept in a chair in the kitchen for about six years. Her name was Lizzy and she was very kind to me. There were no books in the house. And when I say no books, I mean it was an absolutely bookless house. No one would have dreamt of reading anything.

I was a solitary child. I never craved company. But there was a German-Jewish lady called Frieda who lived five or six doors down who became a good friend. I used to get comics from sailors down at the docks. They were the cartoon sections of American newspapers – things like Captain Valiant, which I loved. Frieda helped me make sense of the big square areas of writing. The look of the words fascinated me, but I couldn't read them.

Frieda's house was full of books. They were stacked up the walls, on the floor – hundreds of them, crowded into this tiny space. She gave me *Rip Van Winkle* and *The Little Mermaid* to read, which I found very beautiful and very cruel. The thing I really loved about Frieda's house was the smell – it was the damp mothbally smell of old books overlaid with bitter coffee.

As a child I didn't think of myself as either happy or unhappy. I just accepted that life was the way it was. It's only in retrospect that you realise how good or how utterly appalling things were. The four people in our house hardly spoke to each other. There was always this tension, this sense of 'don't rock the boat', so that they were almost silent around one another. They were people who couldn't articulate, who had let misery and anger and disappointment build up inside them to such an extent that it could never be expressed.

When I was thirteen, my mother made a bid for freedom and remarried. My stepfather was an extremely violent man, a belligerent, unhappy drunk who terrorised us both. The house was full of anger and fighting, and both of us were beaten. I would love to have been less helpless, to have been able to help my mother to leave, but when you're thirteen or fourteen, what can you do? When he died I felt nothing but relief, but I still didn't feel free of him. I remember looking at his body in the undertakers' and it was as if he was still beating her up, still beating us both up. It's something I try not to think about. I feel very uncomfortable talking about it, because it's not as if my experience is unique. In those streets, violence was normal. The world is full of messed-up, inarticulate alcoholics beating up on women and children. I wouldn't want to set myself apart simply because these things happened to me.

There might have been an element of me escaping into my own inner world, but whether I am making that up because it fits in with what I'd like to believe, I don't know. I certainly wasn't precocious. I was the last in the class to learn how to read, always in the C-stream. But when I was fourteen, I wrote an essay that the headmaster liked and he moved me to the A-stream on the strength of it. I realised that I could get out of cross-country running – in reality, across the park to the gasworks and back – by saying: 'Please sir, can I sit here and write a poem instead?' The teachers were all so baffled that someone from my background would want to sit and write anything that they let me. Writing became a way of getting out of other things – maybe it still is.

FROM 'BEST OF TIMES, WORST OF TIMES', *THE SUNDAY TIMES MAGAZINE*, 19 JANUARY 2003

Answer **all** the questions that follow. Each question is worth ten marks.

1 How would you describe the writer's childhood and early life?

2 In your opinion, who was the greatest influence on the author when he was growing up? Give reasons for your answer.

3 What do you understand by the final sentence in the passage?

4 From the evidence of the passage, do you think the author has come to terms with his childhood experiences? Explain your answer.

SAMPLE ANSWERS (Q4)

(i) The author hasn't come to terms with his childhood. He has a lot of angry feelings for his stepfather who was a very violent drunk. He still hates his stepfather a lot and this was seen at the funeral. He should have some feelings for the stepfather if he is watching him in his coffin. It looks like he's still as angry about all the violence. The author felt bad and has not come to terms thinking about the problems of his stepfather and his whole family. He liked complete strangers more than his own family. He hates school a lot and the class he was put in. From the last thing he says, the author hasn't come to terms with his childhood experiences because they were violent.

There is the basis of a reasonable response here, but points are not organised well. The final points about strangers and school are not developed at all. Some references and comments are used but there are no direct quotes. Sentences are awkward and the repetition of the phrase 'a lot' becomes a distraction. A basic grade C standard.

(ii) Although Brian is still hurt and bitter about his tough background, he has accepted the past to some extent. A few of his memories are happy ones, for example, his old friends Lizzy and Frieda. He has good memories of being given comics and books – especially by Frieda, the German-Jewish lady. He feels a bit sentimental about the old days, for example, he says, 'The thing I really loved about Frieda's house was the smell'. This is fairly sentimental.

Brian has bad memories about his own home. It was full of anger and the people there never said much. There was no love in that house. I get the impression he felt bad about the unhappiness of his mother, and still does. But he appears to be happy enough about the headmaster who put him into the good class because he wrote so well at school. Brian even jokes about school and the cross-country route, which wasn't a proper course at all. If he had not accepted growing up in Liverpool, he would be bitter about everything.

This answer includes several relevant points that are clearly stated and well supported. These reflect a good knowledge of the passage and a clear understanding of Brian Patten's attitude towards his past. The final point about the author's sense of humour is an effective one. Grade B.

Carefully read the following article and then answer the questions that follow.

Total Exclusion Zone

Toby turned up for his first day in his Barnsley secondary school in jeans and a jumper instead of his regulation school uniform. He was immediately suspended. His mother, who didn't believe in compulsory dress restrictions, advised him to keep going in, whereupon he was suspended a second time.

Then followed what can only be described as a charade – whenever Toby tried to get into school he found the way barricaded, or if he did manage to get in, he would be removed by the headmaster. Toby was also refused by the eighteen other local schools. They claimed that although he himself did not constitute a threat, what he believed in did. Toby has been educated at home ever since.

Lorraine was fourteen when she was eventually excluded from school in North London for stubbing out a cigarette on another girl's hand. This was the final episode in what had been a catalogue of violent behaviour, including beating up other girls. She now attends a special unit designed for children who cannot be taught in the regular school system.

Expulsion is a powerful weapon, but is it necessary? Mr Smith, headmaster of Bradfield Grammar School, believes it is. 'I don't do it very often – maybe once a year – for something which is a blatant defiance of the school rules, like a bad act of bullying or a major theft. But I never do it without a sense of failure.' Martin Penney, Chairman of the Society of Headmasters, is also a benign disciplinarian. 'I like to think that I have only ever expelled two pupils in my nine years as headmaster. They were for drug trafficking, which I abhor. If people can't co-operate with our very reasonable requests, then I think that it's best for everyone that they should go.'

Jane Wharton, co-ordinator for support services in Lambeth, runs units for children who don't fit into the school system – truants, pregnant teenagers and children who can't cope with school, as well as those who have been excluded from it. 'Permanent exclusion is a negative, but in some cases a necessary, solution. Every school will have different thresholds of what they can tolerate, but if a teacher is consistently threatened and abused, they are not going to wait until they are beaten up before they take any action. Once, a boy in my unit who I had regularly warned for his violent behaviour turned to me, threw every pot and pan he could lay his hands on at me, and then threatened me with a pair of kitchen scissors. I had no other choice but to exclude him, because I could no longer work with somebody who didn't understand that I was in authority. It was an awful decision because after that he had nothing – his father was an alcoholic, his mother was in a wheelchair, and although he was now eligible for individual tuition, we have a waiting list of sixty people for home tutors in Lambeth alone.'

Jane does believe that in some cases exclusion is used badly. 'Some children are excluded for not wearing uniform or for coming in late. Well, I would rather they did that than not come in at all. But teachers aren't sadistic, it's just that the pupil/teacher relationship breaks down. Other children just can't take the hugeness of the schools, and do better in a closer unit.' She quotes one example. 'We had a girl in who had been excluded from school for fighting. She kept phoning the Fire Brigade – until eventually I caught her at it. I put my hand on her shoulder to stop her and she swung round and swore obscenely at me. Then when she had calmed down, she said, "You're lucky, I once knocked a teacher's teeth out for doing that." Because of her violent upbringing, she expected all relationships with adults to be violent, but the closeness of the unit had taught her to respect me.'

However, some people believe that children should never be excluded, and that there should always be a way of looking at each child's individual needs and integrating them in a class.

Temporary exclusion is seen by most people as useful for a period of cooling off, and a breathing space in which school and family can come to some kind of agreement over how best to tackle a problem. But we don't live in an ideal world, and problems aren't always sorted out. Kelly was excluded from her East London school for three days when she was caught in a fight with a girl who had been consistently bullying her. When she returned to school the bullying not only got worse, but she was sent to Coventry by the bully's friends. In the end she decided the only solution was to go to another school.

Anne Wade from Education Otherwise, a support group for parents who decide to educate their children out of school, thinks that the answer lies in flexi-schooling, a system a bit like night school, since instead of forcing children to be at school, they attend because they actually want to.

But, in the education system as it stands, it does seem that exclusion and expulsion are necessary evils.

ARABELLA WARNER, FROM *THE INDEPENDENT*

Answer **all** the questions that follow.

1 In your opinion, did Toby deserve to be excluded from school? Give reasons for your answer. (10)

2 In the concluding paragraph, the writer says that exclusions and expulsions are necessary evils. Do you agree with this view? Give reasons for your response. (10)

3 Arabella Warner's report first appeared in an English newspaper. Do you think it is a fair and balanced piece of journalism? Why? (20)

 SAMPLE ANSWER (Q3)

I think this is not a very good example of journalism. The article does give some information about expulsions, however. There are also different views in the article about expulsions and this is something which good journalism should have, in my opinion. This allows us to make up our own minds. Of course, it depends on whether all the views are given or not.

The head teachers give their viewpoints about expelling certain students, but I think it would have been better if there were more facts and figures given. Jane Wharton has a different opinion. I think she puts up with more bad behaviour and has different standards about when children should be expelled. I think the journalist should have questioned her about this, in my opinion.

What I learn about expulsions is that it's a bit of a mess in England. I think that one school has its rules, another school has totally different ones. I think the writer of the article would be better off coming to some conclusions about why this is such a mess. Why doesn't she interview someone from the government? She could ask them why they won't spend more money on schools.

There are valid criticisms expressed in this answer. A number of thoughtful points are raised, including the selection of views expressed and the lack of statistics. Although there are some language weaknesses and the phrase 'I think' is overused, the questions used to round off the answer are very effective and it would achieve a solid B grade.

READING UNIT ROUND-UP

- Read the passage carefully **at least twice.**
- **Study the wording** of questions very closely.
- **Think about the kind of answer** required. Will you be giving information from the passage or your own opinion?
- Be prepared to answer questions on **the writer's style**.
- Support your main points with **appropriate references or quotations**.
- **Avoid writing mere summaries** and drifting into irrelevancy.

CHECKLIST

Having worked through the Reading unit, you should now feel more confident about the following:
- Knowing what to expect in the Junior Cert Reading section.
- Understanding themes and points of view in writing.
- Non-fiction and literary non-fiction.
- Fact and opinion.
- Travel writing.
- The purpose of a piece of writing.
- Different writing styles and techniques.
- Writing about the authors of Reading section passages.
- Responding personally to writers' views.
- Understanding what is needed to achieve a successful answer.

UNIT 2 **Personal Writing**

OVERVIEW

*Personal writing is writing based on your own experience. In the Junior Cert (Higher Level) English exam, the Personal Writing section carries the **most marks** and you are advised to spend about **one hour** writing a prose composition from a wide-ranging list. This will include personal narrative, descriptive, discursive, imaginative and dramatic writing. It is likely that you will also be given the opportunity to respond to a picture.*

YOUR WORK will be rewarded for:
- A personal approach.
- An appropriate style.
- Liveliness and a good choice of words.
- Organisation and accuracy.

MAKE PLANS

It makes sense to spend up to ten minutes thinking about and planning your prose composition by doing the following:

1 Read all the essay topics carefully.
2 Choose an interesting one that you know you can write about.
3 Think about the main ideas you want to get across.
4 Decide on the form your writing will take (narrative, article, diary, etc.).
5 Start brainstorming.

Example: *A local park is in danger of being used as a site for a new housing estate. How do you react?*

You oppose the development

Trees and wildlife at risk

Used by joggers, the elderly, etc.

Very few parks left

Pupils use park for nature studies

Other building sites available

Summer concerts

Where would owners exercise their dogs?

Safe place for family outings

A place of great beauty

Attracts visitors

Park

When you **brainstorm**, jot down ideas that occur to you. You don't have to use all of them. Indeed, you will probably add to these points while you are writing.

Now organise your essay paragraphs into the order in which you will write them.

- **Introduction:** Describe peace and beauty of the park – contrast with the noisy town.
- **Paragraph 1:** Importance for families – pleasant, safe environment – nature study area.
- **Paragraph 2:** Used also by older people, pet owners, joggers, visitors, etc.
- **Paragraph 3:** Summertime activities – sports, concerts, tourists.
- **Paragraph 4:** Local community needs park facilities – other building sites exist.

- **Paragraph 5:** People should protest – letters to papers, contact politicians, etc.
- **Conclusion:** This park has special meaning for you – memories playing there as a child.

When you have finished planning your main paragraphs, you can then start writing the actual essay.

TITLES

It is worthwhile studying the lists of recent titles and becoming familiar with the various types of essays you can expect.

This is a typical list of titles:

1 How I see my life ten years from now.
2 A clash of personalities.
3 Write a short story entitled *I Wish I Could Just Turn the Clock Back*.
4 The trip of a lifetime.
5 *Young people nowadays are too easily led.* Write out the speech you would make for **or** against this view.
6 The journey to school in summer **or** winter.
7 Sisters **or** brothers.
8 Write a composition inspired by the photograph below.

DECISIONS, DECISIONS!

As the writer, it is up to you to pick a **title** and decide on a **format** (story, article, diary etc.).

Of course, some questions (such as questions three and five above) specify the format that your writing must take. In most cases, however, you make the choice about how you write.

You will find that titles can fit into a number of categories, and there can even be an overlap with the questions in the Functional Writing section. In the sample list above, for example, a diary format could be successfully used for several of the essays, while question two could be a personal narrative, descriptive, dramatic, imaginative, etc. It's quite common for top-grade essays to show control of a range of writing styles.

Because exam time is strictly limited, it is important to choose a title fairly quickly. Read all the questions through and make a shortlist of the ones you might be able to do. It makes sense to pick a topic that you find particularly interesting, otherwise you might run out of things to say.

You will already have done successful written assignments, so **build on your strengths**. You may like writing directly from personal experience, or perhaps you are good at speech-writing, descriptive essays or can produce memorable stories. As a general rule most people seem to find personal writing easiest, but don't forget to talk to your teacher. He or she will be glad to advise you about the type of essay you should concentrate on.

WHERE DO I START?

You should spend up to **ten minutes preparing** your work. Planning helps you to get your ideas organised before you start the actual answer.

HOW DO I PLAN?

Begin planning by looking closely at the question and underlining or highlighting the **key parts**. Here is a typical example.

You have been given the opportunity to address your <u>year group</u> on an <u>issue you feel strongly about</u>. Write your speech trying to <u>persuade your listeners</u> to support your views.

The **form** of the writing is a speech to an **audience** of young people who are your own age. **Brainstorm** the question by jotting down any ideas that come into your mind about subjects that concern you, such as:
- School topics (pressure, rules, examinations, etc.).
- Social topics (racism, injustice, sexism, etc.).

- Current affairs (politics, crime, corruption, etc.).
- Pet hates (litter, TV, animal rights, authority, etc.).
- Youth issues (exploitation, attitudes to teenagers, etc.).

After thinking about all these ideas, let's say you decide on one final issue you feel strongly about: **how teenagers are badly treated**. This is the topic you are going to write about in your speech.

You now **brainstorm specific ideas and points** that will be the basis of your speech. You will probably find that one idea will spark off another. For example:
- Prejudice against young people (negative media image on TV, etc.).
- Attitudes in shops, discos, etc.
- Confusion over age limits (when exactly am I an adult?).
- Prices (cinemas, public transport, designer labels, etc.).
- The generation gap (authority, family, etc.).
- Exploitation – part-time jobs, etc.

Although you might not use all these ideas, you can begin to place them in order. Decide on a strong opening – in this case, perhaps the confusion over the legal situation. Nobody seems to know when a person becomes an adult. What happens when you turn twenty-one? Why do we celebrate?

Organise main points into separate **paragraphs** and use evidence to support your views – actual examples from personal experience will make an

impact. Remember that you are trying to **persuade your audience** that it is unfair for adults to treat teenagers like adults only when they can make money out of them.

Don't forget that you will be expected to give your writing the feel of an actual speech. It should not be too formal or altogether serious. At the same time, you need to **show that you feel very strongly** about what you are saying.

You might end on a positive note by appealing for a more tolerant attitude towards teenagers. Suggest ways to improve the situation that will benefit society as a whole.

CONVERSATION PIECE

A title that occasionally appears in the Personal Writing section asks you to write a short dramatic scene. For example, you might be asked to write a **conversation** between two people in a photograph, or the **dialogue** between an adult and a teenager who are having an argument.

Dialogue is easy to write because it is simple to punctuate if you follow the system of putting the names of the speakers on the left (as seen in the various **drama extracts in Unit 5**). Put any brief directions, such as the speaker's mood, in brackets immediately after the speaker's name. If you need to include any additional directions, keep these as short as possible and preferably put them at the beginning of a scene.

Writing a short dramatic scene needs to be carefully planned. It is **another way of telling a story** so there has to be a beginning, middle and end to the drama. The speakers' personalities should be reflected in what they say and how they say it. If two speakers sound exactly the same, the scene will probably be unrealistic and unconvincing.

WHAT MAKES A GOOD ANSWER?

A good answer is easy to understand and interesting to read, which means that it must be clearly written in sentences and paragraphs, and fit the purpose and audience for which it is intended.

BE A MODEL STUDENT

Successful writers use all the help they can get. They learn from other writers and often 'borrow' ideas. It makes sense to learn from others, so don't be afraid to model your essays on writers whose work you admire. Keep on the lookout (in books, magazines and newspapers) for fresh ideas, new words and expressions that will help you develop your own style of writing. Look back over the extracts in the **Reading section** and check if some of these could be used as models for your Personal Writing.

DESCRIPTIVE WRITING

Your main aim when writing to describe something is to create pictures with words to help readers vividly imagine the person, scene or situation that you are describing. Effective description involves controlling your use of language to avoid being overly elaborate. It's best not to overdo the description with fancy or impressive-sounding words.

Look at these four short sentences. One stands out because it is forced and overly descriptive.

1 The sky was growing grey with menace.

2 The dark, ominous sky was heavily laden down with gloomy precipitation.

3 The clouds were growing darker and more menacing.

4 Rain was just a mile or so away.

Three of these sentences avoid fancy language but help the reader to visualise the weather. They use words that are more interesting than those we might have thought of straightaway. By contrast, the second sentence is a little over the top. After all, why make a fuss when all you want to say is that it looked as though it might rain?

MAKING DESCRIPTIONS VIVID

Good descriptive writing brings people, places and events to life. In this example, words and images are carefully chosen to describe an old castle.

> **The ancient castle, its harsh grey stone partly covered with green and gold lichen, loomed above them. In places, the walls had tumbled into piles of random boulders, while the towers, still dark and tall against the pale blue spring sky, were ragged with holes; they looked like the arms of an old, worn-out jumper stretching towards the clouds.**

The more detail you use, the easier it will be for the reader to see what is being described.

The author's use of detail and colour helps us visualise the place. We also get a sense of the castle's atmospheric setting when the towers are compared to old sleeves. You can make your own writing more effective by using the following:
- Vivid imagery, such as similes and metaphors, to help readers recreate the scene or experience in their imaginations.
- Interesting sound effects.
- Varied sentences and rhythm patterns.

DESCRIBING PLACES

In this short extract from *Hard Times* by Charles Dickens, notice the writer's detailed description of Coketown, a nineteenth century industrial centre.

> **It was a town of red brick, or of brick that would have been red if the smoke and ashes had allowed it; but, as matters stood it was a town of unnatural red and black like the painted face of a savage. It was a town of machinery and tall chimneys, out of which interminable serpents of smoke trailed themselves for ever and ever, and never got uncoiled. It had a black canal**

in it, and a river that ran purple with ill-smelling dye, and vast piles of buildings full of windows where there was a rattling and a trembling all day long, and where the piston of the steam-engine worked monotonously up and down, like the head of an elephant in a state of melancholy madness. It contained several large streets all very like one another, and many small streets still more like one another, inhabited by people equally like one another, who all went in and out at the same hours, with the same sound upon the pavements, to do the same work, and to whom every day was the same as yesterday and tomorrow, and every year the counterpart of the last and the next.

Dickens' use of colour imagery, especially red and black, emphasises the unnatural atmosphere of the dreary industrial town. He also uses metaphors and similes to suggest the monotony of this dreadful place. What do the serpents of smoke make you think of? What other place is the writer associating this old Victorian town with?

Repetition is used to show the routine lives of the workers. Do you get a sense of their drudgery from the wearisome rhythm of the final sentences?

Dickens also uses language that relates to our senses, such as 'ill-smelling dye' and 'there was a rattling and a trembling all day long'.

DESCRIBING PEOPLE

Whether real or fictional, the people you describe should be believable and convincing. Keep their personalities in mind as well as their appearance. Try to imagine the background of all the characters you describe. As you write about them, ask yourself if this person would really behave this way.

Read the following extract (also from *Hard Times* by Charles Dickens) about Mr Bounderby, an important factory owner in Coketown, and see if you agree with the comments that follow about the author's descriptive skills in bringing his character to life.

He was a rich man: banker, merchant, manufacturer, and what not. A big, loud man, with a stare, and a metallic laugh. A man made out of a coarse material, which seemed to have been stretched to make so much of him. A man with a great puffed head and forehead, swelled veins in his temples, and such a strained skin to his face that it seemed to hold his eyes open, and lift his eyebrows up. A man with a pervading appearance on him of being inflated like a balloon, and ready to start. A man who could never sufficiently vaunt himself a self-made man. A man who was always proclaiming, through that brassy-speaking trumpet of a voice of his, his old ignorance and his old poverty. A man who was the bully of humility.

Dickens adds the phrase 'what not' to the list of Bounderby's occupations. This suggests that he controlled almost everything – and everybody – in Coketown. The phrase is often used as shorthand for a long list, so Bounderby presumably has a list of all the important positions he holds in the town.

Most of the adjectives used to describe Bounderby paint him in an extremely unattractive light. His features are 'loud', 'puffed', 'coarse' and 'strained'. His voice is like a 'brassy-speaking trumpet'. Every detail Dickens uses emphasises Bounderby's negative and unpleasant character.

The author uses the simile 'inflated like a balloon' to describe Bounderby's self-important personality. Balloons are full of air and have very little substance. The comparison succeeds in conveying Bounderby's shallow character. There is little of worth beneath the extrovert appearance.

We learn that Bounderby likes to boast about 'his old ignorance and his old poverty'. By concentrating on his humble background, Bounderby's success will seem even more impressive – or so he hopes. The extract ends with a wonderful paradox (an apparent contradiction) when Dickens describes Bounderby as a 'bully of humility'. We can easily imagine this boastful character boring his workers with tales of his own humble origins in the hope that they will admire him even more. Throughout this short descriptive extract, Dickens makes it very clear that he wants readers to dislike Bounderby.

DISCURSIVE WRITING

Discursive essays consider different points of view about a particular topic. Titles may vary from discussing the pros and cons of examinations to the rights and wrongs of Third World aid.

Before you decide to do a particular question, ask yourself these two questions:

- Do I know enough about this topic to write about it at length?
- Do I care enough about it to make it sound interesting?

It is common practice to consider **both sides** of the question before stating your own viewpoint. However, you can also argue strongly for **or** against a given subject throughout a discursive essay as long as opposing arguments are discussed.

PLANNING DISCURSIVE ESSAYS

1 Take time to plan and brainstorm. Think out your points clearly and begin with an interesting introduction. **Do your best to avoid being bland or dull. Try to get the reader's attention**

somehow. For example:

- Start with an **anecdote** – *Hare-coursing has always disgusted me ever since I watched a TV documentary about the sport when I was about ten years old.*
- **Appeal** to the reader – *Despite the hysteria surrounding the debate over so-called blood sports, there are a number of convincing arguments to be made in their favour.*
- Be **provocative** – *No intelligent human being could seriously approve of blood sports.*
- Begin with a **question** or two – *Do animals have feelings? Do rabbits and hares feel pain?*
- Use a **quotation** – *Oscar Wilde once described fox hunting as 'the unspeakable in pursuit of the uneatable'.*
- Create a **scene** – *On a beautiful October morning, a small, terrified animal is savaged by a pack of baying dogs.*

2 What is **your own position** on the topic? Let the reader know whether you're 'for' or 'against' it.

3 Consider both sides of the argument (the pros and cons). Remember to add supporting **evidence** to back up points and always organise main points into **paragraphs**.

4 Link ideas. A well-written discursive essay will avoid repetition and flow as one continuous piece despite being made up of different arguments. Key **linking words**, especially at the beginning of paragraphs, can be useful. Some examples of linking words are as follows:

- **To develop a point** – furthermore, in addition, similarly, moreover.
- **To add emphasis** – without doubt, unquestionably, absolutely, without question.
- **To show contrast** – conversely, however, on the other hand, nevertheless, yet, on the contrary.
- **To conclude** – overall, thus, therefore, in conclusion, in brief, to sum up.

5 Conclusions. In the concluding paragraph, you might weigh up the arguments and sum up your own thoughts on the topic. It is quite possible that you will not completely agree or disagree with the statement you have been discussing and it is perfectly acceptable to agree (or disagree) *up to a point*. Be confident but realistic and explain your own opinions as honestly and clearly as you can.

Read the following two essays by Third Year students and see if you agree with the examiner's comments. Then complete the follow-up exercise.

(i) Television is a Bad Influence on Young People Today

Television. Love it or hate it, you can't avoid it. Most homes have at least one set and some have a TV in every room.

There is an ongoing debate about the influence of television on the lives of young people. It is estimated that the average teenager watches three hours a day of television. Sitting passively in front of a box with remote control in hand is not exactly healthy.

Television can be a good medium if used correctly. The quality of the programmes we watch determines the influence. There are a variety of programmes to entertain and educate. For entertainment purposes, there are dramas, films, soaps, comedy and sport. The highlight of many young people's evening is their favourite soap opera. There is also a wide choice of sport on our screens, anything from Sumo wrestling to netball. For film addicts, television is a dream come true with endless movies and plays. For fun lovers there are comedy and variety shows, not forgetting MTV with its constant music and celebrity gossip. Television is also good for educational purposes. Most channels provide us with news on the hour, giving the viewers the latest updates of events unfolding throughout the world. Documentaries and science programmes provide insight and knowledge to young minds. For example, on Discovery Health, there are many types of medical programmes.

On the contrary, television can be a negative influence on the young. It is known to affect concentration as a result of the constant changing of channels. Young people want instant entertainment. At school, teenagers find it difficult to pay attention. This can have a dramatic effect on their education. Watching TV can also cause a teenager to become lazy – instead of playing sport or going for a walk, some teenagers prefer to stay inside in front of the television screen.

Another disadvantage would be the lack of communication, thus causing less talking and less listening. Some families don't even eat together anymore as many meals are eaten in front of the television. This leads to a breakdown in communication within the household.

What causes television to be a bad influence is what young people watch and the period they watch it for. The official figures show an average of three hours of television per day, but for many young people it could be six, even seven hours. If the seven hours were spent watching something constructive, like educational programmes, it would not necessarily be bad, but this is usually not the case. Disturbing films, etc. could be viewed. This could cause violence at home or at school as a result.

In America, some high school shootings have been attributed to watching certain films. If we carefully choose what we watch and plan our own evening's viewing, unquestionably television can have a positive influence on the lives of the young.

In conclusion, I feel that the benefits of TV outweigh the negative effects, and television, if viewed in moderation, is worthwhile in our lives.

This is a solid discursive essay that attempts to consider both sides of the subject. Worthwhile types of TV programmes are listed in a general way, but with little discussion about their positive effects on teenagers. The negative aspects are dealt with more successfully, although vagueness is a problem throughout. The essay would probably benefit from a more direct personal approach and more illustrations. For example, the point about family meals could have been developed with some interesting observations from the writer's own experience. Although the expression is a little awkward in places, the essay is structured quite well and achieves a basic grade B standard.

(ii) Television is a Bad influence on Young People Today

Television has killed the minds of young people today. The ability to expand the mind has declined since the invention of the television. Whatever happened to a family discussion or reading a good novel? Oh yes, I know what happened, they started to make programmes like Friends and The Simpsons. Man has evolved from ape to couch potato. People are now so lazy they won't move from the couch. They seem to have lost all power of movement.

Although the television does have a good educational programme or film on every so often, most of the channels are swamped with either murder or if it's not that extreme, the use of bad language, cursing and swearing, which encourages people to repeat what they hear as they think it's OK because it's the television and Tom Cruise or Meg Ryan or somebody famous who is on it said it. When parents let their children watch the television, they want to know that their children will not be exposed to bad language and violence while watching something as simple as Tom and Jerry because television is most likely to affect the younger child as a child at the age of under ten years old picks up information that they hear on television whether it's good or bad or even very bad violence which isn't suited to young children due to its bad example.

Television these days is all about looking good, no matter who you are, if you appear on television you must look good. This can depress teenagers who have a lack of self-confidence and may cause them to go on crash diets and sometimes cause anorexia and even death. Teenagers may also be influenced by the trend or style that's in fashion at the time even if it's against the will of their parents. On the other hand, television has been a great advertiser to teenagers, advertising the latest fashions worn by famous stars.

Many people these days have idols who inspire them not to waste their lives and to seek a good career and life. Many of these idols are portrayed as characters on television and this gives many children faith in themselves to do something better with their lives despite the background they may come from. Idols are a thing that were always around back in the old days. It's nothing new, e.g. sports.

Television also raises awareness to teenagers these days about advertisements which may be shocking and sometimes even horrific but they get to the point. The point that they are getting to is that drink driving kills, smoking kills and drugs kill and everyone knows with the help of television that these things are not to be taken advantage of, or they will be hurt. Also, there is the thing about teenagers becoming rebels and doing the opposite of their parents and many blame television for the rebellion of their teenage sons and daughters.

I do agree that television is mostly a bad influence which has many disadvantages, more than advantages which lead me to say that young teenagers, even though they do enjoy good programmes on it, are not getting the right example which they should need from its very bad influence.

This essay attempts to consider some worthwhile points about the negative effects of television. The opening was lively and made good use of rhetorical questions, but there were times when the writing drifted away from the influence of TV on young people. The paragraph on idols was vague and lacked development, and the final paragraph was ineffective. Essays should end on a strong note. Overall, the expression was weak and there was a general lack of control – the second paragraph is a good example of where sentences ran into one another without punctuation. Grade D.

EXERCISE

Study both essays closely and make a list of at least five suggestions (in note form) that would raise the standard and improve their grades. Try to say something about every paragraph. When you are ready, you can compare your own ideas with the rest of the class.

For example, for the first essay you could make the point that the opening paragraph is too short – the writer could have given some details about the number of TVs at home in his/her house. Possible suggestions for the second essay could be that the fourth paragraph should focus on teenagers instead of people in general and the ideas could be more clearly thought out and expressed. In addition, the last sentence would sound better without so many 'ands'.

PERSONAL EXPERIENCE ESSAYS

Writing about personal experiences, feelings and reactions is popular simply because everyone has something interesting to say. Such essays can also suggest something about society or human behaviour in general.

Most of the exam titles involve a great deal of personal response. Always take account of the **key words in the title** so that your essay fits the purpose of the task you have been set. Don't get caught up telling an anecdote or personal story and then forget the question.

Look at the following titles and decide which of them suits a **personal response**.

• The holiday of a lifetime.
• Being short of money.
• Favourite toys.
• The best time of year.
• A clash of personalities.
• Weird relatives.
• What friends are for.

You've probably guessed that *all* of these titles allow for personal insight and feelings.

When you are looking through lists of essay titles in past papers, think about how you could plan interesting responses. A good **autobiographical**

or **diary** piece might concentrate on events or feelings that have remained with you (these don't have to be earth shattering). Old photographs or toys you have kept, a time when you were really happy or upset or a moment when you felt very close to someone in your family are much more interesting than how big your hotel in Spain was!

Of course, there's nothing wrong with writing about a foreign holiday, but concentrate on the aspects that really affected you. Readers don't need every detail about the trip to the airport and all the usual travel arrangements.

WHAT WILL THE EXAMINER BE LOOKING FOR?

• Write with an overall emotion in mind – happiness, excitement, disappointment, sorrow, fear, shock – and plan your language to match.
• Try to make the reader share in the experience or feeling you are describing.
• Don't bother including boring details. If something doesn't add to the feeling you want to create, why include it?
• As with all types of writing, the examiner will be looking at the way you use language, e.g. spelling, punctuation, sentences and paragraphs.

Read this sample Personal Experience essay from a Third Year student and check if you agree with the examiner's comments. Then answer the follow-up question.

The Journey to School in Winter or Summer

I trudge wearily through the freezing winter wind and rain, my schoolbag – weighing half my own bodyweight – lying heavily on my tired shoulders, my old blue uniform getting soaked through as I continue the 'March of Dread' to The Bus Stop.

Here, I must wait in anticipation of a bus that never seems to arrive. The only mornings it ever comes on time are the ones when I don't. Along with my comrades, I stand beside the run-down, rickety bus stop, decorated with tribal inscriptions, such as TRACY LUVZ SEAN 4EVA", and fight with my friends for a position under the hallowed umbrella of someone with sense.

We while away the hours imparting nuggets of wisdom to the young of our tribe: 'If you ever dare go into the Third Year toilets, they'll kill you.' Here, we exchange witty repartee with our contemporaries: 'Argh! No! I forgot to do my Geography homework! Oh, God – I'm dead!' and 'Ha! Too right you are.'

Sleep clouds our eyes as we think we spot the bus on the horizon. No – wait! It's just a noisy, articulated truck, probably bringing innocent, young lambs to the abattoir ... actually, that could easily be our bus. We rest awhile, leaning on someone's schoolbag for as long as they let you, i.e. until they realise that actually they now really have twice their bodyweight lying on their shoulders. Suddenly they pull away from under you, so you wake with a nasty jerk.

Eventually, our school transport arrives and there is a mad rush to get on the bus and out of the rain. Everyone fumbles in their pockets, looking for the right change. Naturally, the bus driver ignores us as the people at the back shout at him to wait a second. They can see somebody running towards the stop as fast as her school shoes, schoolbag, Art folder and PE bag will let her. Cruelly, the bus pulls away and the forlorn figure of the latecomer is left looking up at the evil driver.

We sit in the brown seats and look out at all the other sad cases going to school. We listen to the conversations of the people sitting behind us and have conversations of our own – even though we know the people in front are listening to us. Before long, we begin to contemplate our dreaded destination. 'Why me?' everyone asks. 'Why did we have to try Junior Cert Higher Level?'

The bus brings students to every other school before ours. We see hordes of other pupils getting off similar buses, going into similar school buildings to do the very same things as us. They all wear similar uniforms, they all look alike…Oh, how the wonders of education become apparent on a rainy winter's morning at 8:15 am.

By 8:30 we reach our wonderful school, the bus empties and we shuffle into the bee-yooo-ti-full mint green and beige corridors, ready for another day's learning, plus – joy of joys – homework to follow. Evidently, a winter's journey is a joyous, sprightly stroll…

Hmm…let's try summer instead. OK, here goes…

I trudge through the freezing summer wind and rain, my schoolbag – weighing half my own bodyweight – lying heavily on my tired shoulders…ahem! Yes…Oh, well.

This is a very enjoyable piece of humorous writing based on personal experience and achieves a high grade A standard. Using lots of lively illustrations, the writer closely observes – and exaggerates – the absurdities of human behaviour on the daily trek to school. The essay also raises one or two serious points, such as the dull uniformity of school life. At roughly 550 words, it's just about the right length to suit the comic content of the writing. Indeed, the jokes might well have been laboured if there had been longer anecdotes and additional detailed description. The short, snappy style and the clever ending are appropriate to an imaginative, satirical essay that takes a sideways look at the world.

EXERCISE

Write a prose composition on **one** of the following titles.
1 True friends.
2 My kind of music.
3 The day I thought would never end.
4 The joys of technology.
5 Regrets? I've had a few.
6 A surprise party.
7 My worldly goods.
8 You have arranged a meeting with your school's careers teacher. Write the dialogue that takes place between you.

SHORT STORY WRITING

The short story (sometimes called a narrative) has long been a popular type of fiction. Writing that deals in completely new story-lines is said to be fiction. Although fiction means that the story is made up, it is often based on real experiences. Unlike a novel, where the author has time to develop characters and show many events in their lives, a short story usually takes characters at important times in their lives and gives us **a snapshot of a significant moment**.

You will already have read a variety of short stories in English class. Most of these stories (like the one you will read in Unit 7) are likely to be much longer than anything you could write under exam conditions, but if story writing is your strong point, then you should go for it. Fiction and personal narrative provide opportunities to write imaginatively and entertain the reader.

MAKING THE GRADE

To produce your own grade A story, you need to:
- Create engaging characters, setting and atmosphere.
- Write with flair and originality.
- Interest the reader from start to finish.

There are no rules in short story writing, but here are some guidelines that will help you improve.

Plot
Something of significance has to happen in a short story, but it is best not to have too many events taking place. **Keep the story-line simple.**

Keep in mind that a significant event doesn't have to be wildly dramatic or violent. Your characters do not have to be abducted by evil aliens, nor do you necessarily need international terrorists to create excitement.

An important event or incident is one that **changes the main character in some way**. It does not have to be exaggerated or unusually dramatic.

Characters
Every good story needs characters, whether they're humans, animals or aliens, but **keep the cast small**. It's better to have a few key characters who are really needed to tell the story. Suppose your story is set on a boat in a storm – focus on the personalities and feelings of one or two characters. You don't need to tell the life stories of half the passengers.

Concentrate on bringing the main characters to life through **detail**, but don't feel you have to provide lots of background information. Use their actions and words as clues and let the reader's imagination fill in the details.

Characters should be consistent if they are to be convincing. Remember not to tell your reader about the characters — instead, **show** them what characters are really like through their appearance, actions and dialogue.

Don't spend too long establishing characters, otherwise you won't have time to describe the central incident. **Let the characters develop naturally** as the story unfolds. For example, if you write 'Maria took another deep breath, steadied her trembling hands on the ship's controls and spoke clearly into the microphone', you have already given the reader strong hints about her personality.

Point of View

An important decision is whether to write in the **first person**, where one of the characters is referred to as 'I', or in the **third person**, where the writer is an unseen observer.

There are advantages to both styles. First person narrative perspective makes it easier to express thoughts and feelings, while third person allows you to move freely from one character or place to another, for instance, from the ship's engine room to a lifeboat.

You need to decide on which point of view to take depending on which is best for your story. If a story is not working, it might be helpful to change from third to first person narrative or vice versa.

Setting

The setting of a story is **where** and **when** it happens. Always try to give the reader a clear sense of setting. It is easier to set the story in a place you are familiar with, since your description is likely to be more realistic when set against the background of your everyday life.

As you will read later in the Drama and Fiction sections, writers like to use settings to create **special atmospheres** and to influence the way readers feel. Compare these two examples.

(i) The candlelight cast soft shadows around the room. I stretched out lazily in the old armchair by the fire.

'Dinner is served,' the butler announced. At that moment, the Count breezed into the room and suggested we move to the dining room.

(ii) The candlelight cast huge shifting shadows on the mossy walls. The wind howled through the chimney, tossing sparks around the room.

'Dinner is served,' the butler announced. The Count took my arm and silently led me towards the dining room.

Although it's the same dinner date, the first setting is much more pleasant and relaxed. By contrast, the second one is creepy and the Count might well be having his guest for dinner – in more ways than one.

Dialogue

Dialogue is another word for speech. When characters speak they come alive. Make sure that the dialogue you write sounds **realistic** – read it aloud to check that it does.

We get to know characters by what they say and how they say it. Remember that dialogue should reveal a person's style, so try to bring out that individual's personality through the character's speech. In a short story, you have limited time so don't waste dialogue. And, of course, you should **write dialogue carefully**, using inverted commas around the actual spoken words and starting a new paragraph for every change of speaker.

Order

A story doesn't always have to be told in the order of events as they actually happened. Writers experiment with chronological order to keep us interested. For example, **flashbacks** are often used. In other words, the story is going along in the present and suddenly the scene goes back in time. **Foreshadowing** is a more subtle technique. This is where the reader is given clues about what will happen later on in the story.

Openings

Stories can start off in various ways, such as description, dialogue, reflection, etc.

The main thing is to **get the reader hooked** and get into the story quickly, so avoid long and complicated openings. Tell the readers only what they need to know.

This is the beginning of a short story called *Baby Overboard* by Gregory Maguire.

Here's how it happened. Are you listening?

The baby was naked as a boiled egg. In fact, the clothes it had wriggled out of looked like bits of eggshell left behind; white socks, white hat, white bib, clean white nappies. Out of its overturned basket the baby rolled, like an egg wobbling along a ledge. Only the baby then found its feet – something boiled eggs rarely manage to do. And the baby toddled towards the railing of the cruise ship.

Notice how the author **demands our attention** from the start. He doesn't waste time on names and family background. We really want to know what is going to happen next, and that's why this is such an effective opening.

Endings

Whatever kind of story you write, decide on your ending and include it in your plan. That way you can build towards it and avoid anti-climaxes.

You have many options as to how any story ends. It is up to you to decide, for example, should it be **happy or sad**? You make it happen. The great thing about stories is that they can end either way and people read them for this very reason – to find out.

You also have to strike a balance between giving the reader a sense that the story is complete while avoiding the urge to tie up every loose end in the main characters' lives.

An effective ending will be in keeping with the rest of the story. Forget about using an alien spacecraft that suddenly appears and takes the drowning passengers to another galaxy. There's no law to say that your story has to have a clever twist-in-the-tail ending. Finally, never end off with the old cliché *'And then I woke up and it was all a dream!'*

Read this short story written by a Third Year student and see if you agree with the examiner's comments. Then complete the follow-up exercise.

A Clash of Personalities

Jason annoyed me from the moment I first set eyes on him. I wanted to grab him by his cool spiky hair. I wanted to push him through the window. It was the start of the school year. We had returned to school. There were new fellows in the class. It was early September. The new term was just started. I thought Jason was just too perfect. Too good to be true. His new uniform was just what the principal wanted, that's all the principal ever thought about.

When the form teacher brought him into the class, he made a big fuss about introducing Jason O'Kane. Jason seemed to love the attention. He played the part of the good student, smiling at all the vice principal's totally unfunny jokes. I knew I wasn't going to like him.

As soon as the teachers were not looking, Jason scowled at the rest of us. Then a day or so passed and most of the time Jason kept to himself with his head stuck in his books. All tries by the rest of our class to talk to him bar the teachers (who loved him) were met with these grunts. One day I was being very charitable and decided to break the ice.

'Hi. How are you doing?' I asked.

'OK,' he grunted without even looking at me. I mean, did I suddenly not exist or something?

'What do you think of the place?' I said, trying to be cheerful.

'It's OK,' he said, 'and if you don't mind, I'm working. Or are you blind as well as dumb?' Hey, friendly or what?

'Sure,' I said, 'but you're not worth talking to anyway.'

Later on that same day, I told some of my mates about what had happened. Some of them wanted to get him but I made them forget it. I wasn't going to get into trouble over him. He just wasn't worth the trouble.

For weeks we scowled at each other big time. He would scowl at me and I would give as good as I got. He was a bit of a loner whereas I always had people around me and was very popular. I guess this made Jason real jealous.

Then one day during PE, some of our gang were outside cooling off from an indoor soccer match. A few of the lads started messing about, throwing water bottles around the place. Naturally, I got involved. I flung a water bottle straight at Conor but it went past his head and guess who it happened to hit right in the face? Yeah, right first time – Jason.

He scowled at me and slammed me against the nearest wall. I grabbed his shoulders and pushed him back so that he fell to the ground. Then I pinned him to the floor as he glared up at me, unable to move a muscle.

A crowd soon gathered and the PE teacher arrived on the scene to stop me doing serious harm to Jason. Before we knew it, the principal was grounding us both for the rest of the week. When we came back to school, we didn't fight much of the time. In fact, we had gotten it all out of our systems. And the strange thing is that Jason and I have gotten to become friends, but we never mention the fight.

Although this isn't a particularly original story, it is well structured. The writer has sensibly kept the plot simple and focused on two characters only. The story begins well and is realistic throughout. The dialogue adds a little extra drama and is a welcome break from the first person narrative. It's also correctly punctuated. While some of the American slang might be off-putting, there is a good build-up to the PE confrontation and the ending is effective. A basic C grade.

Read the story again closely and then write down at least five suggestions (in note form) that you think would improve the overall standard. (Use the guide notes in this section to come up with some good ideas.) For example, the opening paragraph has too many short sentences. Some of these could be joined to make one or two longer ones to add variety. We are also told about the start of a new term several times. Omit some of these references.

PERSUASIVE WRITING

In your examination you may be asked to write a **speech** for or against a debate motion.

Typical examples are:
- Mobile phones are more trouble than they're worth.
- Prison life is not harsh enough.
- Today's teenagers have it easy.

If you have already practised writing successful speeches, it makes sense to choose a debate topic in the exam. You should do even better if the topic is an issue you feel strongly about.

Traditionally, debating speeches begin formally, e.g. 'Chairperson, ladies and gentlemen, fellow students…'.

Nowadays, however, they tend to be less formal but it all depends on the audience you are addressing. You don't have to be quite so formal when writing a speech in an examination. It's acceptable to begin with a simple 'Fellow students' or to omit the address altogether.

Plan your speech carefully:
- Capture the attention of your audience at the start.
- Develop your main ideas using convincing arguments.
- Get your facts right. Your opinions will be more convincing if you are well informed and appear to know what you are talking about.
- Sum up key points at the end.
- Find a final, particularly persuasive note on which to end.

Make your writing more persuasive by using:
- Emotive language to appeal to the reader's feelings, e.g. 'the unfortunate victims', 'stunning beauty', etc.
- Repetition of key words and phrases to make a strong impact.
- Rhetorical questions that involve the readers and make them think.
- Varied sentence length (short sentences can really make a point).
- Exaggeration to add emphasis (but be careful not to over-exaggerate).
- Humour to get the readers on your side and make points more memorable.

Read the following sample essay and see if you agree with the examiner's comments. Then complete the follow-up exercise.

Prison Life is Not Harsh Enough

I would fully agree with this. The stories you hear about the easy life they have would make you want to apply to Mountjoy for what they have rather than study hard for a hard life for years at school. The food they get is fantastic and the prisoners don't seem to do much work. It is supposed to cost about €50,000 a year to keep a criminal inside. Why should ordinary workers pay so much for keeping muggers and crooks in an easy life?

I have no time for these people who want to make prison into easy street. Have they ever been mugged or attacked in the street? Dublin is becoming a dangerous place. A few months ago, a cyclist was nearly killed off Grafton Street. He was coming home late at night and he was suddenly attacked by thugs who left him for dead. Why should such people get a life of luxury in jail when they are supposed to be learning a lesson? It is just encouraging them.

If prison worked, there would not be as many going back there. It is a well-known fact that the same people commit offences over and over again. Joy riders you read about in the paper have ten or twenty past offences. What does this prove? It just goes to show that they have no fear about going back to jail. This is because jail is no problem for them. In fact, it's more like a holiday camp. I have even heard about one man who said that he really liked the life in jail. He had a roof over his head and it was just like a holiday – a free holiday.

I am not saying that all prisoners go back or that all jails are easy. Some of them are violent and it stands to reason that there will be prisoners who learn their lesson and go straight. The sad thing is that many of them go straight all right – but it is straight back to robbing houses and dealing drugs on the street.

I know of a family who have three brothers who spend most of their time coming and going to jail. My dad says it's partly the fault of the legal people who are making a lot of money out of all the short sentences. I am beginning to think he is right. When they are out, everyone is afraid of them. They go around with big smiles on their faces and it is very clear to everyone that they couldn't care about jail. Why should my dad pay tax at forty per cent to keep these criminals smiling? It's not right and if the government was any use whatsoever, they would change the system.

I think enough is enough. Prisons should be places of punishment where criminals learn to behave properly. All the rewards and the easy treatment should go. If this happens, the jails will start to do their job and the criminals will fear these places. They won't be looking forward to special meals and video games all the time. It's time to get rid of TVs and video games in their cells and playing snooker in comfortable sports halls every night.

Crime is on the increase and criminals are having a great laugh at their victims. If prisons were a lot tougher, the situation might change. I hope you agree with me that prisons are not harsh enough.

Despite some awkward expression in the opening paragraph, this piece of writing soon settled down to sound more like a public speech and became much more persuasive. There were a number of emotive phrases used, e.g. 'easy street' and 'holiday camp', and the writer uses questions very effectively throughout the speech. The choice of words, e.g. 'criminals' rather than 'prisoners', adds strength to the writing. The speech was also fairly well organised. However, it could have moved more logically from one point to another. Anecdotal evidence, some statistics, touches of humour and repetition all contribute to the success of the speech. Although the use of language could have been more controlled, the aim of convincing an audience is well sustained and the ending is quite strong. Overall, a good C grade standard.

 EXERCISE

Read the speech carefully one more time, and then write down at least five suggestions (in note form) that would improve the writing and bring the grade up to an A standard. Try to comment on every paragraph. When you are ready you can compare your ideas with the rest of your class.

For example, it is not clear who the 'people' are who are mentioned at the start of the second paragraph. In an effort to be more persuasive, the writer could be more specific and refer to 'do-gooders' or 'liberals' instead.

ADDITIONAL PERSONAL WRITING TITLES

The more practice compositions you do, the better. Always try to write timed essays, allowing yourself one hour (uninterrupted if possible) to complete your work. Remember to use the main guidelines suggested in this unit when practising Personal Writing assignments.

Although the following list is sub-divided into broad categories, how you respond to the titles is entirely up to you. Some compositions work best as narrative, others as descriptive or discursive essays.

- The importance of television **or** sport **or** nature in my life.
- My life from five to fifteen years of age.
- Write a dramatic scene (in dialogue form) about a memorable incident at school **or** at home **or** in a department store.
- Image is everything in the modern world.
- Money-making schemes.
- Look through this book and choose a picture that you find interesting. Then write a composition inspired by it. Think up a title for your composition.
- The person I admire most.
- Moving house.
- Saturdays in town.
- Welcome to my world.

- A relationship that went wrong.
- What teachers don't know about students.
- Nightmare neighbours.
- Write a short story beginning: 'You know I'm always right!' said a smug voice behind me.
- Use the following as the start of a narrative: 'When I woke up, everyone had gone and I was left completely alone.'
- Good fences make good neighbours.
- Write a story involving three people, a car and a stolen wallet.
- A space adventure.
- Write a talk to give to your year group entitled 'You need a very good sense of humour to live in Ireland'.
- 'War is sometimes a necessary option.' Write out the speech you would make for **or** against this motion.
- The mobile phone: a blessing or a curse?
- Write a speech for **or** against the view that animals should not be kept in captivity.
- 'Students should be represented on all school management boards.' Write a persuasive article on this subject for your school magazine.
- Today's teenagers are every bit as responsible as teenagers of earlier years. What do you think?

PERSONAL WRITING UNIT ROUND-UP

- **Choose your title very carefully**. You will be writing about it for almost one hour.
- **Don't begin** the actual composition **until you have brainstormed**.
- Keep to the **structure** (order of paragraphs) you planned.
- Try to make your writing **fluent**, i.e. leading your reader smoothly through the writing.
- Read over your work after every paragraph or two to **check relevancy and accuracy**.
- **Write about what you know**. The examination hall isn't the place to experiment with topics you haven't thought about before.

CHECKLIST

Having worked through the Personal Writing unit, you should now feel more confident about the following:

- Knowing what to expect in the Junior Cert Personal Writing section.
- Planning and organising your own work.
- Personal experience writing, e.g. personal narratives and diary writing.
- Using various techniques to make description more effective.
- Writing good discursive essays.
- Matching writing to an audience (the people you are writing for).
- Producing strong persuasive writing.
- Creating successful short stories.
- Making all your writing more interesting and effective.
- Understanding why examiners award different grades in exam compositions.

UNIT 3 Functional Writing

OVERVIEW

Writing for a particular purpose or function is more organised and structured than personal writing. The Functional Writing section of the examination usually involves doing clear-cut tasks such as reports, talks, reviews, brochures, instructions, speech and letter-writing.

EXAMINERS WILL REWARD you for showing that you fully understand the **task** you have been given and that you use the correct **tone** and appropriate **register**. This simply means that what you write has to **suit the context**. For example, a speech welcoming a sports celebrity to your school will be expected to sound like the real thing. It must have the 'feel' of a convincing speech made by a student to somebody famous.

There will be many differences between a fan letter to your favourite film star and an application letter to the local supermarket seeking a temporary summer job. It's not just the **content** that will be different – the **layout** and the **style** will also differ. As always, it is important to think about **audience** and **purpose**. Who are you writing for, and what are you trying to achieve?

For example, if you are writing about school rules for a class of very young children, the language you use will be clear and simple. Describing and entertaining will be more important than analysis or detailed discussion. When writing about the same subject for a more mature audience, such as a group of parents, you would include more detailed analysis, discussion and comment. *What* you write and *how* you express yourself must always suit your audience. Remember to match your vocabulary, content and sentence structure to the **needs of the reader**.

In the exam you should allow about **twenty to twenty-five minutes** for the Functional Writing section, which is worth thirty marks.

REVIEWS

You might be asked to review any one of a range of things, including:
• A film, stage show or concert.
• A book or TV programme.
• A video or DVD.
• A music CD or computer game.
• A fashion show or exhibition.
• A product of some kind.

Although a review is mainly made up of your opinions, you will also need to give the reader some basic information, such as:
• The title and author/director, etc.
• A brief summary.
• Strengths and weaknesses.
• Its suitability for a particular audience.

Read through the film review of *Identity* and think about how effective it is.

Identity (15PG)

Starring: John Cusack, Ray Liotta, Amanda Peet
Director: James Mangold

On a dark and stormy night, a group of seemingly unconnected strangers – including a convict, an ex-cop and an average American family group – are stranded at a place that makes *Psycho's* Bates Motel look like it deserves four stars for safety. Within moments, they are being mysteriously killed off one by one...

It's no surprise that it's typical slasher-movie genre. *Identity's* producer, Cathy Konrod, is behind the highly successful *Scream* films. But beware, for this is one of those grisly fairground rides where nothing is quite as it seems.

So, typical Hollywood fare then? Certainly all of the traditional horror-suspense clichés are present: supposedly sane characters scorn safety to wander off alone to their inevitable doom, while somehow nobody thinks of dashing across the road to check if the diner's phone is working.

Nevertheless, the audience is kept guessing as to what's about to happen – and is fooled every time. There's a major twist two-thirds of the way through, and another in the tail. But the solution to the initially intriguing plot stretches credulity to breaking point and seems blatantly rigged, not least because it allows a sequel. Consequently, the audience will most likely be divided into those who find it ingenious, and those who simply view it as irritating and ultimately deeply unsatisfying.

Throw in some striking visual touches, quite an amount of sparkling dialogue and load it up with fun set-pieces – and what do you get? An entertaining thriller for those who like that kind of thing. Especially since *Identity* is greatly assisted by John Cusack's leading performance as a burned-out cop who, subtle, low-key and edgy, gives to an often unlikely story a measure of conviction.

Now ask yourself the following questions:
- Did the review give basic information (film title, actors' names, genre, etc.)?
- Was there a brief summary of the plot?
- Were the film's weaknesses and strengths pointed out?
- Was the film recommended to a particular audience?
- Is the review itself lively and well written?

If the answers were mostly 'yes', then it's clear that the reviewer has done a good job.

The book review that follows was written by a Third Year student in just over twenty minutes. Even if you're not familiar with the novel, read through the review and see if you agree with the comments that follow.

SAMPLE ANSWER

Write a review of a novel you have studied in preparation for your Junior Certificate English examination. Give the title of the novel and the name of the author at the beginning of your answer. (30 marks)

During the first term, our class read Roll of Thunder, Hear My Cry *by Mildred D. Taylor. The story is about the Logan family and takes place back in the 1930s in Mississippi. Cassie Logan tells the story about how black families struggle to survive against poverty. The whole story is also about racism and especially how one wealthy man named Granger owns a huge cotton plantation where black workers depend on him totally. Most of the black families are still working like slaves for Granger, but the Logans are better off and not under his control so much.*

I found the story interesting because I knew nothing about how people lived back then in the 1930s. It was even better because many of the characters were young, and it was the first time I had thought about how children are affected by things like racism.

I finished the book at home because I wanted to see how it ended, but we took turns reading it out loud in class, and I was able to get to understand how good Mildred Taylor is at describing nature. At the start of the story, the Logans (Cassie and her brothers) are walking to school at the start of the new term. Mildred Taylor describes the dry soil and bright sunlight. It's pretty obvious she's not describing Ireland. She gives a very clear idea of the land all through the story – not just the big cotton plantations, but the dusty red soils during the hot summers. She is a great writer to describe atmosphere.

The scene where the Logans have a traditional Christmas is well done. There is a build-up to the feast of food being prepared, e.g. 'a sea of onions'. The novel takes place back in the 1930s in Mississippi or the Deep South and it is a totally different world. The Logans live simply, but the family have a great Christmas. Their parents work hard and give the children presents that show their love and respect, e.g. books with each child's name written on the inside cover. This was a bit sentimental, but the Logans are very close. The only one of the family I didn't like was Little Man, who to me was far too perfect and fussy. I just couldn't take to him.

The book tells the story of other characters as well as Cassie, but Cassie is the main narrator. What I liked most was that you got to know about different people's lives. T.J. Avery is a sad character. He is a poor black boy who is easily led into crime by two white boys, the Simms brothers. T.J. is funny in ways, although he just isn't smart enough to stay out of trouble. But not all the white people are bad. Mr. Jamison, the lawyer, tries his best to help the Logans hold on to their small farm.

Roll of Thunder is well worth reading, and there are two follow-up books as well, which I would also like to read, just to see what happens when Cassie grows up. She is a lively *character, a tomboy who is able to fight and stand up for herself when she has to. I admired her and enjoyed reading the book.*

This review includes lots of interesting points about the novel's setting, plot, characters and themes. Enough aspects are mentioned to give a flavour of the book and to interest the review's readers. There is some balance as well in the negative criticism of Little Man. While some of the expressions are a little awkward, there is a genuine sense of appreciating Mildred D Taylor's writing skills and engaging directly with the novel. A very good grade A review.

Answer **one** of the following questions. Each question is worth thirty marks. (Allow about twenty minutes to write the answer.)
1 Write a review of a film that you **either** liked very much **or** disliked very much.
2 Your school librarian has asked you to give a talk to First Years about reading novels and short stories. Write out the talk you would give, suggesting some good books that their age group would enjoy.
3 Write a letter to a favourite pop group or singer whose music you really like. Explain why you are the group's (or singer's) number one fan and mention some of the songs or albums that you enjoy most.

WRITING TO ADVISE

There's no shortage of advice around. We are constantly giving or seeking advice of one kind or other. It may be advice on personal problems, career choices, fashion, what to see at the cinema and so on. **Advice comes in many different forms**, and often whether we want it or not.

There is verbal advice spoken by friends or relatives or that we hear on radio or TV. Advice is also written in magazines and newspapers, rulebooks, leaflets, books, posters or on the internet.

Instructions can sometimes be difficult to understand. Most of us have problems working out the mysteries of the brand-new DVD player, reading bus timetables or giving travel directions.

Whatever kind of advice is being given, though, the main purpose is to **communicate ideas clearly** and effectively. Most written advice is likely to have certain key features that you need to know about.

- The language should be clear and simple.
- The advice should be divided into clear sections.
- Each section should deal with a particular point.
- Illustrations may be used to help reinforce the point.

When writing to advise, always use language in an appropriate way to communicate ideas to your audience.

Now look at the example about protecting your mobile phone. Think about the purpose, audience, use of language and layout.

How to Hang on to Your Mobile

Mobile phone theft has become increasingly common and young people are especially vulnerable. By taking these simple precautions you can reduce your chances of being a victim of this form of crime.

- Keep your phone hidden by storing it in a zipped pocket or bag when you're not using it, and never leave your phone unattended.

- Lose the catchy ringtone when you're out and about. Switch your phone to vibrate instead, so even if you can't hear it ring you'll know you have a call.

- **If you have to answer your phone in the street, be aware of what's going on around you. That means not only who's in the area, but also watch out when crossing busy roads.**

- **It's almost impossible to text and pay attention at the same time. Don't be distracted sending messages, and if you have to text, keep it short!**

- **Make sure you keep a note of your phone's details, including the handset security code (which you can find by dialling star and then #06#) and the PIN which locks your handset. This information will be very useful in tracing your phone if it is stolen.**

Not all advice makes sense or is completely serious. For example, this set of 'directions' made up the blurb of *Dr* *Fegg's Encyclopaedia of All World Knowledge* by Terry Jones and Michael Palin.

How to Destroy this Book

Apart from the obvious ones – like ripping it apart or getting a huge wolf to come in and rip it to pieces – there are several other ways of getting rid of/breaking/smashing/giving what for to this book.

(i) Go to the end of the pier. Tie an ENORMOUS rock around your wrist. Hold the book firmly and jump into the water. Release the book.

(ii) Yes...yes...I know...very clever of you to spot it...smarmy little creeps...but don't you dare laugh at yerluvinuncle Bert when he makes a little mistake...or ELSE!

(iii) Go to the end of the pier. Tie an ENORMOUS rock around *the book*. Hold the book firmly and jump into the water. Release the book.

(iv) Take the book to a steamroller testing centre. Place the book in front of the LARGEST steamroller you can find. As the driver approaches the book, run out and stop him, pointing to the book. When he gets out, nip round the other side and into his cab. Pinch his address book, and find the address of the people he used to work for. Go round and see them and find out what his name is. Using *his* name, go back to the steam-rolling centre and say you want to borrow a LARGE STEAM-ROLLER. Keep your face averted and give them *his* name. When they have given you the keys to the steam-roller, drive the steamroller OVER the book.

(v) Take the book to the zoo. Find the piranha fish tank. Push your grandfather into the tank, and while everyone watches the terrible struggle, slip the book into someone's handbag and turn them over to the police. The police will get rid of the book for you.

HOW TO DESTROY THIS BOOK

Apart from the obvious ones – like ripping it apart or getting a huge wolf to come in and rip it to pieces – there are several other ways of getting rid of / breaking / smashing / giving what for to this book.

(i) Go to the end of the pier. Tie an ENORMOUS rock around your wrist. Hold the book firmly and jump into the water. Release the book.

(ii) Yes . . . yes . . . I know . . . very clever of you to spot it . . . smarmy little creeps . . . but don't you dare laugh at yerluvinuncle Bert when he makes a little mistake or . . . ELSE!

(iii) Go to the end of the pier. Tie an ENORMOUS rock around *the book*. Hold the book firmly and jump into the water. Release the book.

(iv) Take the book to a steamroller testing centre. Place the book in front of the LARGEST steamroller you can find. As the driver approaches the book, run out and stop him, pointing to the book. When he gets out, nip round the other side and into his cab. Pinch his address book, and find the address of the people he used to work for. Go round and see them and find out what his name was. Using *his* name, go back to the steamroller testing centre, and say you want to borrow a LARGE STEAMROLLER. Keep your face averted and give HIS name. When they have given you the keys to the steamroller, drive the steamroller OVER the book.

(v) Take the book to the zoo. Find the piranha fishes' tank. Push your grandfather into the tank, and while everyone watches the terrible struggle, slip the book into someone's handbag and turn them over to the police. The police will get rid of the book for you.

ISBN 0-413-56430-4

9 780413 564306

PRICE NET
£4.99
IN UK ONLY
A METHUEN PAPERBACK
HUMOUR

When writing serious instructions, of course, you should note the following:
• Before you write anything, make a rough plan of the main tasks that have to be done in the correct order so that you are clear about the instructions.
• Then start by writing a short intro-duction explaining what is to be done, the time it will take, the main benefits and the costs involved.
• Bullet points can make specific pieces of advice stand out clearly.
• Make a list of materials needed, e.g. equipment, special clothing, safety gear, etc.
• Clearly explain any technical terms that will be used.
• Use bold or capital letters to warn of any dangers involved. It's also helpful to use key words such as *Caution!*

- List the actual instructions in short, clear sentences.
- Write in a straightforward, informal style.
- Look for instructions that come with new machines and DIY items. Newspaper and magazine advice columns also help readers cope with a variety of problems.

Answer **one** of the following questions. Each question is worth thirty marks.

1 Write an advice leaflet aimed at teenagers about the dangers of **either** alcohol abuse **or** gambling arcades.

2 Explain the advantages of buying a new computer to an older person who has just retired.

3 Create a tourist leaflet about places of interest (historical buildings, festivals, parks, etc.) in your area. Aim at promoting a positive image that will attract visitors.

FACT-FINDING REPORTS

Fact-finding reports contain information based on research. They **examine important issues**, such as traffic problems, and usually come to **conclusions** and make **recommendations**.

A good report should be **clear, factual, precise** and **logical**. It will have no real value if it is one-sided or incomplete. The readers will wish to know why the report is being done and who is doing it. If there are any opinions expressed in the report, then these should be clearly pointed out to distinguish people's personal views from actual facts.

Most reports could be structured as follows:

- Introduction that explains the reasons for the report.
- Outline stating exactly what the report is about.
- Factual description of what is happening.
- Conclusion and recommendations.

REPORT LAYOUT

Reports vary greatly. Some are simple typed files, others are huge and expensive documents issued by large companies or governments. The layout of formal reports varies, but will usually include these basic sub-divisions.

Title
Your title should be clearly stated. You might also need to add who the report is for, such as 'A report on … for the consideration of …'.

Terms of Reference
This section should give relevant background information explaining why the report is being written.

Methods
Describe how you went about finding your information, for example reference material, interviews, questionnaires, etc.

Findings
Relevant facts should be presented in a logical way. Language should be clear and direct. Include any visual material that will support the points you are making.

Conclusions
Give a brief summary of your findings based on the evidence.

Recommendations
Present your practical proposals for change and improvement based on the report's findings. End with your signature and the date.

Study the example below before trying one of the questions that follow.

Title

A Report on School Library Facilities at Hillview Community School.

Terms of Reference

This report was commissioned by the Hillview Community School Board of Management and the school librarian. The report aims to investigate the present usage of the school library and how this can be increased in future years.

Methods

Interviews with the school librarian, senior English teachers and principal. All thirty-two classes in the school were asked to fill in a questionnaire and their responses were collated. Other school libraries in the area were visited to inspect their facilities.

Findings

The librarian stated that the school library was busiest during break times and lunchtimes, especially on rainy days. There was a fall-off in usage during the final school term (April and May). Most Junior English classes used the library for one class period throughout the whole school year.

Students from all year groups reported that they used the library for research purposes on a regular basis. Transition Years considered the library a very important resource. Over twenty per cent of students said that the books and magazines were old-fashioned, and that their favourite authors were not easily available. Almost thirty per cent complained that the library was cold at times. More than ninety per cent said that they enjoyed visiting the library and always found the librarian to be very helpful.

Two other school libraries were found to be much better stocked with modern, up-to-date literature and non-fiction, videos and full internet facilities. However, three libraries were smaller, poorly stocked and unattractive.

Conclusions

The Hillview Community School library would benefit from being restocked with up-to-date literature, non-fiction and magazines. The room itself could be better heated and ventilated and its services extended.

Recommendations

- Student committee to advise on the purchase of new stock.
- Immediate investment in new books and magazines.
- Four additional radiators to be fitted.
- The room to be redecorated during holidays.
- Two computers to be installed to help with research projects.
- Visiting writers to be invited to visit the library to give readings.

Signed: *J K Roland*

30 April 2004

Answer **one** of the following questions. Each question is worth thirty marks.

1 Write a report about the problem of litter in your school.

2 Compile a news report on the decision by your local council to sell playing fields to make way for a new motorway.

3 Write a report for publication in your school magazine about the typical TV viewing habits of Third Year students in your school.

LETTERS

In the exam you may be asked to write a letter for a particular purpose, for example to offer or seek information, to keep in touch with a friend or relative, to provide a character reference, to act as an 'agony aunt', to complain, to persuade or to express your opinion. Most of these can be classified as either **informal** or **formal**.

INFORMAL LETTERS

Very few people write informal or personal letters and post them off to their friends nowadays, but personal messaging is increasing all the time – through e-mails, mobile phones and texting. These are the latest forms of informal communication, so be prepared to see questions about them in the Functional Writing section.

For exam purposes, you will need to give a letter some shape and think carefully about the contents. All informal letters will have the ring of speech about them. In writing to friends, include plenty of gossipy news about what you have been doing, the places you have visited, the people you have met and any strange or amusing incidents that have happened. It's also important to show an interest in the person to whom you are writing.

Personal letters are just ways of meeting and talking freely on the page. Begin by imagining that the person you're writing to is sitting opposite you. If you still don't know where to begin, start with the present moment: *I'm writing this on the floor in my bedroom on a very wet Sunday afternoon. The house is completely empty, except for my sleepy cat, Sox, who has spent the last hour ignoring me completely.* A simple description of the present moment can lead you to something more important.

While there are fewer rules about the layout of informal letters, always write the full address and date in the top right-hand corner. You usually begin and sign off in a more personal way, e.g. 'Dear Anne/Uncle Jack/Aunt Sally,' etc., and the ending will be 'Yours sincerely, Sincerely, Kind regards, Love,' etc.

You will find exceptions to most rules about letter-writing, so don't worry too much if you come across slightly different guidelines about layout and so on. The most important thing is to get the tone right and to communicate effectively.

Write a letter to your godparents thanking them for letting you stay in their home last weekend. (30 marks)

52, Avenue Road,
Cork.

22 July 2004

Dear Una and Paul,

Thank you for letting me stay with you last week – it was absolutely great and I loved every minute of my time in Dublin. It was very thoughtful of you to get me a ticket for the Eminem concert – I know they are expensive – and I really enjoyed spending time with Michael and his friends. I have been telling everyone in my class about all these brilliant guys in Dublin.

I hardly ever eat in Chinese restaurants, but I thought our meal out on Friday night was terrific. The food was delicious and I am now a total addict of bamboo shoots and roast chestnuts! And I must say that I was very impressed with Paul's unusual 'rap' singing in the taxi home. He might even have a future career as a professional if he ever loses his day job!

Of course, being Eminem's biggest fan, the concert at the Point was unbelievable. I hadn't even dreamed of going, so it came as a huge surprise. He was just so cool! He played loads of his old stuff from the early albums as well as this year's songs. I love all of it. Both the supporting acts, 50 Cent and D-12, were also brilliant. Now that I have the t-shirt from the year's best gig, I don't regret spending my last euro in the world and being broke forever.

My parents have made me promise that I'll settle down to my studies for the new year, so I don't think I'll be going to too many concerts for a while. They send their good wishes – and Dad wants to know if you will think about keeping me every weekend for the next two years! If any good bands come to Cork before Christmas, maybe Michael (and his friend, Ken) might decide to visit us.

Thank you both again for every-thing.

Love,
Ciara

P.S. I'm enclosing a (very blurry) photograph showing all of us posing outside the Point.

This is a typical informal letter with a relaxed style throughout. At the same time the letter serves its primary function of expressing thanks. Paragraphs are short and to the point, the tone is casual and chatty and there isn't too much slang. The postscript is a welcome idea that makes the letter more effective. It can be difficult to strike a balance between expressing gratitude sincerely without overdoing the thanks, but the tone in this case has a convincing feel about it. Grade A.

Answer **one** of the following questions. Each question is worth thirty marks.

1 One of your friends has been involved in a car crash and has to stay in hospital for at least three weeks. Write a letter to cheer up your friend, giving him/her all the latest news and gossip.

2 As part of a youth exchange programme you have just returned from a week's visit to France where you stayed in the home of a young person. Write a letter to thank your new friend and invite him/her to visit Ireland during the next school holiday. Outline the activities you plan for this visit.

3 Some close relatives who emigrated to America last year have asked you if you'd like to spend a month's holiday with them in New York next summer. Write an e-mail to them giving your reaction. You might make some suggestions about what you'd like to do during the visit.

FORMAL LETTERS

Formal letters are written to people you don't know or about issues that are not personal. Letters to embassies looking for information or letters of complaint to RTÉ are typical examples.

You usually write a formal letter to arrange something or get something done, such as:
- To make an appointment.
- To buy something.
- To ask for a refund.
- To request information.
- To make a complaint.

You are likely to get a positive response if you **plan** your letter carefully, using the correct **layout** and the right **tone**.

LAYOUT
FOR FORMAL LETTERS

Almost all formal letters are now written on the computer. Your own address goes in the right-hand corner with the date written underneath.

The name and address of the person you are writing to is written on the left. Include the person's title, e.g. Personnel Manager or Principal.

The usual greeting is 'Dear' followed by Mr, Mrs, or Ms. If you don't know the name, write 'Dear Sir or Madam'.

The main part of the letter is then set out in paragraphs.

The ending (or sign-off) should be correctly chosen in keeping with the overall tone of the letter. If you have used the person's actual name, end with 'Yours sincerely'. If you haven't used the person's name, write 'Yours faithfully' (this is the case in the sample letter printed here).

Write a letter of complaint to a holiday company after spending two weeks in one of their Mallorcan hotels. (30 marks)

SAMPLE ANSWER

22, High Street,
Thurles,
Co. Tipperary.

17 August 2004

The Manager,
Happy Holidays,
Henry Street,
Dublin 1.

Dear Sir or Madam,

I am writing to complain about my family's recent holiday in the Hotel Splendido, Porto Paloma, Mallorca, where we stayed from August 1–15. Our booking reference number is M713/03. Your company's brochure promised 'an unforgettable holiday' and that is exactly what we had –

but for all the wrong reasons.

Although our outgoing flight was delayed at Dublin Airport by over three hours, this was actually the best part of our holiday as we were dry, warm and reasonably well treated. The real problems began on our arrival at the Hotel Splendido where my parents, my young brother and myself were shocked to find extensive building work in full swing between the hours of 6:00 pm–11:00 am local time.

Apart from the high noise levels of bulldozers and drills during the thirteen nights of our stay, most of the hotel's promised facilities were not available. The so-called 'state-of-

the-art entertainment centre, spacious gymnasium and exclusive shopping mall' are still weeks away from being ready. The only facility we could find was a makeshift disco in the restaurant area in the late evening. In fact, the builders turned out to be our main form of entertainment throughout the holiday, and we almost began to look forward to their shouts, rude gestures, whistles and occasional singing.

Along with several other Irish families, my parents repeatedly made our feelings known to both the hotel manager, Mr Gonzales, and to your own Happy Holidays rep, Ms Kavanagh. Although both of them were sympathetic, they were unable to solve any of the serious problems that existed, and no alternative hotel accommodation was available anywhere else in Porto Paloma.

As you can imagine, we are all deeply disappointed and annoyed about what happened. Our holiday photographs are a reminder of how terrible the whole experience has been. After enduring a fortnight of sleepless nights, you will surely agree that our summer has been ruined. Considering that we have paid your company almost €3,000, we now feel that we deserve a sizeable refund or some other form of acceptable compensation. Otherwise, we will be immediately forced to seek legal advice about this matter.

I look forward to hearing from you within the next day or two.

Yours faithfully,

Michelle O'Leary

This letter shows signs of careful planning, is set out correctly and is of a high grade A standard. Paragraphs are well organised and the expression is varied and controlled throughout. The letter also succeeds in building to a logical conclusion. The opening gives clear details about when and where the holiday took place. The paragraphs that follow explain in some detail why the complaint is being made, and the letter ends with a strong request for a refund. While the tone of the letter is sarcastic at times, there is no doubt that it is a serious complaint and that the writer expects a favourable response.

Answer **one** of the following questions. Each question is worth thirty marks. (Allow about twenty minutes to write the answer.)

1 Your school principal has introduced a new rule that all students must remain within the school grounds during lunchtime. (Up until now, any student who had permission from home was allowed to leave school at this time.) Write to the principal complaining about the change.

2 You recently had a special birthday meal for a member of your family in an expensive restaurant. Unfortunately, the food and service were very unsatisfactory. Write a letter of complaint to the manager.

3 You recently attended an international soccer friendly in Dublin between Ireland and Belgium. Throughout the game some Irish fans started booing several Belgian players. Write a letter to your local newspaper outlining your views on what you witnessed.

WRITING A SPEECH

One of the Functional Writing questions might be a speech, probably on an issue you feel strongly about. Unlike other forms of writing, debate speeches are designed to be **spoken aloud** so you have to choose words that will sound effective. All of the guidelines about **persuasive writing** suggested in Unit 2 apply to the shorter speeches you might be asked to write in this section.

You must think of the effect of your language on an **audience**. Every speech has a purpose, usually to make the listeners change the way they think, so you have to be careful about what you write.

Successful persuasion depends on using **convincing evidence** and **expressing viewpoints forcefully**. Other useful techniques include the following:

- Questions.
- Repetition.
- Varied sentence length.
- Powerful vocabulary.
- Humour.

You have to get the balance right, of course. If you include too much evidence, people think you're a walking encyclopaedia. If you use too much humour, it can take away from your message. A good speech needs an effective opening that will really grab the audience's attention. Questions or funny one-liners can work well.

Keep the audience involved throughout your speech by using short, snappy sentences that make a point. Emotive language can also get the audience on your side, and make sure to end on a strong note.

Of course, not all speeches are persuasive ones. You might be asked to write a speech welcoming somebody famous to your school, a farewell speech to a teacher who is retiring or a thank you speech at your birthday party. Whatever the occasion, **plan** the speech first, think about your **audience** and get the **tone** right.

Answer **one** of the following questions. Each question is worth thirty marks.

1 Write out the text of a speech you would make to inform your school year group about a deserving charity that you support.

2 *We are right to be proud of Ireland's education system.* Write out the speech you would make for **or** against this debate motion.

3 You have been asked to speak at your best friend's sixteenth birthday party. Write out the speech you would give.

INTERVIEWS

You might be asked to write an imaginary interview in this section of the exam. It will obviously be necessary to set out the dialogue in the usual interview format.

The following example is taken from the *RTÉ Guide* and is fairly typical of the countless 'personality' interviews that are found in many popular magazines and websites.

The Final Say

Ray Walsh interviews Derek Mooney, TV and radio presenter.

Where are you?
I'm in the car park heading into work, but I've pulled in to the side of the road and put you on speakerphone.

Favourite item of clothing?
A Levi's cardigan, with a blue strip across the arm. That, and a pair of jeans, is what I feel most comfortable in. I hate dressing up and I only ever wear a suit when I'm on the telly. I get too confused about which shirt to wear with which suit. It's much easier sticking to jeans.

Favourite drink?
Unfortunately I live on coffee. I've no particular favourite alcoholic drink, though a very cold Guinness is just right depending on the weather. But to be honest, I'm cutting it out completely as it's a great way to keep a check on your weight.

Favourite holiday?
Iceland two years ago. Went to see Keiko, Rekjavik, out in the bay. Just spectacular, best place I've ever been. Drama of the sight, killer whale, volcanic rock.

If they were making a movie of your life, who would you like to see in the starring role?
Strangely enough, I'd have to say Michael Caine. He's always himself in every movie, but I'd go to see anything that he's in.

What were you like at school. Swot or not?
Definitely not. I had a good memory and that's what got me through. I'm able to take a lot of information in and then regurgitate it. With all the natural history and science that we talk about on the radio programme, I take it in but then it's gone.

What was the first record you ever bought?

It was a tape, actually. I was 18 and working for Puma and they'd given me a big company car. I bought a Freddy White tape with the song *Martha* on it, from a little shop in the centre of Balbriggan, and I played it constantly.

Most embarrassing moment on air?

I was presenting a programme on air called Work Space and in the introduction to one piece I just couldn't pronounce one word and started effin and blinding and every word of it went out on air. I wasn't really embarrassed by it, as it got picked up on Playback and even by Vincent Brown and there's no such thing as bad publicity. I was more worried for my job, though. It was back in a time when you just didn't swear on air.

Who would you like to give a good slap to?

To be honest, there's no one that I let bother me that much.

Who makes you laugh?

Two New Yorkers – Jackie Mason and Woody Allen.

Your greatest fear?

If work, particularly my radio work, ended tomorrow.

If your house was on fire, what item would you rescue first?

My cardigan! Material things don't really matter to me.

Current burning ambition?

Always wanted to do a show featuring non-celebrities with talent or something to talk about. I'm not as interested in talking to celebrities.

Now ask yourself the following questions:
- Are the questions long-winded or short and snappy?
- Are the questions trivial or serious?
- Are the answers in-depth or fairly short?
- Is the language simple or complex?
- What does the photograph add to the interview?
- Who is this kind of interview aimed at?
- Why are these kind of interviews popular?

WRITING INTERVIEWS

There are many different interviews you might be asked to write, e.g. incidents in school, getting a part-time job, celebrity interviews, etc.

Always take time to brainstorm ideas about the purpose, content and format. The interview must be realistic and convincing. This means that the words used have to give a sense of the person-alities who are 'speaking'. Write the names of both the interviewer and the interviewee (in capital letters) on the left-hand side of the page to clearly distin-guish both speakers.

Answer **one** of the following questions. Each question is worth thirty marks.

1 Imagine that you are a TV news reporter interviewing the Minister for Education about the pressures of examinations on students. Write out the text of the interview.

2 Write out the interview that might take place between your school's deputy principal and a Junior Cert student who has been having discipline problems during the term.

3 One of your favourite soap stars has agreed to be interviewed for the school magazine. Write out the interview you would carry out with him/her.

FUNCTIONAL WRITING PRACTICE QUESTIONS

Allow yourself twenty to twenty-five minutes when practising any of the following questions. Plan your points and layout carefully, and remember to keep your audience in mind as you write. Each question is worth thirty marks.

1 Write an information leaflet for people who are taking up a new sport or hobby for the first time. The activity can be anything you wish. (Explain what the hobby involves, specialist clothes and equipment needed, training, costs, local clubs, etc.)

2 An RTÉ arts programme has asked you to review a new Hollywood film that is due for release this week. Write out the review that you will broadcast.

3 *People who wear fur products should be ashamed of themselves.* Write out the speech you would give your class **either** for **or** against this statement.

4 With the help of a small group of friends, you have carried out a study of sports and leisure facilities in your local area. Write up the finished report of your findings.

5 Your class has compiled a collection of interesting poems and song lyrics aimed at teenagers. Write the introduction for the book.

6 You are the editor of your school magazine. Write up the interview you have done with one of the following:
  • A well-known TV personality.
  • An overseas charity volunteer.
  • A former prisoner.
  • An Irish politician.

7 The principal of a local primary school has invited you to address parents about ways of preventing young children from being bored during the summer holidays. Write out the talk you would give.

8 Write a letter to a national newspaper expressing your views on the eating habits of modern Irish teenagers.

9 Your school will soon be host to a group of visiting Japanese students. Write a guide for the visitors, telling them a little about Irish life and how they can get the most from their visit here.

10 Compile a web page offering advice on preparing for the Junior Cert.

FUNCTIONAL WRITING UNIT ROUND-UP

- Carefully study the **task** you have been given to do.
- Keep the **audience** in mind at all times.
- Pay close attention to the **tone** of the writing.
- Whatever the type of functional writing, **always plan** it.
- Make sure to get the **layout** right.

CHECKLIST

Having worked through the Functional Writing unit, you should now feel more confident about the following:

- Knowing what sort of exam questions to expect in the Functional Writing section.
- Understanding the importance of writing for a particular purpose.
- Recognising what makes a good review.
- Understanding how to compile an effective report.
- Writing an interesting interview.
- Formal letter writing.
- Informal and official letters.
- How to write different kinds of speeches.
- Writing to advise and give instructions.
- Writing successful answers of a high standard.

UNIT 4 **Media Studies**

OVERVIEW

*The study of media texts is a key part of Junior Cert English. It includes the print media (mainly journalism from newspapers and magazines), television and radio, film, advertising, photographs, cartoons, etc. For the purposes of exam preparation, it is useful to **study as many forms of media as possible**.*

THE WORD *MEDIA* is the plural of *medium* (**a way of communicating**). We normally use the phrase 'mass media' to refer to all the main forms by which information is conveyed, thus TV and newspapers are very important media. The internet has recently become another significant medium.

The messages the media carry are a mixture of entertainment, information and sales. While most of the media are enjoyable and useful, some parts (such as the effects of television violence) are not as positive. Since the media have so much influence, it is important for us to be **media literate**. This means understanding how the media work. It's always worth knowing who owns and controls the papers we read and the TV shows we watch. If we are media literate, we will be able to appreciate, discuss and challenge the media in all their forms.

To do well in the Media Studies section of the exam, you will need to be able to **critically analyse and respond to a variety of media texts**. Over recent years, the emphasis has been on advertisements, journalism, brochures and cartoons, but there have also been general questions about the media. For example, students have been asked to discuss the effects of film cartoons and to compare national and local radio stations.

In dealing with any media text, it is important to show that you understand the following:
• The meaning of the text.
• The purpose of the text.
• The techniques used in it.
• The effectiveness of the text.

As always with texts you are studying in English, it is useful to look at **purpose, audience, technique** and **effect**. These are the most important considerations in dealing with media-based material.

NEWS
AND VIEWS

A long time ago, most news was spread slowly by travelling traders. Urgent messages were carried by messengers on horseback. Then along came printing presses and news broadsheets (early versions of modern newspapers).

Now we find out about our world through the media. However, the media don't simply present us with objective facts, as if we were seeing events ourselves. Instead, the media give us a combination of **fact, opinion, persuasive argument** and **bias**.

IT SAYS
IN THE PAPERS

These are some of the key media terms you will find useful when answering questions about the print media.

Broadsheet: A larger newspaper often referred to as a 'quality' paper, such as *The Irish Times* and *The Sunday Tribune*. Aims to inform and report more than to entertain.

Caption: Words that explain pictures or artwork.

Classified ads: Small adverts without illustrations grouped according to subject area, e.g. pets, cars, lost and found, etc.

Display ads: Large adverts, often with illustrations. They appear throughout the editorial pages.

Columns: Newspapers and magazine articles are set out in vertical sections. Columns break up a page and make it more interesting to look at. Journalists often refer to the regular article they write as their column.

Diary column: Usually a day-to-day personal column or a gossip column.

Editorial: This can refer to all non-advertising material, but it usually means an article.

Exclusive: A story carried by only one newspaper.

Headlines: Headings above news stories that provide basic information or try to grab our attention. In tabloid newspapers, dramatic headlines are often linked to pictures to make up most of the front page.

Hard news: Important news stories about national and international events, current affairs and politics. Most commonly found in the broadsheets.

Human interest story: This concentrates on tragedy, success, failure or people's emotional or private lives. A common feature of the tabloid press and sometimes called 'soft news'.

Layout: The design and look of the page.

Masthead: The newspaper's title at the top of the front page.

Pictures: Used in newspapers to back up articles and dramatise or personalise a story.

Quotations: Direct comments from someone involved in the news story. Reporters are required to be unbiased (to give a balanced account) but the people involved will often be on one side or the other.

Subheadings: Smaller headlines within the main story. They act like signposts and usually contain key words to focus the reader's attention.

Tabloid: Smaller-sized papers, such as *The Irish Star* and *The Sunday World*. Sometimes called 'the red tops', they are usually less serious and aim to entertain as well as carry news stories.

Topic sentence: Often appears at the beginning of a newspaper story. It usually tells you who, what, when and where the story happened.

PAPER ROUND

To answer questions about the print media, you should be able you understand the following:
- How to examine a newspaper article.
- Fact and opinion.
- How to compare different reports.
- How issues are presented.

The newspapers' main function is to **report** news of all kinds to the readers. This covers a wide area ranging from serious issues to unimportant ones. Most of the papers we read include the following kinds of news:
- World events and current affairs.
- Political news.
- Minor news items.
- Entertainment, e.g. TV, film, etc.
- Sports.
- Gossip.

Most newspapers also comment and make judgments on main events and give their opinions.

WHO? WHAT? WHERE? WHEN? WHY?

Good news writing is well organised. The first paragraph of a news story usually contains the most important information – the **who, what, where, when** and **why** (and sometimes **how**). It should also hook the reader into wanting more, but all the basic facts should be clear by the end of the second paragraph.

The reader may read on through the rest of the article for more information, background details, comments, opinions and reaction. Paragraphs in news stories should be short (usually no more than three sentences) and self-contained. Stories are often cut short for lack of space in newspapers, so every paragraph in an article should be carefully written to ensure that it could work as the final paragraph if necessary.

Look carefully at the article 'Salad days for winning gardener' and check if the opening paragraph gives readers enough basic information to encourage them to read on.

Salad days for winning gardener

SARAH MARRIOTT IN LONDON

A landscape designer from Dundalk was awarded a Silver Flora medal at the Chelsea Flower Show in London yesterday. Mr Paul Martin said he was 'delighted' to win a medal for his Lazy Salad Days Garden, in the Chic Garden section of the show.

The surprise of the walled garden is that it is planted with vegetables as well as flowers, grasses and an olive tree. In a 5 metre by 4.5 metre space, Mr Martin successfully creates a relaxing yet practical and contemporary outdoor living room.

Two teak sun loungers, with drink holders conveniently nearby, float above a dense carpet of twenty-five different salad stuffs and culinary herbs. Behind the loungers, which can move along a steel rail to follow the sun, is a raised bed planted in muted creams, greys and purples, including Dryas Octepetala 'Burren nymph', a rare flower discovered in the Burren in 1997 and on its first outing from Ireland.

Mr Martin sourced Irish materials: the steps and lower level are paved in a Donegal sandstone; the plants come from Flit Schram nursery in Co Kildare; the glasses were designed specially by Jerpoint in Co Kilkenny, and the pots by Christine Hughes in Dublin.

Mr Martin, who has been designing gardens for seventeen years, hopes Lazy Salad Days will inspire Irish gardeners: 'It's as trendy to grow salad and herbs as it is to cook them.' The feedback from visitors was 'massive', he said.

FROM *THE IRISH TIMES*, 21 MAY 2003

The opening paragraph sums up the story using the five Ws:

- **Who:** Paul Martin, a landscape designer from Co. Louth.
- **What:** He has won an important design award.
- **Where:** The Chelsea Flower Show, London.
- **When:** Yesterday.
- **Why:** He entered the competition.

You will notice how the story is developed through the rest of the article. Following the high impact of the first paragraph, additional information is given about the prize-winning design. We learn about the size of the garden, its trees, herbs and colours. There are details about particular plants and where they were bought. The last paragraph focuses on Mr Martin and ends with a comment from him about the reaction his new garden has received.

WRITING ABOUT A NEWSPAPER STORY

When you are studying a newspaper report you should think about the following.

Layout

- Where does the story appear on the page? (Does it seem important or is it hidden away?)
- How is the article broken up?
- Is the headline effective? (How much of the page does it take up? Does it use any language devices?)
- What use is made of pictures, captions and subheadings?

Audience

- Who is it aimed at? (Consider age, occupation, class, interests, etc.)

Language

- What kind of words are used – simple or complex?
- Check sentence length and structure.
- Is emotive language used (words that make the reader respond emotionally)?

Tone
- Is the article informative, entertaining, shocking, humorous or sad?

Bias
- Is the article balanced or does it take sides?

Personal response
- How do you respond to this kind of reporting?

Look carefully at the article 'Quake baby saved after 39 hours' and answer the questions that follow.

Quake baby saved after 39 hours
By **STEPHEN WHITE**

A TODDLER WAS PULLED ALIVE from the rubble of the Algerian earthquake yesterday – 39 hours after it struck.

Yousra Hamenniche, aged two and a half, had been buried in the remains of her gran's five storey apartment block.

One rescuer shouted: 'She's coming, she's coming,' before Yousra, dressed only in an orange T-shirt was freed. She was revived with oxygen.

Her dad Samir told the French rescue team: 'I thank everyone, you've done an incredible job.'

One ecstatic rescuer, who had worked all night to free her, replied: 'We told you we would get her out.'

Algerian state radio reported her progress: 'The life of this miraculous baby is no longer in any danger.'

Samir had been told they might have to amputate Yousra's left arm to get her out.

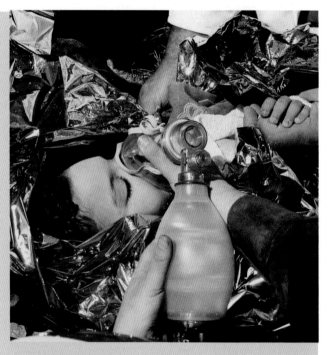

He said: 'They were going to cut her arm. I said don't, so they worked all night. They saved her.'

They drilled through the roof of the block, squashed into one storey, and cut a hole to pull her out.

Six members of his family including his wife and sister, who were having a dinner party in Boumerdes, thirty miles east of the capital Algiers, to plan a wedding, are all thought to be dead. Her rescue was the only bright interlude in a grim day for rescuers as one by one they pulled corpses from buildings.

Teams have flown in from all over Europe including Britain. It is now a race against time to find survivors. The death toll yesterday rose to 1,467 with 7,207 people injured.

Angry locals in Boumerdes, who are using sledgehammers and their bare hands to dig, complained that help had come too late.

Soccer coach Brahim Ramdani said: 'I have no family left.'

'My wife, my daughter, my granddaughter, my son and grandson are dead. I know you can't do anything about natural disasters, but I am angry nobody came to help us.'

In one building, eight members of a family – including a four-week-old baby – were killed sheltering in a cellar.

Reghaia has also been badly hit by Wednesday's quake – the worst in Algeria for twenty years. A ten-storey block crumpled and 250 bodies have been found. Hospitals are overflowing and 10,000 survivors are homeless. People are sleeping in their cars, and in the open for fear of another tremor.

FROM *THE DAILY MIRROR*, 24 MAY 2003

Answer **all** of the following questions. Each question is worth ten marks.

1 What is the effect of the headline that accompanies this article?

2 How would you describe the information presented in the main story? Is it completely factual? Give reasons for your answer.

3 What does the photograph add to the overall effect of the article?

4 How does the reporter capture the sense of alarm caused by the earthquake? Use close reference from the story to support your answer.

SUGGESTIONS FOR ANSWERING

As always, be sensible in using the time available for answering the Media Studies section. For example, if you have thirty minutes to do four 10-mark questions, you would spend roughly five or six minutes studying the text, followed by six minutes writing each of the four answers to the questions.

Remember that questions carrying equal marks should always be given equal amounts of time. Address all questions directly and use relevant reference to support your points.

The suggested answers below would achieve a grade A standard. As you read them, think about what points are being made and the use of evidence.

Q1 This is a dramatic headline that shows the human tragedy caused by the Algerian earthquake. The leading word quake *immediately tells readers what has happened and also explains the picture used in the report. The shorter version of the word* earthquake *is used to add emphasis and drama.*

However, the full headline highlights a positive moment when a young child is found alive. This will help balance some of the sadness felt by the reader, especially as the baby survived for thirty-nine hours. The headline is typical of tabloid news coverage of human interest stories and will encourage readers to continue reading the full report to learn more about this young child's rescue.

Q2 The information in the article is mainly factual, explaining how the child was rescued as well as giving other details about the effects of the earthquake. These include the latest figures for the dead and injured. Although the information, e.g. in the last paragraph, tends to be of a general nature, it still rings true and gives a clear overview of the devastation.

There are also some comments that could be taken as opinion. For example, the report about the child's relatives has not been backed up by facts. However, the fact that much of the story includes comments from named survivors encourages readers to believe that this is an accurate news report.

Q3 The photograph graphically illustrates a close-up view of the little girl being carried from the rubble. The emotive phrase 'pulled alive' in the caption suggests the effort and success of the rescue workers. The child's small hands show her dependence on the adult hands around her.

Q4 The full report – including the picture – about the earthquake and its devastating effects gives readers a vivid impression of the fear and confusion throughout Algeria. The first part of the report focuses on the frantic efforts to save the child. The excited shouts of the rescuer ('She's coming') emphasise the tension at the rescue scene.

Later in the article, angry locals in Boumerdes voice their frustration that nobody came to help them. The last sentence leaves readers with a sense of growing chaos as hospitals struggle to cope. Even as people start to understand the full scale of the tragedy, people live in 'fear of another tremor'.

PUNS: WORDPLAY UPON EVERY SUBJECT

Tabloid newspapers aim to entertain as well as inform. They tend to use emotive language and sensationalise stories.

Headlines in tabloid papers are often humorous and puns are frequently used. For example, a story about a bakery workers' strike might be given the headline 'Bakers Born and Bread'.

Read the newspaper article 'Artist milks public art exhibition for all it's worth' and then answer the questions that follow.

Artist milks public art exhibition for all it's worth

By **SIOBHÁN GAFFNEY**

Have you heard the moos? One hundred and fifty cows are to be let loose on the streets of Dublin next week.

And the most prized asset of this herd is a creature covered with more than €17,000 in cash. No bull.

CowParade is coming to Ireland and Mool-ah, the work of Donegal artist Kevin Sharkey, will take pride of place in the capital's financial district. Since it began in Zurich in 1998, the exhibition of fibreglass cows has travelled the world in celebration of public art.

Hundreds of artists including Ireland's John Rocha – who has designed a cow made out of Waterford Crystal – have put their stamp on Ireland's life-sized cows. But Mr Sharkey's entry surely has to be the most bizarre (and expensive) yet. He said: 'I came up with the idea of covering it with money. So after I worked out how much it would cost to cover it in notes, all €17,555 worth, I approached a backer who surprisingly went for it.'

Mr Sharkey took three weeks to complete Mool-ah including applying five coats of lacquer so no one could make off with the cash. It should create something of a stir when it goes on display – he hopes – in the Irish Financial Services Centre. 'She'll be in fine company there with all the money. Mool-ah needs to be watched around the clock, she's an expensive cow.'

CowParade organiser for Ireland Peter Hanig said: 'It's not meant to be high art – it's first and foremost a public art exhibit that is accessible to everyone.' The cows come in three different poses – standing, grazing and reclining and weigh approximately 100 lbs each. When installed, they will be attached to 500 lb concrete bases for security.

FROM *IRELAND ON SUNDAY*, 1 JUNE 2003

Answer the following **four** questions. Each question is worth ten marks.

1 Comment on the headline used with this story. What impact does it make?

2 What is the effect of the photograph that accompanies this report? What does it add to the story? Briefly explain your answer.

3 What other evidence (apart from the headline) shows that this story appeared in a popular tabloid newspaper?

4 *The tabloids are good fun, but they aren't really newspapers.* What is your opinion of tabloid newspapers?

✍ SAMPLE ANSWER (Q4)

In my opinion, only very snobbish people look down on the tabloid papers as if they are totally inferior. I think you need a balance. It's the same with music or anything else. Some people like opera and others don't. As a young person, I like reggae music and I sometimes read tabloids like The Star *for gossip and sport. There is news in that paper as well. It's not just totally entertainment.*

I think the sports reports are up to date, especially on football. The big papers are too serious and too expensive for a lot of people. If you are on a bus, you would feel totally stupid trying to fold a bigger-sized paper into somebody's face. That's if

you are lucky enough to ever get a seat in the first place. That's why I think tabloid papers are proper newspapers and are popular with readers.

This answer contains a number of strong points in support of the tabloid press. There is an attempt to support the main point in the opening paragraph and some practical advantages of tabloid papers are outlined in the second paragraph. Although the adverb *totally* is overused, most of the writing is lively and the answer deserves a basic B grade.

Look closely at the following newspaper article and then answer the questions that follow.

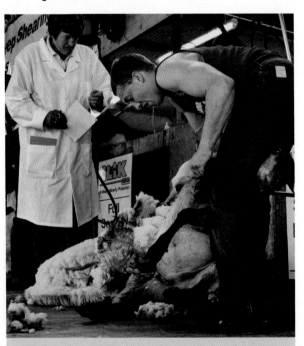

Alister Crawford of Co. Tyrone competing in the junior finals at the National Sheep Shearing Championships in Monamolin, Gorey, Co. Wexford

Close shaves as shearers go into action

SEÁN MacCONNELL, GOREY

'Wolf Pups for Sale' said the sign outside a house north of Gorey yesterday within miles of where the National Sheep Shearing Championships were being held.

Perhaps they were selling sheep in wolf's clothing but it was an odd sign, nevertheless, bearing in mind that the last Irish wolf was destroyed in Ireland in 1850.

From a Wexford hurling point of view there was a serious raider on their territory yesterday, with Kilkenny hurling legend DJ Carey, officially opening the event which was held at the Buffer's Alley GAA Club in Monamolin, Co Wexford.

The chairman of the organising committee, Michael Murphy, said DJ may well be a saint in Kilkenny but as far as the Wexford people are concerned, he is a devil.

Despite that, he was given a tremendous welcome by the thousands of people who came to support the event which is the third largest specialist event of its kind in the country.

Inspectors from the Health and Safety Authority made a lightning inspection of the site to ensure everyone's safety.

There were no signs of any panic at the GAA grounds where 1,500 sheep had been assembled to be stripped of their fleeces in the dozens of competitions to find the best sheep shearers in the country.

With yesterday's unseasonal weather it was easy to be sorry for the poor sheep losing their coats to be sent off pink and exposed into the sea fog which hung over the site.

Few would believe that it was June 1st, only a score of days from Midsummer's Day, not that that detracted from the myriad of events taking place on the site.

The event had shades of the National Ploughing Championships with its muddy carparks which had been churned up by the cars and four wheel drives.

The dozens of marquees, tents and caravans which doubled for stands, were packed with people sheltering from the rain which was relentless.

With the heavy smell of chips and crushed grass were it not for the rain, it might even have been summer.

But shearing is a serious business and shearing faster than anyone else can bring its rewards.

On Saturday night, before a capacity crowd, New Zealander, James Fagan, sheared a sheep in 19.6 seconds before a crowd which included Evelyn Quigley from Rathmore, Co Wexford.

The event has its serious side too. Sheep farmers have to pay €2 a head to have their sheep shorn to prevent them getting pneumonia.

For the last number of years there has been no real return from wool.

However, there was some good news yesterday at the site where farmers were talking about better returns as wool is now being used in the construction industry as insulation and in bedding.

While the organisers were a little bit disappointed at attendances at this, the 50th anniversary of the event, there was a certain satisfaction that it will continue to hold its place in the annual calendar of farming events.

FROM *THE IRISH TIMES*, 2 JUNE 2003

Answer the following **four** questions. Each question is worth ten marks.

1 What is the main purpose of this story? Is it to inform, entertain or both? Give reasons for your answer.
2 How important is the picture to the story? Would the story have been just as interesting without it?
3 What was the atmosphere like at the Sheep Shearing Championships? Which words and phrases are most effective in capturing the atmosphere?
4 Would you be interested in reading this story? Who do you think the story is aimed at?

 SAMPLE ANSWERS (Q4)

(i) Farmers from down the country would read it. Sheep is their thing and it's a cruel business to be at. It says the farmers enjoyed themselves. I wouldn't read this normally. I wouldn't even go to sheep shearing. I'm not a vegetarian but I object. It says the sheep were all stripped of their fleeces in the competitions. It says they were cold in the wet weather. This just annoys me even more. Young people from the towns would just be bored.

(ii) I would not usually read a story like this because I have no real interest in farming and I don't live in the country. However, the headline and the photo got my attention. It's a fairly short report, so I would probably have a quick look at it anyway. As it turns out, the report is interesting enough in that it explains how people in the farming community have special events that are related to their work and that are probably important for their community spirit.

I imagine the story is aimed mainly at the farming community, which would include many Irish people in what are called market towns, such as Mullingar and Gorey. Country people of all ages would probably be interested. Even the kids would like to see the photo of the sheep since young children always seem to enjoy anything to do with animals. I imagine that city folk would be less interested although everyone likes to see how the other half live and townspeople might just have a quick glance at this report out of curiosity and to see what the farmers are getting up to now.

Apart from the first and final sentences, this answer tends to miss the point of the question. The expression could also be greatly improved, e.g. the phrase 'it says' is overused. Grade D.

This is a very good answer that directly addresses both parts of the question. The use of long sentences means that the expression isn't varied or lively, but points are clearly thought out and very well developed. Grade A standard.

SERIOUSLY FUNNY

The two examples of journalism that follow both deal with the same basic story but take contrasting approaches. The first article, from *The Irish Times,* is a **factual report**. The second piece comes from the satirical magazine *The Phoenix* and doesn't take the story at all seriously. This **parody** mimics the original news story in a humorous way. Obviously, the two pieces differ greatly in their purpose, technique and effect.

Carefully read through both pieces and then answer the questions that follow.

O'Connor quits music business

Singer Sinéad O'Connor is retiring from the music business at the age of thirty-six, she has announced on her website, saying she has grown tired of being famous.

Addressing her fans, the singer who once gained notoriety by tearing up a picture of the Pope on live television says she plans to retire in July. A spokeswoman for O'Connor's label Vanguard Records said the statement on the website was authentic, but did not give further details.

O'Connor recently called off a number of concerts in Europe with the British group Massive Attack, citing health problems.

The last recordings she will make will be a track for American country star Dolly Parton's tribute album and a track for accordionist Sharon Shannon's forthcoming album.

She will also release a DVD of a live show and documentary in July entitled *Goodnight, thank you. You've been a lovely audience.*

'I would request that as of July, since I seek no longer to be a famous person and instead I wish to live a "normal" life, could people please afford me my privacy,' she says.

This means, she adds, that she does not want her name or anyone connected with her 'exploited' by newspapers.

'I also mean that [with love] I want to be like any other person in the street and not have people say "there is Sinéad O'Connor" as I am a very shy person, believe it or not,' she writes on the website.

She advises anyone who loves a 'so-called celebrity' to ignore them in the street, not to stare at them, take their picture or bang on restaurant windows if they are inside.

O'Connor's biggest hit was a haunting version of the Prince song *Nothing Compares to U.*

Frank Sinatra threatened to 'kick her ass' after she would not appear at a show in New Jersey if the US national anthem was played prior to her performance.

In 1999, rebel bishop Pat Buckley ordained her in Lourdes as a priest in the controversial Latin Tridentine Church. Subsequently O'Connor, baptised a Catholic, styled herself as 'Mother Bernadette Mary'. – (APP)

FROM *THE IRISH TIMES,* 26 APRIL 2003

SINEAD QUITS SHOCK

'I cannot go on combining the two roles of being a famous artist and a leading campaigner for self-publicity at the same time.' So said Sinead O'Connor as she announced on her website that she is to retire from the music business at the end of the month.

Addressing her fans, O'Connor also revealed that she intends to devote her life from now on to developing her various artistic talents and making controversial, guest appearances on television chat-shows.

Since the shock announcement, tributes to the singer have been pouring in from all over the country. Yesterday, in silent tribute, members of the public queued outside the RTÉ studios to sign the Book of Relief that O'Connor would never be heard of again.

'We shall never see her like again,' said the former *Late Late Show* presenter, Grey Byrne, who is well known himself for having retired completely from our TV screens. (That's enough Retirement – Ed)

SINEAD'S RETIREMENT PLANS
(IN FULL):

June: The Farewell tour 2003
July: RTÉ shows *Nothing Compares 2 Me* documentary
August: *Farewell Double-Album* released
September: Autobiography *My Name is Sinead* on sale
October: *Earth Woman Celtic Cook Book* in shops
November: *Sinead Live DVD*
December: *The O'Connor Christmas Carol Collection* CD
January: *All-time Best of Sinead* (boxed set)
February: The Comeback tour 2004

FROM *THE PHOENIX*, 9 MAY 2003

Answer **all** of the following questions. Each question is worth ten marks.
1 What evidence can you find to show that *The Irish Times* article treats Sinead O'Connor's retirement seriously?
2 In your opinion, is *The Phoenix* story just meant to be funny or is it also making a serious point?
3 A photograph of the singer is included in the satirical article. How does this affect your understanding of the story?
4 Which of the two versions do you prefer? Give reasons for your answer.

This is a much funnier story than the real news one. Most of what is said about Sinead in it is making fun of her and not taking her at her word because she has such a history of doing ridiculous kind of things just to get any sort of publicity to sell her records. I think the writer is being serious in one way by telling us that this is Sinead's latest publicity stunt. She probably won't really retire. As it says, she will be on television all the time talking about not wanting to be famous. The long list of tours and albums at the end also show her up as someone who really loves to have attention.

Although the second sentence rambles on, the answer improves and makes a solid point about this 'latest publicity stunt'. The last sentence offers strong support and the overall length of the answer is quite sufficient for a ten-mark question. A basic B grade.

READING MEDIA TEXTS

Carefully study this radio web page to see how it works as a media text.

Who? This page is aimed at young people interested in entertainment, particularly pop music and films.

Why? It has been compiled to provide information and to advertise 2FM.

How? The text contains up-to-date entertainment details and web links. The

presentation is colourful and attractive.

What? The main idea is that 2FM provides lively entertainment programmes.

Content: There is a balance of fact (programme times) and opinion (claims made for the programmes). Brief news headlines and various web links are also included.

Language: The language is straight-forward and easy to understand, and the tone is friendly and informal throughout.

Layout: A variety of layout features are used. **Pictures** of presenters and celebrities break up the text and give a modern look to the page. **Headings** are used to attract attention to each of the topics. Key words are written in **bold** type and the text is divided into small **sections**, making it quick and easy to read.

MAGAZINES

In a magazine, the use of headings, lists, frames, illustrations, different font styles and sizes will often be more emphasised and eye catching than in, for example, an information leaflet. As a commercial publication, a magazine is out to catch the interest (and the money) of the readers. To get our attention it will aim for **maximum visual effect and the most intriguing headlines**.

Most magazines contain feature articles, which are more like essays than news reports. They draw the reader in from the first line by setting a particular scene or using anecdotes (short personal stories), questions, dramatic descriptions, etc. The focus is very often on human interest.

Tabloid newspapers increasingly resemble magazines. Unlike the broad-sheets, which contain 'serious news', **most tabloids exhibit the qualities found in magazines**, especially photo-graphs, dramatic typeface, short articles, little in-depth analysis and an overall emphasis on entertainment. Look at the kinds of topics and the style used to write features in popular magazines. Are the articles usually serious? Informative? Chatty? Humorous? Sensational? Dramatic?

Of course, there are many exceptions to this. **Special interest magazines**, such as sports, music or current affairs, can go into great detail. The same is true of trade and professional journals, such as medical and business magazines. Always keep the **target audience** in mind when discussing magazines. While you may find a particular magazine boring or trivial, it will probably be the exact opposite to its regular readers.

SPORTS MAGAZINES

Carefully examine the contents page of *Sports Digest* and then answer the questions that follow.

Answer **two** of the following questions. Each question is worth twenty marks.

1 Do you think the contents page of this sports magazine is well presented? Give reasons for your answer.

2 Write **four** new sports items of your own to add to the list on the contents page. These can be about any sport (GAA, soccer, tennis, camogie, etc.). Give each of the new articles a headline and add a summary (twenty to thirty words).

3 In your opinion, do sports magazines serve a useful purpose? Give reasons for your answer.

SPORTS
DIGEST
Volume 3 Issue 2 May, 2003
€2.95 (inc VAT)

inside this issue

Soccer

6 TAKING KERR OF BUSINESS

A difficult six months await Brian Kerr as Ireland continue their quest to reach the Euro 2004 finals in Portugal, writes Paul Hyland of the Evening Herald.

18 COUNT DOWN TO GLORY

This is the time of the season where nerve and verve are the most important commodities in the Premiership, writes Bob McKenzie.

42 REACHING THE GRASSROOTS OF IRISH SOCCER

The Statoil sponsored FAI Junior Cup continues to play a significant role in the lifeblood of soccer throughout the country. Paul Keane reports.

Rugby

12 GRAND SLAM DESPAIR

The 2003 Six Nations Championship ended in despair and disappointment for Ireland at the Grand Slam hurdle, writes George Hook of The Sunday Independent.

Gaelic Games

24 A WONDERFUL SPECTACLE OF GAELIC GAMES

Victories for Nemo Rangers and Birr concluded another exciting AIB Club Championship season, writes Jackie Cahill of the Irish Mirror.

AIB GAA CLUB CHAMPIONSHIPS
ONE LIFE **ONE CLUB**

Motor Sports

28 A NEW ERA DAWNS IN FORMULA ONE

There is a new broom sweeping through F1 racing that is cleaning away the detritus of years of complacency. Declan Quigley of the Irish Independent reports.

Basketball

34 OUT OF THIS WORLD

After a number of traumas that would have beaten a lesser team, Neptune emerged as ESB National Champions. Aidan O'Hara reports.

irishbasketball

Golf

38 IN SEARCH OF TIGER

Charlie Mulqueen of the Irish Examiner explores the new Tom Callahan offering, which discovers the Real Tiger Woods.

Texaco Awards

44 45TH TEXACO SPORTSTARS

Sports Digest salutes the winners of the 45th Texaco Sportstars Awards which took place in Dublin earlier this year.

Regulars

48 GREAT MOMENTS IN SPORT

The Paddy Mullins trained Dawn Run comes from behind to claim the 1986 Cheltenham Gold Cup with Jonjo O'Neill.

50 SPORTING GREATS OF THE 20TH CENTURY

Jackie Cahill acknowledges the contribution of Brendan Mullin to Irish Rugby in a career than spanned between 1984-1995.

49 SUBSCRIBER OFFER

Subscribe to Sports Digest and have Ireland's No. 1 Sporting Magazine delivered to your doorstep each issue.

14 Golf
ANNIKA SHOWS THE MEN
Top Swedish golfer Annika Sorenstam was back at Fort Worth in Texas last week where she showed that she could still compete with the world's top golfers. Aoife Henry reports.

25 Soccer
DUFF'S DELIGHT
In an exclusive interview, soccer superstar Damien Duff talks frankly to Don Thornton about the current Irish team and the future of Irish football.

36 Cycling
WHEELS OF MISFORTUNE
This year's Tour of Belgium ended in confusion after several leading competitors were disqualified after Stage Two. Jim Leahy reports on this troubled sport.

47 Motor Sports
SCHUMACHER KEEPS COOL
Motor ace Michael Schumacher notches up yet another Formula One victory after remaining ice-cool during a pit stop fire at last weekend's Austrian Grand Prix, writes Ben Brady.

Although this might seem like an undemanding question, it is quite challenging to create four convincing items to add to the contents page. This answer really succeeds in keeping within the guidelines of the given task. The four extra news stories cover an interesting variety of sports and fit in very well with the style of the existing contents list. Imaginative headlines are given (especially the third item) in each case. The answer achieves an overall Grade A standard.

TEENAGE MAGAZINES

Most popular teenage magazines include articles on music, fashion, celebrity gossip, horoscopes, advice columns, health issues, reviews and much more. They also tend to be very lively, varied and colourful.

Carefully read this magazine review page and then answer all the questions that follow.

Reviews music

Altogether now:
"Row, row, row
your boat..."

Singles Reviewed by Dom Phillips

Rob regretted
letting Laurence
Llewelyn-Bowen
decorate his home

The fame game

Robbie Williams
Something Beautiful (CHRYSALIS)
Looks like Robbie's got his sense of humour
back. The video to this third hit from the six
times platinum-selling *Escapology* cunningly
parodies *Pop Idol* as legions of wannabes audition to lip-sync
for Robbie in the vid for this single. Filmed at London's Excel
Centre as a fake TV show called *Manufactured Miracles*, the
"auditions" were won by a guy called Peter, who performs in
the video. Got that? Now to the song, which is simply infectious
– a soulful rock number that fires brass lines and Robbie's Elton
John-style choruses over an incessant piano line. ★ ★ ★ ★ ★

A kind of magic

The Coral
Magic And Medicine (DELTASONIC)

In a nutshell: This
critically adored,
multi-faceted Scouse
combo are adept at
incorporating
everything from
bluegrass to stinging blues into their
timeless rock 'n' roll shuffle. And their
second album surpasses even their
Mercury-nominated debut.
What's it like? *Magic And Medicine*
hones their jingle-jangle sound to a taut,
tinny perfection. *Bill McCai* is a bluesy
rocker that tells the tale of a balding
salesman harking back to his youth.

Liezah is a sparkling country love song.
Eskimo Lament swings from sombre,
finger-pickin' guitars to a joyous
Dixieland brass band. *All Of Our Love*
toys with atmospheric blues moods.
And *Confessions Of A.D.D.D.* wraps
things up with a psychedelic Scouse wig-
out, dripping in 60s-style guitar solos.
How many good tracks? Eleven, out
of 12.
Best track: Summery current hit *Pass It
On* is one of this year's best records – but
the rest of the album stands up to it.
Worst track: *Milkwood Blues* drags on.
Verdict: The Coral's deft use of old-time
country flavours gives their indie rock
a special shine. ★ ★ ★ ★ ★ DOM PHILLIPS

Longview
Mercury (14TH FLOOR)

In a nutshell: They
might have one of
the most boring
names in indie-dom,
but scruffily cute
Manchester
quartet Longview's music is far
from nondescript. Highly hummable,
superbly summery single *Further* is
hardly off the radio and rightly so,
as it's one of the tunes of the year
so far. Can they keep up the standard
on their debut album?
What's it like? If you like Doves, Travis
or Coldplay, chances are you'll love this.

Like those bands, Longview deal in
grown-up guitar music with throbbing
drums, tinkly pianos and sensitive-boy-
in-sixth-form lyrics. The album's split
pretty evenly between soppy ballads and
rockier numbers, all lovely enough to
suggest Longview might be here to stay.
How many good tracks? Nine, out
of 12.
Best track: The fabulous *Further* is hard
to beat, but *Still*, *Electricity* and *Can't
Explain* come pretty damn close.
Worst track: There's no total duds
but the album does sag slightly in the
middle, notably with *Nowhere*.
Verdict: Windows down. Stereo up.
Enjoy. ★ ★ ★ ★ MICHAEL HOGAN

Lumidee
Never Leave You (Uh-
Oooh) (UNIVERSAL ISLAND)

One of
this year's
weirdest,
yet most
hypnotic hits
is this New York grass-roots
sensation for 19-year-old
Harlem singer Lumidee.
Never Leave You... scatters
an infectious soul vocal over
the barest Caribbean rhythm
– the result is a rousing
reggae/R&B fusion. ★ ★ ★ ★ ★

Blu Cantrell
featuring Sean Paul
Breathe (ARISTA/BMG)

Blu had a
huge R&B hit
with *Hit 'Em
Up Style
(Oops)* in
2001. For this smash from
second album *Bittersweet*,
her street-soul vocals do
battle with Jamaican toaster
Sean over a snaking reggae-
cum-hip-hop rhythm while
dramatic chords explode
like depth charges. ★ ★ ★ ★

Lisa Maffia
In Love (INDEPENDIENTE)

Can the
second solo
single from
So Solid
Crew's first
lady Lisa match the Number
Two success of her debut *All
Over*? *In Love* is a summery
R&B love song that mellows
out So Solid's infectious
rowdiness with Spanish
guitars, stuttering beats,
electronic birdsong and –
crikey – even harps. ★ ★ ★

Kosheen
All In My Head
(MOKSHA/BMG)

Kosheen
have
ditched
the drum
'n' bass
flavours that defined hits like
Hide U for their second album
Kokopelli (out 11 August). This
first single is a high-energy
rock number with swathes of
guitar – but the soaring, folksy
vocals of Sian Evans are as
potent as ever. ★ ★ ★ ★

WOOLWORTHS

Hurry, until 3 Aug our "Offer of the Week" CD is Stereophonics – You Gotta Go There To Come Back for £9.99

Answer **two** of the following questions. Each question is worth twenty marks.

1 Do you like the layout and presentation of this page? Give reasons for your answer.

2 Write **two** new review items of your own in an appropriate style for a teenage magazine that you read. Each review should be sixty to seventy words long and can be about whatever you wish, such as films, CDs, books, soap operas, videos, concerts, etc.

3 Teenage magazines are sometimes criticised for being shallow and superficial in dealing with important issues. Do you think this is a fair criticism? Give reasons for your answer.

 SAMPLE ANSWERS (Q3)

(i) I do not agree with this question at all. Teenagers have a right to the things they like reading, and their teenage magazines like Bliss *and* Sugar *are what they're interested in, such as relationships and the latest charts. The teenage magazines my friends and I read every week are not meant for the old population who read old-fashioned adult magazines which are meant for their older age group but not for young people.*

I don't care what they read, so they should not be down on us and our magazines. Which they don't pay for because we do so out of our own money that we earn ourselves. Their entertainment is what suits them, like books about cooking and cars.

No one my age would want to go near those magazines for obvious reasons. As far as I am concerned, the teenagers can't win with them because they forget that they were young at one time as well and they don't understand that everything's changed and become more modern, just like the mags we read. Our interests suit us because it's entertainment, such as pop music, gigs, films and clothes. We will be old soon enough and when we are older, we will be reading different kinds of magazines.

The answer attempts to defend teenage magazines in a general way and reflects a clear point of view. However, it does not address the central criticism of the way popular magazines treat important subjects. The expression is awkward throughout and the long, rambling sentences reflect the lack of control. Grade D.

(ii) Some teenage magazines are interesting and entertaining, others are not. It's not right to group them all together. To a more mature teenager doing the Leaving Cert, a magazine aimed at First Years is going to seem silly. Many of these young teen magazines are limited to pop music, posters and famous faces from television. The kids who

buy these are only interested in the charts. Pop music is an important issue for this age group. We all went through it and we move on. So, in one way, it is true to say that there are no serious issues in some teen magazines.

Stereotyping is also a problem in the magazines girls read. There are loads of romantic stories with girls being all dreamy as if their whole lives depended on the latest boy in town. It's almost the same with the way teenage boys are presented. My objection to these magazines is that they are not realistic. Most of the pictures show good-looking 'perfect' types. Girls are beautiful but empty headed. Boys are only involved in sports or forming a band. We all know this isn't the way life really is.

I see a comparison with American TV shows where problems are solved in a few minutes and everybody hugs everybody else. The problem is that a lot of teenagers don't want serious discussions that go on too long. Teenage magazines are similar. They are full of little bits of information and summaries. I think this is a fair point, but it's just the way modern teenagers are.

This is a thoughtful response that makes a number of interesting points directly related to the question. The first two paragraphs are particularly effective and well supported. The final idea (comparing magazines to television) is less successfully developed, but it is still a valid point. A good grade A standard.

READING ADVERTISEMENTS

Advertisements are mostly intended to **persuade** us to buy something, do something or change our opinion about something.

When discussing advertisements, keep these basic questions in mind:

- **Who** is this advertisement aimed at?
- **Why** has it been written?
- **What** is the main message?
- **How** is that message put across?

Who? This advert is aimed at anyone who uses cosmetics, animal lovers and young people who may want to protest about vivisection and cruelty to animals.

Why? It has been written to encourage people to become more aware of animal cruelty and to learn more about BUAV (British Union for the Abolition of Vivisection).

What? The main idea is that animals are suffering and dying due to cosmetic testing.

How? The language is straightforward and both slogans are instructive in tone. The picture of the rabbit and some parts of the text, e.g. 'horrific cosmetics tests', are emotive.

Keep the following in mind when studying advertisements:

- Who is the advert aimed at? Think about the **target audience** (age, sex, class, lifestyle, level of education, etc.). How do you know who the audience is?
- What is the main idea or **message**? What is being promised?
- How is that message put across? What is the main selling **technique**? Advertisers try everything (flattery, sex appeal, positive images, etc.).
- Who or what is in the ad? **How are they presented**? Are they ordinary, perfect, comic, happy, etc.?
- What do the **objects in the background** of the ad suggest about the product?
- What **kind of language** is being used? Is it exaggerated, seductive, exciting? Are certain power words used?

- Were **graphics** used? Any diagrams, maps, charts, graphs or drawings shouldn't just look good and add variety. They ought to complement the written text by making the advertisement more effective and complete.
- The **use of colour** can reinforce messages and feelings. Red is warm and passionate as well as the colour of danger. Blue is colder but can suggest freshness. There is usually a good reason why advertisers choose particular colours.
- **Are you convinced?** Compare the actual function of the product being advertised to the promises that the ad is making for the product. Is there a gap?
- Finally, and most importantly, **is the ad effective?** Look at its overall strengths and weaknesses.

The Dulux paint advertisement pictured here represents an interesting approach to advertising. Carefully study the advert and then answer the questions that follow.

Answer **two** of the three questions that follow. Each question is worth twenty marks.

1 What is unusual and interesting about this advert?

2 Do you think it is an effective advertisement? Give reasons for your answer.

3 From your study of advertising, choose one advert which made an impression on you. Say what the ad was for and explain why you thought it was particularly good.

I found this advertisement interesting because it tells a story, unlike most ads which are just giving the name of whatever is being sold and don't really stand out that they are remembered later on after the ad is forgotten. Most types of paint are alike, so an unusual ad will be more memorable to the customer.

This Dulux Once ad reminds me of a TV ad for coffee I watched where two people are neighbours in an apartment block and they get to know each other from borrowing coffee. There were a series of these ads and the couple gradually got attracted to each other and it's a bit like a soap opera story. This is the first time I've seen this used in a magazine and I like it because it's unusual.

People enjoy love stories and there is also a very modern setting or atmosphere to this Dulux ad. We're all in the EU now and we know some French, so we can get what they're saying. The couple are attractive and customers and target audiences like to imagine a perfect world with attractive people. Maybe women will think that if they ask a painter to decorate their house, this will also happen to them.

I get the impression this will also continue. The handsome Dulux guy will return and they may end up falling in love. There's not very much about the paint in the ad. They don't say it's long lasting or good value. The whole emphasis is on the story.

Also I noticed that the opening pictures were dark while the ending is all soft lilac. Maybe this means that the Dulux painter really brightened up her day.

This is a lively response that shows a clear understanding of the narrative technique used in the advertisement. There are several insightful points made throughout the answer, and the length is sufficient for a twenty-mark question. Had the expression been less awkward, e.g. the clumsy opening sentence, a higher grade would have been awarded. Overall, this is a focused and thoughtful answer that would receive a grade B.

Both advertisements pictured opposite are aimed at the parents of young children. Carefully study the two advertisements and then answer the questions that follow.

Answer **all** of the following questions. Each question is worth ten marks.

1 Do you think the Executive Nannies ad is persuasive? Give reasons for your answer.

2 Discuss the impact of the photograph in the VHI advertisement.

3 Which of the two advertisements do you prefer? Why?

4 From your study of advertising, do you think advertisements should be taken seriously? Give reasons for your answer.

(i) Most of the ads are a joke, a total act. The funny thing is that teenagers still buy designer labels. I think you should be yourself. People shouldn't follow ads to buy designer labels. My friends have a good laugh at the ads. The funny thing is a lot of them then go out and buy the latest mobiles. They also buy other gear that is advertised by certain famous footballers. Nobody wants to stand out. So even though we all know the ads are just a joke and a complete act, we still fall for them every time. Ads have a strong effect on us and they are taken seriously, even though we know they're a total joke and not always telling the truth.

The answer includes one strong point summed up in the final sentence. The power of advertising is fairly well illus-trated, but the expression is a little disjointed and there is some repetition of phrases, such as 'the funny thing' and 'a total joke'. A basic grade C.

(ii) I would think that the majority of people do not take advertisements very seriously. The TV adverts are sometimes entertaining, but I would be very reluctant to believe all the claims they make. For example, ugly-looking men only have to use a particular brand of deodorant and suddenly they're surrounded by beautiful girls. It's the same with those energy drinks. One sip and you're Lara Croft.

I don't really object to these unrealistic adverts, but I could never take them seriously. Most of us realise that exaggeration plays a big part in advertising. Some of these adverts are based on a fantasy world. We are told that if we bite into a chocolate bar, we will experience an escape to a tropical island. Everyone likes to escape now and again – even if we let such adverts fool us that we're not destroying our teeth and putting on weight by pigging out on sugar.

A fluent and interesting personal response that ends with a touch of humour. The comments are intelligent and incisive, and illustrations are effec-tively used to support the main point that advertisers sell dreams. The vocabulary and range of sentence structures add to the high grade A standard.

POSTER CAMPAIGN

Posters are used to advertise everything from soft drinks and school events to new movies and pop concerts, as well as all your 'favourite politicians' at election times. Posters also form part of government health and safety campaigns to encourage people to be more responsible drivers or to have healthier lifestyles. As with all forms of advertising, the language, layout and pictures used in a poster are intended to persuade you or appeal to your emotions.

The poster pictured here is advertising a computer game based on *The Thing*, a famous horror film directed by John Carpenter. Closely study the poster and then answer the questions that follow.

Answer **all** of the following questions. Each question is worth ten marks.

1 Who is the target audience for this game?

2 Is the design and layout of the poster effective? What are its main strengths?

3 What impression of the game is given by the six magazine reviews?

4 If you were asked to redesign and improve this poster, what changes would you make?

SAMPLE ANSWER (Q3)

All these reviews emphasise the horror and excitement of The Thing. *The language is very exaggerated and also very emotive. Words like 'repulsed' and 'paranoia' would appeal to young people who love scary computer games. Also, the questions are very effective in one review. The words 'Terror? Tension? Paranoia?' are very dramatic.*

Also, the repetition of 'Be excited. Be very excited.' adds to the drama. The fact that there are six different reviews printed is very persuasive. They all praise the same game and say how thrilling it is in terms of its graphics and action, and this is also a good way of convincing young people to buy it.

The first paragraph gets straight to the point, mentioning the use of emotive language and questions as effective advertising techniques. Good use is made of direct quotes from the reviews. Although overuse of the word *also* is a distraction, there is a solid grade B standard overall.

Carefully examine the two Amnesty International advertisements and answer **all** of the following questions.

1 What are the main differences that you notice between the two advertisements? (15)

2 In your opinion, which of the two advertisements would appeal more to young people? Give reasons for your answer. (15)

3 Some advertisements use shock tactics, such as pictures of starving people or torture victims, to get our attention. What do you think of such advertisements? (10)

SAMPLE ANSWER (Q3)

Some of the Third World charity ads are definitely shocking. I think it's justified because there's not much point in hiding the facts. I have often opened a magazine and could hardly believe the photographs of old people in rags and young babies with swollen stomachs. In my opinion, we need to be shamed by groups like Concern and Amnesty into doing whatever little we can for people who are worse off than ourselves. I don't think it's all about money, either, because the older I get, the more I

This is a very solid personal response to the question and includes a number of incisive points. The focus throughout is on arguments supporting the use of shock tactics in charity adverts. There is good control of language and some attempt at varying sentence length. Grade A.

see that governments have a lot of power to improve conditions.

So, if charities want to get governments, including the Irish government, involved, they are justified in using shock tactics to raise our awareness. Some of the pictures of AIDS victims are also worth showing as a warning to everyone else. People have to learn not to take risks with their health. Charities are only reflecting the real world. We may not like what we see in photographs of tortured people in Africa, but if that is the reality, then we should be told the truth.

what's your EXCUSE?

In other parts of the world joining Amnesty International can be a dangerous business.

All of the above are real excuses for not joining Amnesty International. There are over 111 countries world-wide where torture and oppression are commonplace. In many of these countries any man, woman or child can be imprisoned, tortured or even murdered just for standing up for their basic human rights. And yet hundreds of people continue to do just that.

In this country, of course, you face no danger whatsoever. Here you are free to show you care about human rights. You are free to join Amnesty International – the world's largest voluntary human rights organisation. All you have to do is fill in the attached form. And that's it. With this one simple step, you can help our work to end human rights violations everywhere. Without any risk to yourself.

Of course you may still have your own excuse for not joining us. But if it's one of the following ones, perhaps we can help you to overcome it.

AMNESTY
INTERNATIONAL
UNITED KINGDOM

READING
PHOTOGRAPHS

In our busy multimedia world, photographs communicate instant messages. Photographs in our daily papers show the faces of people in the news, the horror of war and famine, the joy of children playing, the excitement of sport and the beauty of nature. Photographs fill celebrity magazines such as *Hello*, *VIP* and *Heat*. They also help in police investigations. Every picture tells a story, but whether it's a true story or not is another matter.

Some pictures can be changed or 'doctored' for particular purposes. For example, celebrities go to lots of trouble with make-up and clothes to ensure that they look their best in publicity shots. With modern digital technology, famous people can be made to appear thinner or younger than they really are. A clever photographer can make anyone appear powerful and important or the exact opposite, depending on the background, lighting or camera angle.

When responding to photographs, think about the following:

- **Purpose:** What was the photographer's intention when taking the picture? What story is being told? Does the photo speak for itself or is the photographer making a point using the image?

- **Content:** Who is in the photo? What objects are there and what do they signify?
- **Composition:** How are the objects or people in the photo arranged? What does this arrangement suggest?
- **Angle:** Where is the photograph taken from? How does this affect our reaction?
- **Production:** Is the photo in black and white or colour? Has it been set up or arranged in any particular way? How does this affect us?

The two newspaper photographs shown opposite were taken on the same sunny day in Dublin. Carefully study both of them and then answer two of the following questions. Each question is worth twenty marks.

1 In the case of each photograph, what story is the photographer telling?
2 Photographers pay close attention to how pictures are composed. What differences or similarities do you notice in these two photographs? (Consider the backgrounds, camera angles, facial expressions, use of colour, etc.)
3 Which of the two photographs do you prefer? Give reasons for your answer.

 SAMPLE ANSWER (Q2)

Both these photos are about young people, but they could not be more different. The little boy reaching up

for the ice cream is a real feel-good picture. The whole atmosphere is positive and the colours are bright, except for the road. The photographer has put all the attention on the child who is very young but very determined to reach up for the delicious cone.

The second picture also shows concentration, but in this case it is an unfortunate drug addict. In this photo, the image of the needle in the addict's arm is what I notice most, and it is really frightening. The camera angle is looking down, making the addict seem small. All the dirty brown colours and discarded rubbish around him just add to the image I get of him living a tragic life.

What is really good about the ice cream picture is that it captures a special moment just before the child gets the ice cream. We all know that looking forward to something is often better than actually getting what we want. The camera angle cleverly shows us the view from the child's point of view. It is low and we are looking up just like the child.

In the background, his mother keeps a close eye on him to make sure everything is all right. This is totally different to the drug scene where the other people have their backs to the addict. The two pictures tell very different stories about modern Ireland. It is almost as though the ice cream photographer is telling us that this is the way childhood should be. Kids should enjoy their innocence, being taken for walks in the park in a loving family atmosphere.

This is a well-written and perceptive answer that makes interesting observations about the two photographs. The comparative approach is sustained throughout and reference is made to important aspects of photography, such as background, camera angles and expression. The points are well organised and fluently expressed. Grade A.

Look closely at the four photographs shown here and then answer two of the following questions. Each question is worth twenty marks.

1 Which one of the four photographs makes the greatest impact? Give reasons for your answer.
2 Compare any two of the photographs, paying close attention to composition, background, camera angles, etc.
3 Which of the photographs do you like best? Give reasons for your answer.

I thought the old woman in the field was the most interesting. Her photograph stood out. It wasn't as in your face as the rest. It makes a different kind of impact because it looks so ordinary. I started to think about her life. She must be lonely and not too well off. It's more of a flashback to life out in the country. I liked the way you don't see her face. She could be any old person. The dog seems to be her only company. To me this is kind of sad.

The background is empty. She is walking past an old farmhouse. Nobody lives in it anymore. In class, we read about the way people are leaving the country. This is the message I get from this photo. Some parts of Ireland are empty. The population of farmers isn't there. Things change. There is nothing for young people. It's only for tourists to look at. It's beautiful in a kind of wild way.

The image this photo gives is of a rugged piece of land. It's not even good for farming. But the old people left there still struggle on. All the other pictures were either funny or weird. This one is more Irish. I liked that.

This answer focuses well on the distinctive qualities of the photograph. Attention is given to details such as the disused farmhouse. The expression could be more varied. Apart from the slang ('kind of') there are too many short sentences. However, the ideas are interesting enough to achieve a good C grade standard.

READING CARTOONS

Visual texts are made to convey a **message** of some kind. Many young people go through a comics phase, reading stories about monsters, mutants and men in tights. Cartoons are also texts and cartoonists are making a point, especially in political cartoons. Media Studies questions could also include strip cartoons and extracts from comics.

Cartoons aim to make us **laugh** or make us **think** about the world in which we live. Many cartoonists satirise people by making fun of their behaviour.

Keep the following points in mind when examining a cartoon.

- **Visual:** Who do the characters in the cartoon represent? Are they meant to be real people, or are they stereotypes (such as rich people, taxi drivers, typical students, etc.)? Are the facial features of famous people exaggerated? Is this to make them look silly and ridiculous? How does their appearance, clothing and setting tell us who they are meant to represent?

- **Verbal:** How does the cartoon use speech to convey its message? Speech bubbles, comments, slogans and captions are all used in cartoons.

- **Context:** What is the background or history of the situation that has led to the cartoon? Does the cartoon refer to a specific event or is it making a general comment?

The two cartoons shown here make fun of Irish football fans and Italian players. They are mainly designed to amuse by reminding us about stereotypical behaviour. Although the tone is good-humoured, the cartoonist is also making a more serious point in each case. Some fans travelling to overseas matches have a tendency to overdo the celebrations. It's also true to say that Italian players are sometimes known for exaggerating their injuries during matches.

Study the following cartoons and then answer the questions that follow.

SUPERMODELS

KERBER

"Now children, 'Hedge Schools' were a safe way for
Irish children to get some kind of an education …"

Answer **all** of the questions that follow. Each question is worth ten marks.

1 As well as being funny, cartoonists sometimes make a serious point. Is this true in the case of any of these cartoons? Explain why.

2 What evidence of exaggeration or stereotyping can you find in these cartoons?

3 Some cartoons can be cruel and hurtful. In your opinion, is there cruelty involved in any of these particular cartoons, or are they simply humorous?

4 Which of the cartoons did you like best? Give reasons for your answer.

 SAMPLE ANSWERS (Q3)

(i) I don't think cartoons are cruel, they're just meant to be a total laugh, especially if they go on about superstars and top personalities like famous football stars or the government. I suppose they could hurt some famous people, but they all love the publicity no matter what and they even pay people to help with publicity so they can't have it their own way all the time, especially as they make a fortune out of publicity for their films and other things they sell.

This answer makes a reasonably good point but uses two overly long sentences to do so. There is no direct reference to any of the actual cartoons on p.149, even though this was an important part of the question. Grade D.

(ii) The cartoons making fun of the government are not cruel. These are examples of satire and there is nobody hurt because of the cartoons. They just poke fun at the way governments cannot be trusted. It's the same with the football cartoons because they just make fun of certain types of people, i.e. fans.

The cartoons that name individual people are not the same. These could hurt the people involved. Some famous celebrities have complained about the pressures. Superstars like Victoria Beckham are probably used to all the attention, but I can't see how eating disorders are suitable subjects for cartoons, even if it is meant to be humorous.

This is a thoughtful and focused response. The distinction is made between cartoons that attack stereotypes, such as politicians or football fans, and individuals who might be offended. Reference is made to a number of the cartoons and the points are expressed clearly in a well-organised answer. Grade A.

MEDIA STUDIES UNIT ROUND-UP

- Take time to **study all media texts** very closely.
- Pay particular attention to the **purpose** of the text.
- Write clear, succinct answers that directly **address the given questions**.
- **Develop main points** using reference to the text.
- Always examine the use of **language** in a text.
- Note the effect of features such as **visuals** and **layout** if appropriate.

CHECKLIST

Having worked through the Media Studies unit, you should now feel more confident about the following:
- Knowing what kind of questions to expect in the Junior Cert Media Studies section.
- Examining a variety of media terms and media texts.
- Tabloid and broadsheet news.
- Recognising how news stories are organised and presented.
- Different styles of writing, e.g. factual, persuasive, emotive, satirical, etc.
- The content and style of popular magazines.
- Understanding the main features of advertisements.
- Responding to photographs, posters and cartoons.
- Comparing and contrasting particular media texts.
- Writing successful answers of a high standard.

UNIT 5 **Drama**

OVERVIEW

*In the Drama section of the Junior Cert you will have to answer two questions. The first is on an unseen extract from **either** Shakespearean drama **or** other drama. The second question is on studied drama based on a play you have read and discussed in class.*

WHEN STUDYING DRAMA, think about how it differs from other texts. To begin with, dramatists use **dialogue** to create characters and present a story that will interest an audience. Although stage directions will be some help in understanding a character's mood or tone, you usually have to guess what a character is thinking and feeling.

While characters are central to any drama, there are many other important elements, including plot, setting, themes, language, atmosphere, dramatic devices and stagecraft. Your own impressions will be affected by all of these. Every play also involves **conflict** of some sort, such as fights, battles, disputes, arguments and internal struggles of conscience.

Of course, a play is meant to be seen and heard, not read. In a theatre there will be visual help so that we understand what is happening. When you read a play or an extract from one, you have to use your imagination more. You have to form impressions from reading the lines, and from reading between the lines. Watching videos, DVDs or films of the plays you are studying will also bring the story to life. Try to see more than one version so that you can compare the different approaches.

DISCUSSING DRAMA

These are some of the **main terms** you will find useful when answering questions in the Drama section.

Actions: The behaviour of characters, what they do on stage.

Aside: When a character in a play speaks directly to the audience, as though the other characters cannot hear. Asides are sometimes called stage whispers.

Characters: The people in the play. Characters are the central feature in any drama. An essential part of your study will be to see how playwrights present characters and how they function and develop as the play goes on.

Chorus: A group of characters (or one character) in a play who comment on what is happening.

Comedy: A play that is supposed to make you laugh. Comedies used to be stories with happy endings.

Dialogue: Two (or more) characters talking to each other. We also speak about the 'dialogue of a play', meaning all the words that are spoken.

Dramatic irony: This occurs when a character says something that means more to the audience than to the speaker on stage. It usually happens when the audience knows more about a situation than the character does.

Monologue: A long speech from one character.

Props: Short for properties used in the set, such as ornaments, books, photographs, calendars, etc.

Soliloquy: Thinking out loud. Usually spoken when a character is alone on stage.

Setting: Where and when the story takes place.

Stage directions: What the actors have to do on stage. Directions are usually written in italics (and in brackets), often at the beginning of a scene.

Themes: Ideas or issues that the dramatist explores during the course of the play.

Tragedy: A serious play, usually with an unhappy ending. Tragedies are meant to be moving and many of them have a serious moral or message. Shakespeare's tragedies involve the downfall of the central character and the deaths of others.

SHAKESPEAREAN DRAMA

William Shakespeare is the most highly regarded figure in English literature. His characters, dramatic skills and extraordinary use of language have influenced most writers in English.

When he was writing his plays about 400 years ago, Shakespeare's stories were about the very same issues and feelings that still interest people today. These include love, ambition, jealousy, hypocrisy, fate, confusion, violence, murder, revenge, courage, tragedy, mystery and magic.

The theatres in which Shakespeare's plays were first performed were different from the ones we have today.

- There was very little scenery and no lighting.
- Props and costumes were not seen as important either.
- Music and songs were sometimes used to help create a particular mood.
- Female roles were played by young men.
- Theatres were rowdier places than they are nowadays. Most of the ordinary people in the audience stood in front of the stage, often eating and drinking during performances.

WRITING ABOUT OPENING SCENES

Opening scenes are important in that they introduce us to the world of the play. When we enter this new reality, we meet characters with a story to tell. The opening is important for a number of reasons.

- It is vital to engage the audience's interest.
- Many openings set the scene in some way.
- Characters and the dramatic situation are introduced.
- The action and story-line gets going.

Watch out for how dramatists make opening scenes effective. Whether you are familiar with the play or not, it will be useful to ask some of the following questions:

- What kind of situation is this?
- What do we learn about the characters?
- What kind of mood is established?
- Are there any hints of any likely developments?

The following extract is the opening scene from Shakespeare's play *Twelfth Night.* Carefully read through the scene and the notes that follow it.

Duke Orsino is hopelessly in love with the beautiful **Olivia** and is pining for her. He refuses to hunt and orders musicians to entertain him while he dreams of her. His servant, **Valentine**, reminds him that Olivia does not return his love or even listen to the messages he sends her. We learn from one of the duke's speeches that Olivia is in mourning for her brother, who has recently died. She wears a dark veil and she has promised that no one will see her face for seven years – and she refuses to marry anyone until then.

A room in the duke's palace.
Enter Duke of Orsino, Curio and other lords, musicians attending.

DUKE If music be the food of love, play on;
Give me excess of it, that **surfeiting,**   *being too full*
The appetite may sicken and so die.
That **strain** again! It had a dying fall;   *melody*
O, it came o'er my ear like the sweet sound
That breathes upon a bank of violets,
Stealing and giving odour. Enough, no more
'Tis not so sweet now as it was before.
O spirit of love, how quick and fresh art thou!
That, notwithstanding thy capacity
Receiveth as the sea, nought enters there,

      Of what validity and pitch soe'er

      But **falls into abatement** and low price   *is lessened in value*

      Even in a minute! **So full of shapes is fancy,**   *love is the*

      That it alone is high fantastical.   *most imaginative thing*

CURIO Will you go hunt, my lord?

DUKE: What, Curio?

CURIO The **hart.**   *stag*

DUKE Why, so I do, the noblest that I have.

      O, when mine eyes did see Olivia first,

      Methought she **purged the air of pestilence!**   *purified*

      That instant was I a hart,   *the air*

      And my desires, like fell and cruel hounds,

      E'er since pursue me.

Enter Valentine.

(To Valentine) How now! What news from her?

VALENTINE So please my lord, I be admitted;

      But from her handmaid do return this answer;

      The **element** itself, till seven year's heat,   *air*

      Shall not behold her face **at ample view;**   *completely*

      But, like a **cloistress,** she will veiled walk,   *nun*

      And water once a day her chamber round

      With **eye-offending brine;** all this to season   *sore tears*

      A brother's dead love, which she would keep fresh

      And lasting in her sad rememberance.

DUKE O, she that hath a heart of that fine frame

      To pay this debt of love but to a brother,

      How will she love, when the rich golden **shaft**   *Cupid's*

      Hath killed the flock of all affections else   *arrow*

      That live in her; when liver, brain, and heart,

      These sovereign thrones, are all supplied, and filled

      Her sweet perfections with one self king!

      Away before me to sweet beds of flowers;

      Love thoughts lie rich when **canopied with bowers**

      Nature gives shelter

Shakespeare's **language** can seem difficult and strange at first, but this is hardly surprising considering his plays were written four centuries ago. They are written in a mixture of poetry and prose.

Shakespeare used **blank verse** in much of his dialogue. Blank verse has a regular rhythm (usually consisting of ten syllables in each line) and usually did not rhyme. It sounds grander and much more poetic than ordinary prose and is generally spoken by more important characters, such as the duke in his opening speech: 'If music be the food of love, play on;/Give me excess of it ....'

Sometimes Shakespeare used **rhymed verse** to emphasise a particular kind of atmosphere or to round off a scene. Poetic verse sounds more dramatic and impressive than the rest of the text.

The thing to remember is that there is always a reason for the language Shakespeare used. Ordinary **prose** is used at times by all his characters, but especially by unimportant or comic ones.

Shakespeare's sense of humour is also different from ours. Many of his jokes are **puns** (words with double meanings), such as the lovesick duke's response when asked if he had been hunting: 'That instant was I a hart'. In this case, he is telling us that his heart has been hunted by Olivia.

ANSWERING QUESTIONS ON SHAKESPEARE

In the opening scene from *Twelfth Night* it is clear from what the duke says that he is hopelessly in love.

Other points to consider in this opening scene are as follows:
- Where the scene takes place.
- The way the duke speaks and behaves.
- Curio's thought about the duke.
- What might happen next.

SAMPLE QUESTION (GRADE A)

Describe the atmosphere in the opening scene of *Twelfth Night*. Refer to the text in your answer. (15 marks)

This scene is set in a palace where the duke is listening to music, which he calls 'the food of love'. Although love is in the air, the atmosphere is overly romantic and sickly, especially as the duke seems to be living in a dream world. Everything he says is exaggerated and sentimental, e.g. 'O spirit of love, how quick and fresh art thou!'

In fact, the duke is so caught up in himself that it seems he is putting on a false act as the typically unhappy lover. The mood is dreamlike and a little depressed. At the end, when

Valentine brings news about Olivia, the duke reacts with another flowery speech about how happy he is that she can show her feelings.

Overall, this scene is so dominated by the duke's selfish attitude to love that the atmosphere is both romantic and ridiculous. Perhaps Shakespeare is really laughing at this foolish character.

SHAKESPEARE'S IMAGERY

Shakespeare liked to use figures of speech, i.e. **imagery**, to create vivid pictures in the minds of his audiences. He was fond of using comparisons and his imagery often includes **similes** and **metaphors**. Shakespeare often uses imagery to explore and add emphasis to an idea.

A **simile** compares one thing to another using *like* or *as.* For example, consider Juliet's words to Romeo: 'My bounty is as boundless as the sea,/My love as deep.'

A **metaphor** is a direct comparison (without *like* or *as*). For example, look at Iago's warning to Othello: 'O, beware, my lord, of jealousy!/It is the green-eyed monster.'

Motifs are also a common feature of Shakespeare's plays. These are patterns of images (or themes or characters) that recur throughout a particular text. For example, **disguise** is a running idea in many of the comedies, such as *Twelfth Night* and *As You Like It,* while sleep is a recurring feature in *Macbeth*. After Macbeth kills King Duncan, he feels terrible remorse and begins to hear voices: 'Methought I heard a voice cry, "Sleep no more!"/ Macbeth does murder sleep.' Later on in the story, Lady Macbeth is driven mad with grief and begins to sleepwalk.

Shakespeare usually matches imagery to themes. In *Macbeth,* recurring animal imagery reflects the cruelty and inhumanity of Macbeth and his wife just as sleep imagery is a sign of their guilty consciences.

The extract that follows is taken from *Henry IV, Part 1,* one of Shakespeare's history plays. These were based on important historical conflicts involving kings or leading figures from Roman history. While they often had tragic elements, they also included various comic characters.

Scenes from Shakespeare can be very challenging at first. It's best not to worry about understanding every line completely, but rather, aim to get an overall feeling for the characters and their relationships.

In this scene, we meet Prince Henry (Hal), the young heir to the English throne. Hal wastes much of his time idling and drinking in the tavern with Sir John Falstaff and his friends. Falstaff is a fat criminal but he is also a good-humoured companion who loves the easy life.

Read the extract and then answer the questions that follow.

FALSTAFF	Now, Hal, what time of day is it, lad?
PRINCE	Thou art so fat-witted with drinking of old **sack** *wine*
	and unbuttoning thee after supper, and sleeping
	upon benches after noon, that thou has forgotten
	to demand that truly which thou wouldst truly
	know. What a devil has thou to do with the time of
	the day? Unless hours were cups of sack, and minutes
	capons, and the blessed sun himself a fair wench in *Roast*
	flame-coloured taffeta, I see no reason why thou *chickens*
	shouldst be so superfluous to demand the time of the day.
FALSTAFF	Indeed you come near me now, Hal; for we that take
	purses go by the moon and the seven stars, and not by
	Phoebus, he, that wand'ring knight so fair. And I prithee,
	sweet wag, when thou art a king as, God save thy grace –
	majesty I should say, for grace thou wilt have none –
PRINCE	What, none?
FALSTAFF	No, by my troth; not so much as will serve to be prologue
	to an egg and butter.
PRINCE	Well, how then? Come, **roundly, roundly.** *quickly*
FALSTAFF	Marry, then, sweet wag, when thou art king, let not us that
	are squires of the night's body be called thieves of the day's
	beauty. Let us be **Diana's** foresters, *Diana*
	gentlemen of the shade, *was the moon goddess*
	minions of the moon; and let men say we be men of good
	government, being governed as the sea is, by our noble and
	chaste mistress the moon, under whose countenance we steal.
PRINCE	Thou sayst well, and it holds well too; for the fortune of us
	that are the moon's men doth ebb and flow like the sea, being
	governed, as the sea is, by the moon. As, for proof now: a
	purse of gold snatched on a Monday night and most wastefully
	spent on Tuesday morning; got with swearing 'Lay by', and
	spent with crying 'Bring in'; now in as low an ebb as the foot of
	the ladder, and by-and-by in as high a flow as the ridge of the
	gallows.

FALSTAFF	By the Lord, thou say'st true, lad – and is not my hostess of the tavern a most sweet wench?
PRINCE	As the honey of Hybla, my old lad of the castle – and is not a **buff jerkin** a most sweet robe of durance? *rough jacket*
FALSTAFF	How now, how now, mad wag? What a plague have I to do with a buff jerkin?
PRINCE	Why, what a plague have I to do with my hostess of the tavern?
FALSTAFF	Well, thou hast called her to a reckoning many a time and oft.
PRINCE	Did I ever call for thee to pay thy part?
FALSTAFF	No; I'll give thee thy due, thou hast paid all there.
PRINCE	Yea, and elsewhere, so far that my coin would stretch; and where it would not, I have used my credit.
FALSTAFF	Yea, and used it that, were it not here apparent that thou art heir apparent – But I prithee, sweet wag, shall there be gallows standing in England when thou art king? And resolution thus fobbed as it is with a rusty curb of old father antic the law? Do not thou, when thou art king, hang a thief?
PRINCE	No; thou shalt.
FALSTAFF	Shall I? O rare! By the Lord, I'll be a brave judge.
PRINCE	Thou judgest false already.

Answer **two** of the questions that follow. Each question is worth fifteen marks.

1 Based on your reading of the extract, describe the relationship between Hal and Falstaff.

2 Both characters are naturally witty and fond of word play. What evidence of this do you find in the extract?

3 Costumes tell us about the period in which the story is taking place, characters' social class and their personalities. If you were in charge of costumes for Falstaff and Hal, what would you recommend?

SAMPLE ANSWER (Q2)

Both of these characters seem to enjoy showing how clever they are with words. It is like a game between them. The prince's comparisons are quite funny. He insults Falstaff by saying that he spends all his time eating and drinking. Falstaff would only be interested in the time if hours and minutes were bottles of wine and cooked chickens.

But Falstaff answers back that Hal hasn't enough 'grace' to cook an egg. He uses another pun when he says 'were it not here apparent that thou art heir apparent.' This shows his love of jokes and wordplay, which he might use to impress the prince.

Falstaff also boasts a lot when he pretends that robbers like himself are great romantic heroes. He uses fancy poetic language to claim that thieves are 'gentlemen of the shade, minions of the moon'. There is a battle of wits between them throughout the scene and they both want to impress each other with clever jokes.

This is a very good response that shows a clear understanding of the way language is used by the characters. It is effectively illustrated with carefully chosen reference and quotation, including puns and comparisons. The answer is also well organised and the expression is varied and fluent throughout. Grade A.

CHARACTER STUDY

More questions are asked about **characters** and their **relationships** than almost any other aspect of drama. You learn about characters through:
- What they think, say and do.
- Their appearance, clothes, etc.
- What other characters say about them.
- How they develop and change.
- Stage directions.

While characters come alive through what they say, it is important to examine characters in their full **context**. This means being aware of what is actually happening in the story. What characters say may not always match what they do. It is also worth thinking about the time and place the characters are living in. Characters will be shaped by the many influences of the world around them, including attitudes, customs, laws, etc.

Quite often you will find clear contrasts between characters. As well as highlighting their personalities, **contrasts** usually have other purposes, such as telling the audience more about the themes and ideas in the play. Of course, characters should never be treated as real people. Although they portray human qualities, they have a **dramatic purpose**. Many characters are recognisable as **stereotypes** – villains, heroes, etc. The most realistic and fully rounded characters in Shakespeare's plays are to be found in the great tragedies.

The following (edited) extract from *Othello* involves two key characters, Othello himself and Iago, the old friend he trusts. Othello is a noble North African who has been appointed commander of the armed forces in Venice. He has also just married a beautiful Venetian lady, Desdemona. But Othello is unaware that he has enraged Iago, who feels he should have been appointed as Othello's lieutenant instead of the inexperienced Cassio.

Iago plans his revenge against Othello. He intends to poison Othello's thoughts with suggestions that Desdemona might be unfaithful. In this scene, he begins to sow the seeds of suspicion in Othello's mind.

Carefully read the extract and then answer the questions that follow.

IAGO	My noble lord –
OTHELLO	What dost thou say, Iago?
IAGO	Did Michael Cassio, when you woo'd my lady,
	Know of your love?
OTHELLO	He did, from first to last. Why dost thou ask?
IAGO	But for a satisfaction of my thought.
	No further harm.
OTHELLO	Why of thy thoughts, Iago?
IAGO	I did not think he had been acquainted with her.
OTHELLO	O yes, and went between us very oft.
IAGO	Indeed?
OTHELLO	Indeed? Indeed: discern'st thou aught in that?
	Is he not honest?
IAGO	Honest, my lord?
OTHELLO	Honest? Ay, honest.
IAGO	My lord, for aught I know.
OTHELLO	What dost thou think?
IAGO	Think, my lord?
OTHELLO	Think, my lord? By heaven, he echoes me,
	As if there were some monster in his thought,
	Too hideous to be shown: thou didst mean something.
	If thou dost love me, show me thy thought.
IAGO	My lord, you know I love you.
OTHELLO	I think thou dost,
	And for I know thou art full of love and honesty
	And weighest thy words before thou give 'em breath,
	Therefore these stops of thine fright me the more.
IAGO	For Michael Cassio,
	I dare be sworn, I think that he is honest.
OTHELLO	I think so too.
IAGO	Men should be that they seem,
	Or those that be not, would they might seem none.
OTHELLO	Certain, men should be what they seem.
IAGO	Why then I think Cassio's an honest man.

OTHELLO	Nay, yet there's more in this.
	I prithee, speak to me as to thy thinkings,
	As thou dost ruminate, and give the worst
	Of thought the worst of word.
IAGO	Good name in man and woman's dear, my lord;
	Is the immediate jewel of our souls:
	Who steals my purse, steals trash, 'tis something, nothing,
	But he that filches from me my good name
	Robs me of that which not enriches him,
	And makes me poor indeed.
OTHELLO	By heaven, I'll know thy thoughts!
IAGO	You cannot, if my heart were in your hand,
	Nor shall not, while 'tis in my custody:
	O, beware, my lord, of jealousy!
	It is the green-eyed monster, which doth mock
	That meat it feeds on.
OTHELLO	O misery!

Answer **two** of the following questions. Each question is worth fifteen marks.

1 What kind of person does Othello show himself to be in this extract? Use appropriate reference or quotation when describing his character.

2 Iago is often spoken of as one of Shakespeare's greatest villains. What evidence of this can you find from reading this extract?

3 Imagine you are to produce this scene. What guidelines would you give the two actors about how they should play their parts?

SAMPLE ANSWER (Q2)

Iago is a great hypocrite. He gives Othello the impression that he is sincere, but in fact he is extremely cunning. He first greets Othello with 'My noble Lord' as though he respects him. This seems more like flattery and shows Iago's evil side.

Iago has a subtle way of suggesting things to Othello. He keeps hinting at a secret relationship between Michael Cassio and Desdemona. It is the sly way that he asks questions that annoys Othello. What he ends up doing is making it look as if he does not want to hurt anyone or cause trouble. So when Othello asks if Cassio is honest, Iago answers with another question: 'Honest, my Lord?'

Iago also seems to enjoy controlling Othello and watching his suspicion build up inside him. His evil character grows when he tells Othello, 'I think that he is honest.' At the end of the scene, he pretends to openly warn Othello against jealousy and seems to have taken over Othello's mind completely. As a villain Iago contrasts with Othello, who seems to be naive and easily brainwashed throughout the whole scene.

This is a good grade A answer that uses the text well to illustrate Iago's villainy. There is clear understanding of the subtle way Iago operates. The use of contrast is also included as another way of highlighting Iago's evil ways. While some mention of Iago's mock-hesitant tone would have been welcome, there is a high standard of answering throughout.

ISSUES AND THEMES

Most plays deal with ideas or issues that are explored during the course of the story. These are usually called **themes** because they tell us the dramatist's views and they make us think as well.

Themes can be about anything and there is likely to be more than one in any play. They often touch on important issues to do with our lives, such as love, relationships, ambition, conflict, change, tragedy, revenge, society, etc. Once you have identified the themes in a play, it is worth thinking about how the dramatist has presented them. It is important to work out the writer's point of view – but you don't have to agree with it.

Everything in the play can express the dramatist's ideas. The way the story develops and the way characters are created all reveal the theme. Some playwrights hold strong opinions and they get their message across in their work. Willy Russell is a Liverpool writer who has strong views on the way working-class people have difficulties gaining access to middle-class culture. Injustice is a recurring theme in his plays.

The following extract is taken from *Educating Rita* by Willy Russell. The play consists of only two characters: Rita, a hairdresser who has come for tuition for her Open University course and Frank, a college lecturer.

Carefully read the extract and then answer the questions that follow.

RITA   Is that because of me, because of what I said last week?

FRANK (*laughing*) My God. You think you've reformed me?

RITA   (*going to the window*) I don't wanna reform y'. Y' can do what y' like. (*Quickly*) I love that lawn down there. When it's summer do they sit on it?

FRANK (*going to the window*) Who?

RITA   (*going back to the desk*) The ones who come here all the time. The proper students.

FRANK Yes. First glimmer of sun and they're all out there.

RITA   Readin' an' studyin'?

FRANK Reading and studying? What do you think they are, human? Proper students don't read and study.

RITA   Y' what?

FRANK A joke, a joke. Yes. They read and study, sometimes. (*Pause. RITA dumps her bag on the chair and then goes and hangs up her coat on the door.*)

RITA   It looks the way I always imagined a public school to look, y'know a boardin' school. When I was a kid I always wanted to go to a boardin' school.

FRANK   God forbid it; why?

RITA   (*going to her chair at the desk*) I always thought they sounded great, schools like that, y'know with a tuck-shop an' a matron an' prep. An' a pair of kids called Jones minor an' Jones major. I told me mother once. (*She opens her bag and takes out the copy of* Howard's End, *a ring-bound file, note-pad, ruler and pencil-case, placing them methodically on the desk in front of her.*) She said I was off me cake.

FRANK   (*with an exaggerated look at her*) What in the name of God is being off one's cake?

RITA   Soft. Y'know, mental.

FRANK   Aha. I must remember that. The next student to ask me if Isabel Archer was guilty of Protestant masochism shall be told that one is obviously very off one's cake.

RITA   Don't be soft. You can't say that.

FRANK   Why ever not?

RITA   You can't. If you do it, it's slummin' it. Comin' from you it'd sound dead affected, wouldn't it?

FRANK   Dead affected?

RITA   Yeh. You say that to your proper students they'll think you're off your – y' know…

FRANK   Cake, yes. Erm – Rita, why didn't you ever become what you call a proper student?

RITA   What? After goin' to the school I went to?

FRANK   Was it bad?

(RITA *starts sharpening the pencils one by one into perfect spikes, leaving the shavings on the desk.*)

RITA   Nah, just normal, y' know, borin', ripped-up books, broken glass everywhere, knives an' fights. An' that was just in the staffroom. Nah, they tried their best I suppose, always tellin' us we stood more of a chance if we studied. But studyin' was just for the wimps, wasn't it? See, if I'd started takin' school seriously, I would have had to become different from me mates, an' that's not allowed.

FRANK By whom?

RITA By your mates, by your family, by everyone. So y' never admit that school could be anythin' other than useless.

(FRANK *passes her the ashtray but she ignores it and continues sharpening the pencils on the table.*)

RITA Like what you've got to be into is music an' clothes an' lookin' for a feller, y' know the real qualities of life. Not that I went along with it so reluctantly. I mean, there was always somethin' in me head, tappin' away, tellin' me I might have got it all wrong. But I'd just play another record or buy another dress an' stop worryin'. There's always somethin' to make you forget about it. So y' do, y' keep goin', tellin' yourself life's great. There's always another club to go to, a new feller to be chasin', a laugh an' a joke with the girls. Till, one day, y' own up to yourself an' y' say, is this it?

Answer **two** of the following questions. Each question is worth fifteen marks.

1 *Despite its comic moments, most of this scene is serious.* Discuss this statement, supporting your answer with reference to the extract.

2 Comment on how Rita reveals her character by her choice of words and the way she expresses herself.

3 The scene takes place in Frank's university room. How would you create this setting on stage? (Refer to sets, props and costumes in your answer.)

SAMPLE ANSWER (Q3)

I think Frank's room would be very cluttered and untidy – a real bookworm's room – with piles of papers and notes all over the place. The room would be a bit dark and the curtains would be half-drawn. The idea would be to show the audience that he is more caught up in his work than in keeping the room looking nice.

He is an English tutor, so there might be a lot of shelves piled with books behind him and maybe a few arty posters on the walls. His desk *should be a bit of a mess really – with a computer and stacks of files to show that he does a lot of reading. Chairs would be covered in magazines, newspapers and books, for example. Another good idea would be to have a couple of waste-paper bins piled high with papers.*

Frank himself would be a typical sort of college tutor, not very careful about his clothes. He would probably be dressed casually, open shirt, baggy trousers, even unmatching socks to show he's a bit absent-minded. He seems to be the sort of person who is often in a world of his own.

Rita would be in jeans and a leather jacket – as she is probably trying to look a bit younger than her real age. She would have lots of scarves and woolly tops in layers – as if she was knitted. The two of them are a fairly odd couple as if they don't really fit in anywhere. This should be how they should appear to the audience in this scene.

This is an interesting response that comes up with some very imaginative ideas about setting and costumes. The answer remains focused on the question throughout and includes detailed sugges-tions about creating the sense of a typical college room. The casual expression is slightly careless in places, but the answer is lively and always considers audience expectations. A good A grade.

QUOTE UNQUOTE!

Most questions ask you to use textual references to support your points. Answers are likely to use **reference** (in your own words) and **quotation** (extracts taken from the text).

Your answers will be much more successful if you use **quotations** correctly.

- Put inverted commas at the beginning and end of the quotation.
- Write the quotation exactly as it appears in the original text.
- Avoid using a quotation that repeats what you have just written.
- Check that the quotation supports the point you are making.
- Try to fit the quotation into your own sentence.
- Keep quotes short.

For example, the extract ends on a sad note with Rita admitting that 'one day, y'own up to yourself an' y' say, is this it?'

Remember that quotations should be used to develop points. The fact that Rita describes the students who attend university full time as 'proper students' shows us how inferior she feels.

When you use quotations in this way you are showing examiners that you can make use of the text to support your ideas.

CONFLICT

Drama always includes conflict of some sort. People disagree, families fight, battles are waged. But the conflict does not have to be so obvious. It can sometimes be internal as characters struggle with their consciences.

Whenever a difference of interest occurs between characters, a conflict follows. In **comedy**, conflicts are resolved and there is a happy ending. In **tragedy**, the conflicts are more serious and are frequently only resolved by death.

Conflict creates tension and engages the audience by making it get involved with a character who is facing a crisis. It is only natural to sympathise with certain characters and take sides in disputes. All dramatists are keen to use conflict and tension to hold the audience's interest.

The following extract is taken from *Teechers* by John Godber. Mr Nixon is a new drama teacher at Whitewall High, a large English secondary school with a tough reputation. Mrs Parry is the Head, Mr Basford is Deputy Head and Miss Prime teaches PE. At the start of the extract, two of the students, Gail and Hobby, are chatting with Mr Nixon. Notice that the characters sometimes act as narrators.

Read the extract and then answer the questions that follow.

HOBBY	Do you like it at this school, sir?
NIXON	Yeh, it's OK, you lot are awkward, but OK.
HOBBY	Sir, what do you think it's most important for a teacher to do?
NIXON	Well, I think a teacher should have a good relationship, if he hasn't got a relationship he can only ever be a teacher, never a person.
GAIL	What about Mr Basford, he hasn't got a good relationship with the kids...
NIXON	Well, I can't speak for Mr Basford, can I?
HOBBY	Sir, the bell's gone...
NIXON	You'd better go and get it then – and go quietly.
	(A pause)
	It was a trip to see *The Rocky Horror Show* that got me really close to those three, although I had to watch my step with Gail, she kept putting her hand on my leg during the sexy bits...
HOBBY	Science fiction...Whooooo. Double Feature.
GAIL	Doctor X has built a creature.

Hobby becomes Mr Basford.

NIXON   Mr Basford, you wanted to see me?

BASFORD   Mr Nixon, I understand you took a group of fifteen-year-olds to see a play featuring transvestites from Transylvania? I can imagine what educational value that has.

NIXON   A black mark from Basford. Mrs Parry had omitted to tell me about the joys of doing cover... Usually a student would appear like the ghost of Caesar and present you with a pink slip, this would tell you where to go and who to cover for. Mr Basford was in charge of the cover rota.

BASFORD   Nixon N.1. to cover for Fisher F.1. third year games... And the best of luck.

The Gymnasium

PRIME   All right, all third year deadlegs from Mr Fisher's group shut up, said Miss Jackie Prime. If you want to watch the nineteen seventy-four World Cup Final on video, to the lecture theatre with Mr Clarke's group. Those who want to play pirates in the gym get changed, you without kit better see Mr Nixon.

HOBBY   A whole line of kids wearing anoraks came forward... Mr Nixon looked staggered, he'd been left to deal with PE's castoffs.

GAIL   And amongst the throng was the legendary Barry Wobschall. Barry never did sport. He hated games.

HOBBY   Barry was fifteen but had the manner of an old man, he lived with his grandad and spoke with all the wisdom of someone four times his age. Every day for the past two years he had worked on a milk round.

NIXON   Where's your kit?

RON   Sir, my shorts don't fit me.

NIXON   What about you?

PIGGY   Sir, my mother put my shorts in the wash and they got chewed up because the washer has gone all wrong...

NIXON   Oh yeh.

PIGGY   It's true, sir, honest.

NIXON	What about you, Barry Wobschall, have you got any kit?
BARRY	No, sir.
PIGGY	He never brings any kit, sir.
NIXON	I wasn't asking you, was I, Simon Patterson.
PIGGY	No, sir.
NIXON	What about a note, Barry? Have you brought a note?
BARRY	Sir.
NIXON	Oh let's have it then.
GAIL	Barry handed him the note. It was small and crumpled. Barry looked in innocence as Nixon opened the piece of paper.

Gail hands Nixon a piece of paper.

NIXON	*(reading)* 'Please leave four pints and a yoghurt this Saturday.'
BARRY	It's the only note I could get, sir.
NIXON	I tried to talk Barry Wobschall into changing his options. His sort of humour in a drama class would have been dynamite. But he wouldn't change, he said he preferred doing geog, because it was peaceful and he liked copying maps.

Answer **two** of the following questions. Each question is worth fifteen marks.

1 In your opinion, does Whitewall High represent a realistic picture of a modern secondary school? Give reasons for your answer.

2 From the evidence in the extract, describe the kind of person you think Mr Nixon is.

3 John Godber is known as an inventive dramatist. In your view, how does he manage to keep the above extract fast-moving and lively?

SAMPLE ANSWER (Q3)

There are no long speeches in this extract. The conversation is made up of everyday language and is realistic, the way people normally speak. Gail and Hobby ask a lot of quick questions. The language is quite normal – what you would normally expect in real life.

The actors are also narrators. They tell us who they are, e.g. Miss Prime. This saves time and keeps the story going without stops. The actors also play different characters. Hobby becomes Basford. By using this sort of quick direction, the writer is keeping the play moving at a fast speed without waiting for changes of scenery or new actors to come on playing new characters.

There are a number of good points here and the question is directly addressed. However, the overall expression could be improved. Some mention might have been made of the way John Godber manages to condense so much into such a short sequence. An average grade C.

NATURALISTIC WRITING

During the second half of the twentieth century, plays tended to be about ordinary people in everyday situations. Characters were likely to use realistic or colloquial speech. Such 'kitchen-sink' drama contained a great deal of 'naturalistic' dialogue.

To make speech seem natural, dramatists had to reproduce the rhythms of everyday conversation, including hesitations, slang and clichés. The use of **pauses** can create a distinctive dramatic atmosphere. The playwright Harold Pinter often uses repetition, hesitations and silence in his dialogue, which can create a feeling of tension and unease.

As you read through the following scene from Pinter's *The Caretaker,* ask yourself what each of the characters is thinking and doing during the moments of silence.

Read the extract and then answer the questions that follow.

MICK   Uuh...listen...can I ask your advice? I mean, you're a man of the world. Can I ask your advice about something?

DAVIES You go right ahead.

MICK   Well, what it is, you see, I'm...I'm a bit worried about my brother.

DAVIES Your brother?

MICK   Yes...you see, his trouble is...

DAVIES What?

MICK   Well, it's not a very nice thing to say...

DAVIES *(rising, coming downstage)* Go on now, you say it.

[MICK *looks at him.*]

MICK   He doesn't like work.

[*Pause*]

DAVIES Go on!

MICK   No, he just doesn't like work, that's his trouble.

DAVIES   Is that a fact?

MICK   It's a terrible thing to have to say about your own brother.

DAVIES   Ay.

MICK   He's just shy of it. Very shy of it.

DAVIES   I know that sort.

MICK   You know the type?

DAVIES   I've met them.

MICK   I mean, I want to get him going in the world.

DAVIES   Stands to reason, man.

MICK   If you got an older brother you want to push him on, you want to see him make his way. Can't have him idle, he's only doing himself harm. That's what I say.

DAVIES   Yes.

MICK   But he won't buckle down to the job.

DAVIES   He don't like work.

MICK   Work shy.

DAVIES   Sounds like it to me.

MICK   You've met the type, have you?

DAVIES   Me? I know that sort.

MICK   Yes.

DAVIES   I know that sort. I've met them.

MICK   Causing me great anxiety. You see, I'm a working man. I'm a tradesman. I've got my own van.

DAVIES   Is that a fact?

MICK   He's supposed to be doing a little job for me...I keep him here to do a little job...but I don't know...I'm coming to the conclusion he's a slow worker.

[*Pause*]

          What would your advice be?

DAVIES   Well, he's a funny bloke, your brother.

MICK   What?

DAVIES   I was saying, he's...he's a bit of a funny bloke, your brother.

[MICK *stares at him.*]

MICK   Funny? Why?

DAVIES Well...he's funny...

MICK   What's funny about him?

DAVIES Nothing.

[*Pause*]

MICK   I don't call it funny.

DAVIES Nor me.

MICK   You don't want to start getting hypercritical.

DAVIES No, no, I wasn't that, I wasn't...I was only saying...

MICK   Don't get too glib.

DAVIES Look, all I meant was –

MICK   Cut it!

Answer **two** of the following questions. Each question is worth fifteen marks.

1 After reading through this scene, how would you describe the relationship between Mick and Davies?

2 It has been said that lack of communication is the major theme in Harold Pinter's plays. What evidence can you find in the above scene to support this view?

3 Imagine seeing this scene being acted on stage. Do you think it would be highly charged and dramatic? Give reasons for your answer, supporting them with references.

SAMPLE ANSWER (Q2)

There is hardly any communication between these two men in this scene. Mick asks advice in the way someone would look for it from a complete stranger. If anything, the lack of communication is the basic cause of all the tension and suspicion between Mick and Davies. The two men don't really know each other. There are a lot of awkward moments between the pair of them.

Their conversation turns nasty when Davies says, 'Well, he's a funny bloke, your brother.' This is where Mick seems to take offence. It seems obvious that Davies means no harm, but Mick gets really upset about this comment and takes it as an insult.

The word 'funny' can mean different things. Davies is probably sorry he ever used it. Mick then turns on Davies, saying, 'Don't get too glib.' Either he doesn't understand Davies or else he only wants to pick a fight.

This is a reasonably solid response that illustrates the lack of understanding between the two characters. The opening paragraph is strong, although an example or two of their awkwardness would have helped. The pauses and hesitant tone could have been mentioned. Overall, a competent B grade.

HUMOUR

It is always difficult to define or explain humour. In drama, some situations are funny or ridiculous in themselves. Some comedy is purely verbal and is based on what characters say. Humour can also result from what happens in a scene. **Farce** is built completely on the **humour of action** – characters are suddenly discovered where they shouldn't be or self-important people trip over themselves and are humiliated in public. When you are reading a comic scene, look out for the unexpected, the accidents in a situation as well as the characters and language.

Some scenes depend on **witty dialogue**. A character may use a particular catch phrase that the audience enjoys. In Shakespeare's time, Elizabethan audiences loved **puns**. They found them humorous and clever.

Writers use everything they can think of to make us laugh. If you are asked to discuss the techniques used to create humour, look out for surreal situations, contrasting characters, special effects, exaggeration, speech mannerisms and clever use of language in comic scenes.

Peter Cook (1937-1995) was widely known for his comic writing and performances. Like most comedians, he didn't worry too much about political correctness. The sketch that follows is about a one-legged man auditioning for an important film role. Here Cook plays the part of the theatrical agent while Dudley Moore took on the role of the one-legged man, Mr Spiggott.

Read the extract and then answer the questions that follow.

One Leg Too Few

COOK Miss Rigby! Stella, my love! Would you send in the next auditioner, please, Mr Spiggott, I believe it is.
(*Enter* MOORE, *hopping on one leg.*)
Mr. Spiggott, I believe?

MOORE Yes – Spiggott by name, Spiggott by nature.
(MOORE *follows* COOK *around the room.*)

COOK Yes…there's no need to follow me, Mr Spiggott. Please be stood. Now, Mr Spiggott, you are, I believe, auditioning for the part of Tarzan.

MOORE Right.

COOK Now, Mr Spiggott, I couldn't help noticing almost at once that you are a one-legged person.

MOORE You noticed that?

COOK I noticed that, Mr Spiggott. When you have been in the business as long as I have, you get to notice these little things almost instinctively. Now, Mr Spiggott, you, a one-legged man, are applying for the role of Tarzan – a role which traditionally involves the use of a two-legged actor.

MOORE Correct.

COOK And yet, you, a unidexter, are applying for the role.

MOORE Right.

COOK   A role for which two legs would seem to be the minimum requirement.

MOORE Very true.

COOK   Well, Mr Spiggott, need I point out to you where your deficiency lies as regards landing the role?

MOORE Yes, I think you ought to.

COOK   Need I say with overmuch emphasis that it is in the leg division that you are deficient?

MOORE The leg division?

COOK   Yes, the leg division, Mr Spiggott. You are deficient in it – to the tune of one. Your right leg I like. I like your right leg – a lovely leg for the role. That's what I said when I saw it come in. I said 'A lovely leg for the role.' I've got nothing against your right leg. The trouble is – neither have you. You fall down on your left.

MOORE You mean it's inadequate?

COOK   Yes, it's inadequate, Mr Spiggott. And to my mind, the public is just not ready for the sight of a one-legged ape man swinging through the jungly tendrils.

MOORE I see.

COOK   However, don't despair. After all, you score over a man with no legs at all. Should a legless man come in here demanding the role, I should have no hesitation in saying, 'Get out, run away.'

MOORE So there's still a chance?

COOK   There is still a very good chance. If we get no two-legged character actors in here within the next two months, there is still a very good chance that you'll land this vital role. Failing two-legged actors, you, a unidexter, are just the sort of person we shall be attempting to contact telephonicly.

MOORE Well...thank you very much.

COOK   So my advice is, to hop on a bus, go home, and sit by your telephone, in the hope that we will be getting in touch with you. I'm really sorry I can't be more definite, but as you realise, it's really a two-legged man we're after. Good morning, Mr Spiggott. (*Exit* MOORE, *hopping.*)

TRAGICALLY I WAS AN ONLY TWIN BY PETER COOK

Answer **two** of the following questions. Each question is worth fifteen marks.

1 Which of the two characters do you find funnier? Give two reasons for your answer.

2 Examine the sketch closely to explain the methods used by the writer to make it humorous.

3 If you were directing this sketch, what advice would you give the two actors about using facial expressions and gestures to make the scene as funny as possible?

 SAMPLE ANSWER (Q3)

The agent, Cook, is the main character in this sketch. Although what he says is funny, he would be even funnier if he was to act very seriously throughout the whole scene. I would advise him to keep a really straight face during the interview. It would be a good idea for him to have a really concerned expression, especially when he is explaining things that are obvious, e.g. 'You are deficient – to the tune of one.'

Mr Spiggott seems to be stupid and naïve, so his facial expression would be blank right the way through. He believes everything Cook says, so I would ask Spiggott to imitate Cook, e.g. nodding in agreement when Cook nods, or shaking his head in disagreement when Cook shakes his head, such as

when they both say that one leg is 'inadequate'.

I see the agent as a slightly crooked character, moving around a lot. He should cast suspicious glances at Spiggott every so often. At the same time, Cook does not want to hurt Spiggott's feelings, so I would suggest that he act as though he is concerned about him, and reassure Spiggott by speaking in an enthusiastic voice or patting him on the shoulder.

This is an imaginative response that manages to make worthwhile suggestions about both characters. A clear distinction is made between the naïve Spiggott and the more streetwise theatrical agent. The answer uses references to highlight moments when certain facial expressions or gestures could add to the comedy. Overall, a gallant attempt at a fairly tough question. Grade A.

ABSURD DRAMA

In this extract from Samuel Beckett's best-known play, *Waiting For Godot,* all we know is that two characters are on a country road. There is a tree and it is evening. They spend their time 'waiting for Godot' who, of course, never comes. They seem very concerned about the passing of time.

There's no denying that Beckett's plays can be hard to understand. His work is often described as being part of the 'theatre of the absurd'. The setting, characters and dialogue are unrealistic. The world doesn't always make sense, and playwrights like Beckett wrote about people's ridiculous behaviour. He also had a strange sense of humour; perhaps that's one reason he gave the characters such off-putting names.

Read the extract and then answer the questions that follow.

ESTRAGON	People are bloody ignorant apes. (*He rises painfully, goes limping to extreme left, halts, gazes into distance off with his hand screening his eyes, turns; goes to extreme right, gazes into the distance. Vladimir watches him, then goes and picks up the boot, peers into it, drops it hastily.*)
VLADIMIR	Pah! (*He spits. Estragon moves to centre, halts with his back to auditorium.*)
ESTRAGON	Charming spot. (*He turns, advances to front, halts facing auditorium.*) Inspiring prospects. (*He turns to Vladimir.*) Let's go.
VLADIMIR	We can't.
ESTRAGON	Why not?
VLADIMIR	We're waiting for Godot.
ESTRAGON	(*despairingly*) Ah! (*Pause.*) You're sure it was here?
VLADIMIR	What?
ESTRAGON	That we were to wait.
VLADIMIR	He said by the tree. (*They look at the tree.*) Do you see any others?

ESTRAGON	What is it?
VLADIMIR	I don't know. A willow.
ESTRAGON	Where are the leaves?
VLADIMIR	It must be dead.
ESTRAGON	No more weeping.
VLADIMIR	Or perhaps it's not the season.
ESTRAGON	Looks to me more like a bush.
VLADIMIR	A shrub.
ESTRAGON	A bush.
VLADIMIR	A –. What are you insinuating? That we've come to the wrong place?
ESTRAGON	He should be here.
VLADIMIR	He didn't say for sure he'd come.
ESTRAGON	And if he doesn't come?
VLADIMIR	We'll come back tomorrow.
ESTRAGON	And then the day after tomorrow.
VLADIMIR	Possibly.
ESTRAGON	And so on.
VLADIMIR	The point is –
ESTRAGON	Until he comes.
VLADIMIR	You're merciless.
ESTRAGON	We came here yesterday.
VLADIMIR	Ah no, there you're mistaken.
ESTRAGON	What did we do yesterday?
VLADIMIR	What did we do yesterday?
ESTRAGON	Yes.
VLADIMIR	Why…(*angrily*) Nothing is certain when you're about.

FROM *WAITING FOR GODOT* BY SAMUEL BECKETT

Answer **two** of the following questions. Each question is worth fifteen marks.

1 Which of the two characters do you think is more dominant in the above scene? Explain your choice by close reference to the text.

2 In what ways does this example of Beckett's work differ from other types of plays? In your answer, consider the way the characters relate to each other and the plot (story-line).

3 In your opinion, who or what do you think Godot might be? Give reasons for your answer.

SAMPLE ANSWERS (Q1)

(i) I think Vladimir is a stronger character. He does most of the answering to Estragon's annoying questions. It is also Vladimir who refuses to leave. He is much more decisive. He is first to say, 'We're waiting for Godot.' In my opinion, it is Vladimir who believes more that Godot will soon come. He gets angry with his friend and almost tries to pick a fight. 'What are you insinuating?'

At the very end, Vladimir gets fed up with Estragon and says, 'Nothing is certain when you're about.' I think this is the whole point of the scene – and it took Vladimir to see it.

This is an intelligent response to a very challenging question. Writing about characters and scenes from Beckett can be difficult at any time. The answer makes a number of worthwhile points and is well supported by quotation. Shorter answers are more acceptable to demanding questions like this one, and this thoughtful response achieves a grade B standard.

(ii) I don't think either of them is dominant. At the start of this extract, Estragon seems slightly more confident as he complains about Godot not turning up as arranged. His comments about the place are quite sarcastic. Even though he calls it a 'charming place', he can't wait to go.

But Vladimir stops him. For a short while, he is the one in control. He stops Estragon leaving. He is the one answering Estragon's questions. But the balance keeps changing. Near the end, it is Vladimir who seems to be under Estragon's control when he says, 'You're merciless.'

The last line – 'Nothing is certain when you're about' – is puzzling and suggests that Vladimir is always confused by Estragon. He seems to be in Estragon's shadow. On balance, neither of these two strange characters is dominant.

An excellent response to this difficult question. It shows awareness of the odd and subtle relationship between two characters who seem to be unaware of each other at times. The changes in the scene are well illustrated, and points are presented in a concise and organised way. Grade A.

SETTING

Nearly all plays have a setting that tells us the time and place of the story. The setting creates the **social context** within which the action of the drama takes place. Many dramas reflect everyday life. For example, a story could be set against a background of college, home, work, town or country or any combination of a wider range of settings within which we live our lives.

Educating Rita and *Teechers* take place in educational settings located in modern urban environments. Other settings, particularly in Shakespeare's places, are historical, often taking place in exotic foreign cities, royal castles or in bustling Elizabethan taverns. Some settings are more imaginative. For instance, a science fiction story may well be set aboard a spacecraft or on an alien planet.

The set is usually the first thing the audience sees and it should make a strong impression. As well as giving a sense of place, it should also suggest something of the mood or atmosphere that is to come. Every play is a new reality. **Whatever the setting of a story, it must be appropriate.** Settings that do not ring true will not engage the audience. However, an effective setting, with convincing scenery, lighting and special effects, is crucial to compelling drama.

The following extract comes from *The Long and the Short and the Tall* by Willis Hall. The play involves a group of British soldiers on patrol in the Malayan jungle during World War Two. In this case, the playwright has given detailed stage directions and his instructions are precise.

Read the extract and then answer the questions that follow.

WHITAKER	(*notices the radio which is still standing on the table*) **Sarge! The set!**
MITCHEM	**O God, lad! Get it! Quick!** (**WHITAKER** *moves as if to cross the table, but changes his mind and hugs wall in terror.*) **Get the set!** (**WHITAKER** *is still afraid to move.* **SMITH** *is about to fetch the radio when we hear the sound of feet on the wooden veranda.*) **Too late!** (*The members of the patrol squeeze up against the wall as* **MITCHEM** *edges away from the window out of sight.* **JOHNSTONE** *tenses himself. The* **JAPANESE SOLDIER** *can be heard clattering on the veranda for several seconds before he appears at the left-*

hand window. He peers into the room but fails to see the patrol and is just about to turn away when he notices the radio on the table. He stares at it for a short while and then moves out of sight as he crosses along the veranda towards the door. A further short pause, JOHNSTONE raises his hands in readiness. The door opens and the JAPANESE SOLDIER enters. As he steps into the room JOHNSTONE lunges forward and grabs the JAPANESE, putting an arm round his throat and his free hand over the soldier's mouth. MITCHEM, holding the sten gun at his hip, darts out the door and covers the jungle from the veranda. JOHNSTONE and the JAPANESE PRISONER struggle in the room).

JOHNSTONE Come on then, one of you! Get him! Quick!...Evans! Do for him! (EVANS *crosses and raises his rifle, releasing the safety catch.*) No, you burk! You want to do for me as well? Come on lad! Use your bayonet! In his guts! You'll have to give it hump. (EVANS *unsheathes his bayonet and approaches the struggling figures.*) Sharp then lad! Come on! Come on! You want it in between his ribs. (EVANS *raises the bayonet to stab* THE PRISONER *who squirms in terror.*) Not that way lad! You'll only bust a bone. Feel for it first, then ram it in. Now, come on, quick! (EVANS *places his bayonet point on the chest of* THE PRISONER, *who has now stopped struggling and is cringing in the grip of* JOHNSTONE.) Come on! Come on! I can't hold on to him forever! Will you ram it in!

EVANS (*steps back*) I...I can't do it, Corp.

JOHNSTONE Stick it in! Don't stand there tossing the odds! Just close your eyes and whoof it in!

EVANS I can't! I can't! Corp, I can't.

MACLEISH Not me!

JOHNSTONE Smith! Take the bayonet! Don't stand there gawping. Do the job!

SMITH For God's sake do it Taff. Put the bastard out of his misery.

EVANS	(*offering the bayonet to* SMITH) You!
BAMFORTH	(*crossing and snatching the bayonet from* EVANS) **Here. Give me hold. It's only the same as carving up a pig. Hold him still.** (BAMFORTH *raises the bayonet and is about to thrust it into the chest of the prisoner as* MITCHEM *enters, closing the door behind him.*)
MITCHEM	**Bamforth! Hold it!**
BAMFORTH	(*hesitates, then moves away*) **I'm only doing what I'm told.**

Answer **two** of the following questions. Each question is worth fifteen marks.

1 After reading the extract, what do you learn about Johnstone's character? Support the points you make by referring closely to the text.

2 Do you agree that this is a very tense scene? In your opinion, what are the main elements that make the scene highly dramatic?

3 Imagine you were designing the set for a school production of this scene. Suggest the scenery, props and costumes you would use in staging it.

SAMPLE ANSWERS (Q1)

(i) *Johnstone is the main leader of the patrol. He gives out to everyone. 'Don't stand gawping.' I think he's also a bit of a bully. Maybe he's afraid himself. He asks the other people to kill for him. I don't like Johnstone because he's just a coward. He has no bravery to kill the Japanese himself. He's not a good leader. In fairness, he knows what to do but won't do it himself. His soldiers don't do what he says to them. In a war, a good officer would be obeyed. This proves he's unpopular as a commander of the soldiers. I think maybe Johnstone's had some bad experiences in the war. This has made him evil.*

This is a basic grade D answer that could be greatly improved if the points were developed and expressed more fluently. Only one quotation is used, and it is carelessly done. Repetition is also a problem and there is a general lack of focus and control throughout.

(ii) *Corporal Johnstone is a tough, experienced soldier. The stage directions clearly show that he has positioned himself in preparation to attack the Japanese soldier if he enters the room. Johnstone is a disciplined professional who is ready for action the moment the door* opens. *He also knows how to silence his enemy effectively by 'putting an arm round his throat and his free hand over the soldier's mouth.'*

Johnstone has no hesitation about ordering Evans to kill the Japanese. He realises that it is necessary to bayonet the man. The brutality of such a killing does not affect him. His main concern is efficiency. His sadistic side is seen when he says, 'In his guts. You'll have to give it hump.' Johnstone is a realist who knows that humanity has no place in vicious war and he shows no sympathy at all for those around him.

This is a well-written grade A answer. Points are perceptive and clearly expressed. The vocabulary and control of language is very impressive throughout. Good use is made of succinct reference and quotations. The final sentence says a great deal about Johnstone's character.

MOOD

What characters say is the most obvious starting point to examine mood. Some scenes are relaxed and happy while others are tense and violent. Moods can vary from subdued to menacing, jovial to tragic, etc. **Dialogue expresses characters' moods.** It is worth thinking about the tone of voice used by a character. This will help you to read between the lines and understand characters' attitudes when they speak.

The most difficult tone to catch is the ironic one because the character says one thing and means another. Sometimes a character's words have a different meaning for the audience because the audience knows more about the situation than the character. This is called **dramatic irony**. There can also be irony in the unexpected way that events turn out.

In the scene below, adapted from *Macbeth* by William Shakespeare, the bad-tempered row between the two main characters creates a tense mood and the **atmosphere** is uneasy throughout. Shakespeare often uses imagery to explore and emphasise a particular mood. Death, darkness, secrecy, witchcraft and evil are nearly always present in *Macbeth*. Here, Lady Macbeth's vicious comments make a deep impression on her husband – and on the audience.

Macbeth, a respected Scottish lord, has become obsessed with his dream of becoming king. Lady Macbeth is equally ambitious. In this scene, Macbeth is suddenly having second thoughts about killing King Duncan, who is a guest in his castle. In response, Lady Macbeth accuses her husband of cowardice and weakness.

Carefully read the extract and then answer the questions that follow.

MACBETH	We will proceed no further in this **business.**	*murderous*
	He hath honoured me of late; and I have bought	*plan*
	Golden opinions from all sorts of people,	*great respect*
	Which would be worn now in their newest gloss,	
	Not cast aside so soon.	
LADY MACBETH	Was the hope drunk	
	Wherein you dressed yourself? Hath it slept since?	
	And wakes it now to look so **green and pale**	*hung over*
	At what it did so freely? From this time,	
	Such I **account** thy love. Art thou afeard	*measure*
	To be the same in thine own act and valour,	
	As thou art in desire? Wouldst thou have that	
	Which thou esteem'st **the ornament of life,**	*the king's*
	And live a coward in thine own esteem,	*crown*
	Letting I dare not wait upon I would,	
	Like the poor cat i' the **adage.**	*proverb*
MACBETH	Prithee, peace;	
	I dare do all that may become a man;	
	Who dares do more is none.	
LADY MACBETH	What beast was't then	
	That made you break this **enterprise** to me?	*agreement*
	When you durst do it, then you were a man;	
	And to be more than what you were, you would	
	Be so much more the man. I have given suck, and know	
	How tender 'tis to love the babe that milks me:	
	I would, while it was smiling in my face,	
	Have plucked my nipple from his boneless gums,	

	And dashed the brains out, had I so **sworn**	*promised*
	As you have done to this.	
MACBETH	If we should fail?	
LADY MACBETH	We fail!	
	But screw your courage to the sticking place,	
	And we'll not fail. When Duncan is asleep,	
	Whereto the rather shall his day's hard journey	
	Soundly invite him, his two **chamberlains**	*bodyguards*
	Will I with wine and **wassail** so convince	*celebration*
	That memory, the warder of the brain,	
	Shall be a fume; When in **swinish sleep**	*asleep like pigs*
	Their drenched natures lies as in a death,	
	What cannot you and I perform upon	
	His **spongy** officers, who shall bear the guilt	*drunken*
	Of our great **quell.**	*murder*
MACBETH	Bring forth men-children only,	
	For thy **undaunted mettle** should compose	*fearless spirit*
	Nothing but males. Will it not be **received**	*interpreted*
	When we have marked with blood those sleepy two	
	Of his own chamber and used their very daggers,	
	That they have done't?	
LADY MACBETH	Who dares receive it other,	
	As we shall make our **griefs and clamour roar**	*show*
	Upon his death?	*of regret*
MACBETH	I am settled and bend up	
	Each corporal agent to this terrible feat.	*all of me*
	Away, and **mock the time** with fairest show,	*deceive*
	False face must hide what the false heart	*everyone*
	doth know.	

Answer **two** of the following questions. Each question is worth fifteen marks.

1 After reading through the extract, what is your impression of Lady Macbeth?

2 In your opinion, what qualities – if any – does Macbeth have? Support your answer by reference to the text.

3 There is a violent atmosphere throughout this scene. How is it suggested in the language used by the two characters?

SAMPLE ANSWERS

Q1 *Lady Macbeth is pure evil. She is bad to him and she tells him he is green and pale. She is in a bad mood with him and lets him have it. She is bad news all the way through and even calls him a cat. The way she keeps speaking is violent. I can imagine her nagging the husband. He asks her to stop going on at him because he is the opposite to her. 'Prithee, peace.' But Lady Macbeth won't let it go. She is up for finishing off the king. The most violent thing she says is about throwing her own baby on the ground. 'And dashed the brains out'. You couldn't get much worse than this. To be fair, she keeps at it and does not give up until Macbeth agrees to do everything she wants him to. 'We will not fail' is what she says and he agrees to her scheme. Then he also gets in on the act and talks about using the daggers. The two of them end up alike – pure violent.*

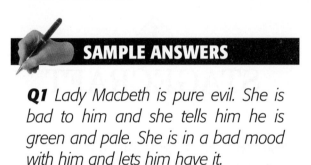

This short answer includes some good points about Lady Macbeth's violent nature and how this contrasts with Macbeth at the start of the scene. An attempt is also made to use relevant quotations. The expression could be better controlled and there is too much slang used. If standard English had been used, the answer would have achieved higher than an average Grade D.

Q3 *It is not just the violent language that makes this scene very violent. The way in which Lady Macbeth mocks her husband so much also contributes to the aggressive atmosphere. She insults him, asking, 'Was the hope drunk wherein you dressed yourself?'*

When Lady Macbeth uses the disturbing image of dashing out her child's brains, her brutal words not only shame Macbeth, but they must also send a shiver through the audience watching. It looks as if she is capable of doing just about anything, no matter how cruel and inhuman.

Macbeth is altogether different. He seems passive as though overpowered by his wife. All he can do is listen and agree with everything she says. Near the end of the extract, he shows his admiration for her murderous plan, saying, 'Bring forth men-children only.'

This violent mood is heightened further when she tells Macbeth her plan to blame the murder on the chamberlains. There is a sense of sadism in her words, e.g. 'Screw your courage to the sticking place.' Perhaps she is thinking of the actual act of murder, when the dagger goes into the victim. Lady Macbeth seems almost deranged at times, someone who takes great delight in violence to get what she wants, and this is clearly suggested by what she says.

A very fine answer, focusing clearly on the use of violent language in creating an unsettling atmosphere. Points are organised into paragraphs and relevant references are well worked into the critical observations. The writing is confident throughout, with flowing expression, a wide-ranging choice of words and varied sentences. A good grade A standard.

STAGECRAFT

Stagecraft is a general term for the playwright's skill at writing for the stage. Of course, everyone involved in the drama — the director, actors, backstage workers, etc. — will also all be using their own particular skills in the play's production.

Stage directions are often used to give more details about the story. They explain how the playwright wanted scenes to look. Along with the dialogue, stage directions show how characters are supposed to look and sound, what the time is, what the weather is like and anything else that is important.

You might be asked to suggest the most suitable kind of stage for a particular scene. An **end-stage** (or proscenium stage) is the traditional stage at one end of a hall with rows of seats facing it. It is usually raised and has a curtain to hide the 'picture'. End-stages are best for plays that have bigger fixed sets, such as a shop or living room.

Plays are increasingly being staged **in the round** (an arena stage). The audience sits around the stage area and is in much closer contact with the actors. Instead of elaborate sets, simple props are likely to be used to suggest settings. Stage directions will help you decide the best way to stage a scene.

There are many backstage workers (usually known as the crew) involved in a drama production. One of these is the **stage manager**, whose job is to take overall charge behind the scenes and to make sure that everything is in place and runs smoothly on the stage. In the extract that follows, taken from *Our Town,* a well-known American play by Thornton Wilder, the playwright has had the original idea of including a stage manager as one of the characters in the play.

Read the following extract and then answer the questions that follow.

The setting is Grover's Corners, New Hampshire. It is just after dawn on 7 May 1901.

STAGE MANAGER So – another day's begun. There's Doc Gibbs comin' down Main Street now, comin' back from that baby case. And here's his wife comin' downstairs to get breakfast.

[MRS GIBBS, *a plump, pleasant woman in the middle thirties, comes 'downstairs' right. She pulls up an imaginary window shade in her kitchen and starts to make a fire in her stove.*]

STAGE MANAGER Doc Gibbs died in 1930. The new hospital's named after him. Mrs Gibbs died first – long time ago, in fact. She went out to visit her daughter, Rebecca, who married an insurance man in Canton, Ohio, and died there – pneumonia – but her body was brought back here. She's up in the cemetery there now – in with a whole mess of Gibbses and Herseys – she was Julia Hersey 'fore she married Doc Gibbs in the Congregational Church over there. In our town we like to know the facts about everybody. There's Mrs Webb, coming downstairs to get her breakfast, too – that's Doc Gibbs. Got that call at half past one this morning. And there comes Joe Crowell Junior, delivering Mr Webb's *Sentinel*.

[DR GIBBS *has been coming along Main Street from the left. At the point where he would, he stops, sets down his imaginary black bag, takes off his hat, and rubs his face with fatigue, using an enormous handkerchief.* MRS WEBB, *a thin, serious, crisp woman, has entered her kitchen, tying on an apron. She goes through the motions of putting wood into a stove, lighting it, and preparing breakfast. Suddenly* JOE CROWELL, *eleven, starts down Main Street from the right, hurling imaginary newspapers into doorways.*]

JOE CROWELL	Morning, Doc Gibbs.
DR GIBBS	Morning, Joe.
JOE CROWELL	Somebody been sick, Doc?
DR GIBBS	No. Just some twins born over in Polish Town.
JOE CROWELL	Do you want your paper now?
DR GIBBS	Yes, I'll take it – anything serious goin' on in the world since Wednesday?
JOE CROWELL	Yessir. My schoolteacher Miss Foster's getting married to a fella over in Concord.
DR GIBBS	I declare – how do you boys feel about that?
JOE CROWELL	Well, of course, it's none of my business – but I think if a person starts out to be a teacher, she ought to stay one.
DR GIBBS	How's your knee, Joe?
JOE CROWELL	Fine, Doc. I never think about it at all. Only like you said, it always tells me when it's going to rain.
DR GIBBS	What's it telling you today? Goin' to rain?
JOE CROWELL	No, sir.
DR GIBBS	Sure?
JOE CROWELL	Yessir.

| DR GIBBS | Knee ever made a mistake? |
| JOE CROWELL | No, sir. |

[JOE *goes off*. DR GIBBS *stands reading his paper*.]

| STAGE MANAGER | Want to tell you something about that boy Joe Crowell there. Joe was awful bright – graduated from high school here, head of his class. So he got a scholarship to Massachusetts Tech. Graduated head of his class there, too. It was all wrote up in the Boston paper at the time. Goin' to be a great engineer, Joe was. But the war broke out and he died in France – all that education for nothing. |

Answer **two** of the following questions. Each question is worth fifteen marks.

1 From your reading of the extract, what are your impressions of Grover's Corners?

2 Imagine that you are directing a classroom production of this scene. How would you advise the actor playing Doc Gibbs to play the part? You might refer to costume, tone of voice, body language, etc.

3 The stage manager is an important character who is central to this scene. How would you sum up his role?

 SAMPLE ANSWER (Q3)

The role of the stage manager is like a circus ringmaster who is narrating the story and linking everything together for the audience. He introduces the characters and tells us about their lives.

He reminds us that we are watching a play on the stage, not real life. He also makes us think at the end when he says that Joe Crowell's life was ruined by the war: 'All that education for nothing.'

The stage manager seems to be standing in for the playwright. He is not a character in the play but he comments on what is happening and what has already happened. He is not affected by time because he can tell the future as well. For instance, although the time is 1901, he tells us that Doc Gibbs died in 1930.

The stage manager is able to act as a guide for the audience. His easy-going style of speaking helps to make the small town of Grover's Corners interesting and convincing. We are being reminded that this is a very close community where Doc

Gibbs knows everybody and even has time to talk to the boy who delivers the newspapers.

This is a very impressive response that makes a number of well-supported and perceptive points about the different functions of the stage manager, who acts in the traditional manner of the chorus. The ideas are clearly expressed and useful rererences are naturally integrated into the comments. A well-deserved grade A.

STUDIED DRAMA (QUESTION TWO)

You have probably read and studied at least one play already in class, either a popular Shakespearean text such as *Romeo and Juliet* or *The Merchant of Venice,* or some other play by a more modern playwright, such as J B Keane or Willy Russell.

Exam questions are often about **character** and **relationships** and **your reactions** to them. You may also be asked about **a key scene**, perhaps one that was a turning point in the story. Questions about the main **themes**, the **language, atmosphere** and **staging** of a play are also likely to be asked.

STRUCTURE AND PLOT

All plays have a plot and some kind of structure. The **plot** is the basic story that the play tells and the **structure** is the way the story is organised and put together. Most Shakespearean plays follow a similar structure, as outlined below.

1 Introduction to the situation and characters.
2 Something happens to set off a series of events.
3 Problems and confusion follow.
4 The story reaches a climax – a happy outcome in comedies, suffering and death in tragedies.
5 Everything settles down to a new beginning.

Most people know the story-line of *Romeo and Juliet.* Its structure is typical of Shakespeare's plays.

1 We are introduced to the two feuding families, the Montagues and Capulets.
2 Romeo and Juliet fall in love.
3 Problems arise as they try to keep their marriage secret.
4 The play reaches a climax when Romeo believes that Juliet is dead. Not wishing to live without her, he kills himself. In despair, Juliet also takes her own life.
5 As a result of the tragedy, the Montague and Capulet families make peace.

ENDINGS

Plays' endings are also important. They leave audiences with final impressions, so an effective ending will do a number of things:

- Draw together the various story-lines.
- Answer outstanding questions.
- Create a dramatic climax.
- Resolve conflict.
- Form a natural conclusion.
- Often suggest a fresh start.

WRITING ABOUT STUDIED DRAMA

- Closely study the wording of every question and ask yourself **what is expected of you in your response**.
- Always show that you've understood the play and that you are familiar with the **characters**, including the minor ones.
- Write the full **title** of the play you have studied and the playwright's name at the beginning of your answer.
- **Quote** short but important parts of the text to back up your points and illustrate your knowledge of the play.
- Show you know that plays should be watched on stage (and not read). Always keep the **audience** in mind when answering questions. Be sure to let the examiner see that you appreciate **stagecraft**.

- Go into detail on the writer's **style and language** where possible. You might mention imagery, repetition and the dramatic effects created by the playwright.
- When discussing themes, show that you understand the **significance** of the play. Most plays say something about society and human nature.
- Don't be afraid to suggest **ideas** of your own when the opportunity arises, but be sure to support your ideas with evidence from the text.
- Your answer will usually be in essay form, based on three or four **key points**. It should be organised into **paragraphs** and supported by references or quotations that are relevant to the question.

SAMPLE ANSWER (STUDIED DRAMA)

Choose a main character you have studied. Do you think an audience would respond sympathetically to that character as presented in the play? Give reasons for your answer. (30 marks)

The Merchant of Venice *by William Shakespeare*

First impressions of Shylock could never be very positive. He is a miser, obsessed with money and self-pity, and he bullies his own daughter. Worst of all, he tricks Antonio, the naïve merchant, with a crafty agreement (the so-called 'bond') that reflects his truly evil nature.

Yet even at the start, there are some signs that Shylock himself has been mistreated. When Antonio first tries to arrange a loan, he reminds him of the insults he has received from Christian merchants on the Rialto: 'You call me misbeliever, cut-throat dog'. And Antonio freely admits that he is certain 'to spit on thee again, to spurn thee too.'

It is likely that in Shakespeare's time, Shylock would have been seen as a completely bad character. Four hundred years later, we take a more tolerant approach. While no one denies that he is cold-blooded and merciless, modern audiences are likely to view Shylock with greater understanding. Young people especially see him both as victim and villain. Indeed, at a recent stage production of the play in Dublin, the largely teenage audience of Irish students applauded loudly after Shylock's moving speech about prejudice ('Hath not a Jew eyes?').

There are other times in the story when it seems right to pity Shylock. The loss of his daughter, Jessica – and his precious jewels – is one such example. While it is easy to condemn him for his divided loyalties, there is something tragic about his confusion and most contemporary audiences would have some pity for a bitter man who is so out of touch with his own daughter.

This is certainly the case when he hears that Jessica has been foolishly wasting his money. Whether or not he deserves to suffer, it is hard not to feel some sympathy for Shylock when he is obviously upset by the gossip he hears from Tubal: 'Thou stickest a dagger in me.'

Of course, it is in the dramatic court scene (where the tables are so neatly turned on the overconfident Shylock) that the audience's attitude is finally tested. Both the duke and Portia make it clear to the audience that the moneylender's nature has been bitterly twisted by revenge. Antonio has also been deeply wronged and 'the quality of mercy' is obviously absent in Shylock.

But Shakespeare does not let us forget that Christian hypocrisy is also alive and well. The duke is forced to admit that Venice still has its slaves, and there is very little mercy shown to Shylock in the end. Today's theatregoers would probably feel strongly that two wrongs still do not make a right. So, they would feel sorry for Shylock - especially when he is so humiliated by being forced to become a Christian. Whatever about the beliefs and prejudices in Shakespeare's day, Shylock could expect a great deal of sympathy on the modern stage.

This is a well-written answer that shows a close understanding of the play and clearly focuses on all aspects of the question. The changing reactions of audiences is central to the answer and significant references are taken from a number of key moments throughout the story. The writer has made good use of seeing a stage production and this adds weight to the view that many young people see Shylock as a victim just as much as a villain. This is a well-organised answer – points are supported and developed and the expression is varied throughout. It could expect to receive a high grade A mark.

DRAMA UNIT ROUND-UP

- Always read and **study plays** (and extracts) closely.
- **Avoid summary answers** in response to questions.
- All answers need to **be clear** and to the point.
- **Use paragraphs** – a separate one for every main point.
- **Develop the main points** you make by using references and key quotations.
- **Note the marks** allocated for questions so that you spend the correct amount of time on the answers.
- **Use common sense.** A typical ten-

mark question will have a shorter answer (usually consisting of two main points) whereas a fifteen-mark question will be longer (usually three points).
- If at all possible, try to **see stage performances**. Otherwise, watch a video of plays you are studying.

CHECKLIST

Having worked through the Drama unit, you should now feel more confident about the following:
- Knowing what to expect in the Junior Cert Drama section.
- Experiencing a wider range of drama scripts.
- Naturalistic writing.
- The language and style of Shakespeare's plays.
- Understanding how dramatists bring plays to life.
- Mood, atmosphere and humour in drama.
- Recognising and using key critical terms, such as dramatic irony, contrast, etc.
- Discussing important aspects of any play, especially characters and themes.
- Understanding setting and stagecraft.
- Being able to write successful answers of a high standard.

UNIT 6 **Poetry**

OVERVIEW

The very mention of the word poetry makes some of us feel faint with dread. Other people love reading poems, probably because poets have an interesting way of seeing things. Like other writers and artists, poets keep offering us new ways of seeing the world and our experiences.

POETRY IS PROBABLY the most challenging kind of writing, so don't worry if you find it difficult at times. Reading a new poem involves some detective work as you look for clues beneath the surface. Remember that poems can be open to many interpretations and examination questions do not have 'right' or 'wrong' answers. However, you will be expected to explore your own ideas about the poems.

The Junior Certificate Higher Level Poetry section is divided into two parts. In **Question One**, you are asked to write an answer on an unseen poem. **Question Two** asks you to write about poetry you have already studied during English lessons.

WRITING ABOUT UNSEEN POETRY

Explore the poem by reading it at least three times. The **title** should be considered closely – why did the poet pick that particular title? Other questions you might ask as you read include the following:

- Where and when is the poem set?
- What is happening in the poem?
- Who is the speaker or speakers?
- What is the speaker's attitude to this topic or theme?
- Does the poem tell a story?
- What point is the poet trying to make?
- What is your own response to the poet's views?

The actual **exam questions** (immediately following the poem) will also give you useful clues to help you understand what the poem is about. Of course, your first opinion of any poem may change as you study it in greater detail.

Successful poetry answers depend on knowing:
• **What** the poem means.
• **Why** it was written.
• **How** the poet uses language.

Some poets use straightforward vocabulary and can be taken literally. At other times they use language figuratively (metaphorically) and you get the feeling that there are hidden meanings in the poem. There is very little to be gained in thinking about right and wrong answers in interpreting poetry. The main thing is to have **ideas** about possible meanings and to respond to the poems in an imaginative and intelligent way.

All of the poems in this unit will give you **useful practice** in preparing for the unseen poem in **Question One** of the Junior Cert Poetry section. Guideline suggestions and follow-up questions are based closely on recent exam papers.

In addition, many of the poems are likely to suit **Question Two**, the studied poetry question. Common themes examined in recent years include nature, childhood, love, conflict, places, relationships, social issues, poetry, etc.

You will find that the poems vary from the straightforward to the challenging.

Like all interesting poems, of course, they are usually worth reading simply for enjoyment. They will make you think about things and some of them might even affect your feelings.

DISCUSSING POETRY

When you write about poetry you must closely examine the language and use various poetic terms. The glossary below might seem a little daunting at first, but you will probably find that you have already been using most of these **key words** in your English classes. The more poems you read and discuss, the easier it will be to use such terms, which will be very helpful in answering examination questions.

Alliteration: The repetition of the same consonant sound, usually at the beginning of several words used together, e.g. road, roof and railing.

Assonance: The repetition of identical vowel sounds in order to achieve a particular effect. Broad vowels (*a, o* and *u*) can slow a line down, making it sound sad and weary, such as the last line of Seamus Heaney's 'Mid-Term Break': 'A four foot box, a foot for every year'.

Content: The content is simply what the poem is about – its themes, ideas and story-line. For example, in Seamus Heaney's 'Mid-Term Break', the poet remembers coming home from boarding school to attend his young brother's funeral. In the poem he recalls the confusion and deep sadness of the experience.

Enjambment: When a sentence runs from one line of poetry into the next line without any punctuation marks. Run-on lines help to emphasise meaning, often suggesting movement or excitement. This example is from another Heaney poem, 'Blackberry Picking':

'You ate the first one and its flesh was
  sweet
Like thickened wine: summer's blood
  was in it
Leaving stains upon the tongue and
  lust for
Picking.'

Emotive language: Words or phrases that cause an emotional response in the reader, e.g. the defenceless kittens seemed scared.

Form: How is the poem structured or organised? What are the effects of this particular shape? In a sonnet, for example, the poet confines thoughts and feelings to fourteen lines. This condensed form usually means that the feelings in the poem are more intense.

Imagery: The pictures in the poem. Many poets use comparisons to help us more clearly understand what is being said. Writers often use *similes, metaphors* and *personification* to create vivid images (see below).

Lyric poem: A poem that centres on a significant experience in the poet's life, usually about the emotions created by an event. Poets reflect on all kinds of things, such as seeing a field of wild daffodils (William Wordsworth's 'I Wandered Lonely As A Cloud') or being bullied when young (Stephen Spender's 'My Parents Kept Me From Children Who Were Rough').

Metaphor: A direct comparison (without using the words *like* or *as*), for example, 'The fog came on little cat feet'.

Mood: The mood refers to the atmosphere in the poem and is closely linked to the tone. It could be happy, sad, tense, positive, romantic, etc.

Onomatopoeia: The sound of a word or phrase that is similar to the sound being described by the poet. Many words echo their meaning in sound, e.g. *miaow*.

Personification: This is when poets treat objects or something in nature (such as time, death or the sea) as if they are alive, e.g. the door groaned on its hinges.

Repetition: A common feature of poetry, e.g. Wordsworth's 'The Solitary Reaper':

> 'Behold her, single in the field,
> Yon solitary Highland Lass!
> Reaping and singing by herself.'

Poets often add emphasis to what they are describing by using words with similar meanings several times. Sound effects, such as rhyme and alliteration, are also types of repetition.

Rhyme: Matching sounds, usually at the end of lines. Poets use rhyme to emphasise and draw attention to certain words. Robert Frost's poem 'Stopping by Woods' ends with these lines:

> 'The woods are lovely, dark and deep
> But I have promises to keep,
> And miles to go before I sleep,
> And miles to go before I sleep.'

Rhythm: Rhythm is the beat or pace of the words. It can be regular or irregular, slow or fast, depending on the effect the poet wants to create. In W H Auden's poem 'Night Mail' the fast-moving rhythm gives the impression of a powerful train moving through the countryside:

> 'This is the Night Mail crossing the Border,
> Bringing the cheque and the postal order,
> Letters for the rich, letters for the poor,
> The shop at the corner, the girl next door.'

Simile: A comparison using the linking words *as* or *like,* e.g. light as a feather, sleeping like a baby.

Sound effects: Poets choose words very carefully and they pay close attention to their sound as well as their meaning.

Stanza: A section of a poem, sometimes called a verse (particularly if it rhymes).

Symbol: A type of image in which something is used to represent something else. For example, a snake may be used as a symbol of evil.

Tone: This is the tone of voice we can imagine when reading the poem. It could be serious, sincere, angry, mocking, sad, persuasive, etc.

Voice: This is the speaker in the poem – either the poet's own voice or a character created by the poet.

From your study of poems so far you will be aware that all these features of poetry are closely linked together to produce a unified effect. It's not a good idea to use technical terms if you're unsure what they mean. The aim is not to use poetic terms to impress people or to pick out examples of enjambment, but to enhance the quality of your response to poetry.

Carefully read through 'Slow Reader' and see if you agree with the general commentary that follows.

Slow Reader

He can make sculptures
And fabulous machines
Invent games, tell jokes
Give solemn adult advice
But he is slow to read.
When I take him on my knee
With his *Ladybird* book
He gazes into the air
Sighing and shaking his head
Like an old man
Who knows the mountains
Are impassable.

He toys with words
Letting them grow cold
As grisly meat
Until I relent
And let him wriggle free –
A fish returning
To its element
Or a white-eyed colt
Shying from the bit
As if he sees
That if he takes it
In his mouth
He'll never run
Quite free again.

VICKI FEAVER

COMMENTARY

From reading the poem we learn that the speaker – probably the boy's mother – has mixed feelings about her young son's reading difficulties. She begins by listing some of the boy's talents. In the opening lines, the **tone** is one of great pride. The child appears advanced for his age. He makes 'sculptures'. The machines he makes are out of the ordinary – 'fabulous'. He can even mock the 'solemn' adults around him.

But the **mood** changes when the poet describes the boy's disinterest in reading. There is a vague sense of underlying sadness when the child is compared to 'an old man'. This feeling is carried through to the second stanza when the poet likens the unread words to 'grisly meat'. Again, there is something disturbing about this unusual **simile**. We wonder if the mother resents the pressures that learning to read place on her son.

Eventually, the mother stops forcing the child and the poem ends with a series of **metaphors**. The child is compared to a fish that has been allowed to 'wriggle free' and to a frightened 'white-eyed colt'. All the mother's sympathies are now with the child, perhaps because she doesn't fully understand what he is feeling.

QUESTIONS AND ANSWERS

While it would be wonderful just to read poetry out of interest, the reality is that students are required to study poems critically – analysing and discussing them closely in examinations. When trying to make sense of a poem for the first time, it is useful to identify who the speaker is. This helps us understand the tone, mood and overall intention of the poem.

Always study the **wording** of the question and ask yourself: *what are the examiners expecting in the answer?* Find the **key words** in the question and underline or highlight them, as in this sample question: Vicki Feaver touches on a *number of themes* in 'Slow Reader'. Using *evidence* from the poem, identify what you think the main themes are.

THEME QUESTIONS

- Remember that the theme is the central idea in a poem.
- There may be a number of important ideas or issues raised in a poem.
- Readers decide for themselves what they consider to be the main theme.

The following is an example of a Grade A answer on the **theme** of 'Slow Reader'.

All of the themes in 'Slow Reader' are linked to the difficulties some children have in learning to read. In this case, the poet is suggesting that the mother is as distressed as her young son, especially when he is on her knees and 'gazes into the air'. She knows that he is very intelligent in other ways and is clearly concerned for him. But she also seems to accept the fact that she is unlikely to ever solve his reading problems.

As the poem progresses, reading – and perhaps the whole idea of school – is seen in a negative way, restricting the child's natural sense of freedom. This is the main theme in the poem. The second stanza gives a strong impression of the boy's deep discomfort as he resists learning to read. Like a beautiful young horse 'shying from the bit', he is reluctant to do something he dislikes and does not want to be 'trained' like an animal.

By the end of the poem, we are in no doubt that the education system needs to be more sensitive to children's needs. The poet makes it clear that every child is an individual and that learning can sometimes cause serious stress for some children and their families.

SEEING THINGS

There are many ways to explore a new poem. One key question always worth asking yourself is: *what is the emotional tone of the poem?* Try to imagine whether the poet sounds happy, sad, angry, reflective, sentimental, cool and controlled, etc. Poets are a little like tourists in a new land – everything is new and exciting so they look at things twice as closely.

In 'Cataract Operation' by Simon Armitage, the poet is watching from his window and **seeing things in a fresh way**. We do not know for sure why Armitage suddenly sees ordinary things in a new light. Perhaps he did have a cataract operation to remove an obstruction from his eye, or maybe he is imagining what it would be like to see everything so clearly.

The poet certainly seems to be delighted with the world around him. He uses a mixture of **metaphor** and **personification** to describe the washing line. Each item on the line takes on a characteristic movement of something else from another country.

For example, the crimson towel becomes a flag at a Spanish bullfight while the ra ra skirt dances a cancan, like a French woman. Such imagery makes the washing line come alive. It is as though the breeze is shaking us as well, so that we really open our eyes and **appreciate the wonders around us**.

Carefully read the following poem and then answer the questions that follow.

Cataract Operation

The sun comes like a head
through last night's turtleneck.

A pigeon in the yard turns tail
and offers me a card. Any card.

From pillar to post, a pantomime
of damp, forgotten washing

on the washing line.
So, in the breeze:

the olé of a crimson towel
the cancan of a ra ra skirt

the monkey business of a shirt
pegged only by its sleeve,

the cheerio
of a handkerchief.

I drop the blind
but not before a company

of half a dozen hens
struts through the gate,

looks round the courtyard
for a contact lens.

SIMON ARMITAGE

Answer **all** of the following questions. Each question is worth ten marks.

1 In your opinion, what is the main point being made by Simon Armitage in this poem?
2 Using close reference to the text, comment on the poet's writing style.
3 What evidence can you find to suggest that the poet experiences the world through a child's eyes?

SAMPLE ANSWER (Q2)

The poet's style is lively and very economical. He uses very few words to create a series of short scenes. His writing is imaginative throughout the whole poem. Simon Armitage creates a little drama outside his own window. He uses the key word 'pantomime' to compare the washing line to an outdoor performance. This metaphor is developed as the various 'characters' are introduced to perform their colourful party pieces. It is just like an open-air concert. The flapping shirt does its 'monkey business' swinging from the line. The poet seems to like comparisons, e.g. the opening simile comparing the sun to a head popping out of a sweater.

The poet's style is also comical. The pigeons behave like magicians doing card tricks. The hens are like search parties. These are comic images which make me think of things from the point of view of the animals for a change. The poet even jokes about his eye operation at the end when he says 'I drop the blind'.

The first paragraph is exceptionally good, effectively illustrating Armitage's use of figurative language and sense of drama. The point about the poet's humorous style is also well developed. Although the answer ends somewhat abruptly, the standard is very high throughout and deserves an A grade.

RESPONDING TO TONE QUESTIONS

- Try to imagine the poet speaking as you read through the poem. Is it serious or humorous? Sympathetic or angry? Concerned or sarcastic?
- Ask yourself: *what is the poet's attitude to the subject?*
- Tone may change as the poem progresses. It can vary from stanza to stanza, and sometimes single lines have a marked tone of their own.
- However, it should be possible to find the poem's main or dominant tone.

The following poem is a good example of a lyric. The poet, Moira Andrew, remembers an incident from her childhood that made a lasting impression on her.

Carefully read the poem and then answer the questions that follow.

Child with a Cause

My grandmother was chicken-plump
She wore long earrings, smelled of
Pear's soap and lavender water.
She kept cream in a jug under
a blue-beaded net.
Grandfather kept us both
on a short rein, our place
at the kitchen sink. When Gran's mind
slipped slightly out of gear
I was her memory.

Nearly always, that is. She peeled
potatoes once, put them ready
for Grandfather's tea and forgot
to light the gas. He was furious.
I saw Gran's tears.

Upstairs, in the narrow hall
I waited, **scuffing** the turkey-red rug.
He took his time. The flush thundered.
His shape vultured against
the door. I was raw

as **carrion.** 'It's not fair.
You made Gran cry.' He lunged at me.
'How dare you, child? How dare you
Speak to me like that?' Picked clean
by anger I ran.

'Don't mind him,' my grandmother said.
'He likes his tea on time.' The matter
was closed. Grandfather tore into
his beef stew and mashed potatoes.
I pushed my plate away.

MOIRA ANDREW
SCUFFING: SCRAPING   **CARRION:** DEAD ANIMAL FLESH

Answer **two** of the following questions.
Each question is worth fifteen marks.

1 How does the poet show the tensions in the relationships between the characters in the poem?

2 Animal imagery plays an important part in this poem. Choose two examples of animal imagery and comment on how effective each one is.

3 How would you describe the tone of this poem? Does the tone change at all in the course of the poem? Support your answer by using close reference or quotation.

SAMPLE ANSWER (Q3)

The tone of the first part of the poem shows the poet's love for her grandmother. She sees her as a larger-than-life person and a bit of a character, smelling sweetly of 'Pear's soap and lavender water'. But in contrast, a harsh tone is shown towards the grandfather. He felt that women all belonged 'at the kitchen sink'.

The short sentences show him being angry and thick just because his tea is a bit late – 'He was furious', 'He lunged at me'. The poet uses more harsh words, like 'thundered' and 'tore'. This shows the sharp tone of the old man and his bad temper.

Also, there is a lot of resentment shown towards the grandfather, but the poet's main tone is one of great sympathy for her grandmother. The

images and sounds at the end are gentle sounds. She is being dead honest at the end of the poem – 'I saw Gran's tears' and 'You made Gran cry' show the love. The young child wants to protect her gran.

This is a good grade B answer that focuses on tone throughout and uses many examples of relevant textual support very well. The references to sentence length and sound effects are particularly good. There are minor weaknesses (in expression and the use of slang), but the overall standard is above average.

Carefully read the following poem and then answer the questions that follow.

My mother has gone and bought herself a piglet
because none of us comes to visit anymore.
George has good manners and is clean in his ways:
he is courtly, thoughtful, easy to amuse.
He goes to mass with her, and sits sweetly
while she trots up to receive. He doesn't stray.
She has made a cot for him in the kitchen
where he turns in on our old clothes cut to size.

One Sunday I call on the way to somewhere else.
She props him up beside me in the high chair
and he fixes me with those dreary dark blue eyes.
When I tell him I'm glad he's there when I can't be,
he answers 'thank you' in a voice too like my own,
then bids me sit and make myself at home.

VONA GROARKE

Answer **all** of the following questions. Each question is worth ten marks.

1 In your opinion, what is the main point the poet is making in this poem?

2 The poem contains a great deal of fantasy. Do you find this humorous or disturbing? Explain your view.

3 Do you like this poem? Give reasons for your answer based on evidence from the poem.

SAMPLE ANSWER (Q3)

This is an unusual poem that makes me ask a number of questions after reading it. The relationship between the writer and mother seems strange. Why does the mother buy a piglet for company? It's as if the poet is making fun of her. In line six, the poet says that it is not the piglet but the mother who 'trots up to receive'. In my opinion, this adds comedy but also cruelty to the poem. I like the scenes where the pig is treated exactly like a child in a cot and in a high chair. The funniest part is when the piglet stares at the poet. The idea of the pig glaring angrily with its dark blue eyes adds humour. I also like the poem because it is about the serious idea of old people being left alone and forgotten by their relatives. This seems very sad, especially where the poet says 'I'm glad he's there when I can't be'.

This answer shows a good, personal response to the poem. The relationship between the poet and her mother is very interesting, but the point is not developed. The humour in the poem is well illustrated, as is the final point about elderly people. Grade B.

A **fable** is an old story with a moral or message. This one comes from Hungary and was translated by the English poet, Ted Hughes.

Carefully read through the poem and then answer the questions that follow.

Fable

Once upon a time
there was a lonely wolf
lonelier than the angels.

He happened to come to a village.
He fell in love with the first house he saw.

Already he loved its walls
the caresses of its bricklayers.
But the window stopped him.

In the room sat people.
Apart from God nobody ever
found them so beautiful
as this child-like beast.

So at night he went into the house.
He stopped in the middle of the room
and never moved from there any more.

He stood all through the night, with wide eyes
and on into the morning when he was beaten to death.

 JÁNOS PILINSZKY

Answer **all** of the following questions. Each question is worth ten marks.

1 What kind of story is suggested by the opening lines of the poem?

2 Comment on the writer's use of contrast in the poem.

3 This narrative poem feels as if it has a moral. What do you think the moral of the story is?

 SAMPLE ANSWER (Q2)

'Fable' shocks us because of its brutal conclusion. Up until the last line, the poet has led us to expect a happy ending. Janos Pilinszky has built up a picture of a gentle wolf compared to 'a child-like beast'. The wolf has no fear of the human beings. 'He fell in love with the first house he saw.' The contrast comes in the final line after the wolf has waited all night 'with wide eyes'. I was totally shocked that in the morning 'he was beaten to death'. We can see the most contrast in that the people inside the house are not to be trusted at all. These people are in contrast to the wolf's trust.

This is a grade B answer which clearly addresses the question. Effective use is made of quotations to illustrate the contrast in mood, but some reference to contrasting tone would be welcome. The expression could also be improved, particularly at the end.

ANSWERING QUESTIONS ABOUT RHYTHM

Rhythm (or beat) is closely linked to sound and punctuation. It can be regular and measured or broken and uneven. The rhythm will match the mood of a poem – fast, lively rhythms usually add excitement or happiness while slow-moving rhythms are associated with sad situations. Run-on lines (enjambment) also suggest enthusiasm and eagerness.

Remember that a poem's rhythm pattern has an important influence on the overall effect the poem creates.

Carefully read the following poem and then answer the questions that follow it.

Woman Work

I've got the children to tend
The clothes to mend
The floor to mop
The food to shop
Then the chicken to fry
The baby to dry
I got company to feed
The garden to weed
I've got the shirts to press
The tots to dress
The cane to be cut
I gotta clean up this hut
Then see about the sick
And the cotton to pick.

Shine on me, sunshine
Rain on me, rain
Fall softly, dewdrops
And cool my brow again.

Storm, blow me from here
With your fiercest wind
Let me float across the sky
'Til I can rest again.

Fall gently, snowflakes
Cover me with white
Cold icy kisses and
Let me rest tonight.

Sun, rain, curving sky
Mountain, oceans, leaf and stone
Star shine, moon glow
You're all that I can call my own.

MAYA ANGELOU

Answer **two** of the following questions. Each question is worth fifteen marks.

1 What is your impression of the narrator of this poem? (Think about where she lives, her lifestyle and feelings.)
2 Do sound effects help us understand the heavy workload of the narrator? In your answer, refer to some of the sounds in the first stanza.
3 How does the rhythm of 'Woman Work' add to your understanding of the poem?

 SAMPLE ANSWER (Q3)

I like the opening of the poem where the rhythm is very regular and abrupt. There is a steady, regular rap beat – 'The floor to mop/The food to shop' – this is like a person chanting. It is easy to imagine hearing the different jobs being rhymed off. This gives me an understanding of the woman's daily work routine.

The repetition produces an emphatic tone, which emphasises both the message of the poem as well as the mood created. She is under pressure but can find no way of escape. Then suddenly, at the start of the second verse, the rhythm changes completely and the woman says 'Shine on me, sunshine/Rain on me, rain'. Everything slows down and the tone gets more gentle. The woman seems to be seeing the brighter side of her life here.

She begins to daydream – 'Let me float across the sky' – and the rhythm is easier. In the final stanza, the mood is gentle and dreamlike: 'Star shine, moon glow/You're all that I can call my own'. In contrast to the harsh rhythm of her working life, the poem ends quietly. It is more subdued and I can imagine her escaping into a trance.

This is an excellent answer to a demanding question. Close references and quotations are used effectively to illustrate the contrasting rhythms in the poem. There is a clear understanding of how rhythm contributes to the varying moods and the overall theme of the poem. A well-written grade A standard.

John Agard was born in Guyana in 1949. He moved to England in 1977 where he became well known as a performance poet. *Caste* is an old-fashioned word meaning the racial group you are born into. The term *half-caste* (like *half-breed*) is used to describe people of mixed race.

It can sometimes imply rejection and disrespect. This poem deals with the issues of language and prejudice.

Carefully read through the poem and then answer the questions that follow.

Half-Caste

Excuse me
standing on one leg
I'm half-caste

Explain yuself
what yu mean
when yu say half-caste
yu mean when picasso
mix red an green
is a half-caste canvas
explain yuself
wha yu mean
when yu say half-caste
yu mean when light an shadow
mix in de sky
is a half-caste weather
well in dat case
england weather
nearly always half-caste
in fact some o dem cloud
half-caste till dem overcast
so spiteful dem dont want de sun pass
ah **rass**
explain yuself

wha yu mean
when yu say half-caste
yu mean tchaikovsky
sit down at dah piano
an mix a black key
wid a white key
is a half-caste symphony
Explain yuself
Wha yu mean
Ah listening to yu wid de keen
Half of mih ear
Ah lookin at yu wid de keen
half of mih eye
an when I'm introduced to yu

I'm sure you'll understand
why I offer yu half-a-hand
an when I sleep at night
I close half-a-eye
consequently when I dream
I dream half-a-dream
an when moon begin to glow
I half-caste human being
cast half-a-shadow
but yu must come back tomorrow
wid de whole of yu eye
an de whole of yu ear
an de whole of yu mind

an I will tell yu
de other half
of my story

JOHN AGARD
RASS: WEST INDIAN SWEAR WORD

Answer **two** of the following questions. Each question is worth fifteen marks.

1 Comment on the comparisons used in this poem to show that it is wrong to label anyone by using the expression *half-caste.*

2 Comment on the rhythm used throughout the poem. Is it similar to some kinds of popular music?

3 Did you like or dislike this poem? Give reasons for your answer based on evidence from the poem.

 SAMPLE ANSWERS (Q3)

(i) 'Half Caste' is sort of unusual. It showed me how outsiders feel when they try to settle somewhere new. It's like a poem that was probably written for a play. The comparisons are spot-on. They show that the country is made up of lots of mixtures, like, even the weather is a great mixture.

Also, I enjoyed the way the poet seems to be really having a good laugh to himself as he pretends to be sorry for being half-caste: 'Excuse me/standing on one leg'. He is funny and sarcastic through the whole thing. I liked it because it's exactly what I also believe. I think John Agard is dead clever the way he just laughs at the prejudice of people.

This is a lively personal response that makes some good points about the theme and writing style in the poem. The answer is short, however, and could benefit from additional reference, comment and development of ideas, and less slang. Grade C.

(ii) The language is hard at the start. It's strange as well, but I soon got used to it. John Agard mixes West Indian expressions with standard English. The usual rules we have for proper punctuation and capital letters are not there in the poem. By writing in this way, I think he is really showing us the poem's theme – what it means to be half-caste. Foreign people can't be expected to give up their own culture and way of speaking.

The poem finishes on a really high note, full of repetition as if Agard is chanting. I liked the whole rhythm of it. The poet got across the idea of how sad it is that we don't under-stand people from other countries.

By repeating 'half-a', he makes this point that it is the narrow-minded people who need to start seeing the 'whole' picture. I fully agree with John Agard. He is completely right when he says that it is the spiteful racists who need to learn 'de other half/of my story'.

There is lots of personal engagement here. The answer views the text clearly and makes some relevant observations. The challenging point about West Indian and standard English is handled well. Rhythm is also mentioned but not discussed. The final paragraph makes a clear point and successfully uses textual reference to achieve an average grade B standard.

Some poets write poems to highlight issues that concern them. In the following poem, Roger McGough creates a disturbing picture of our modern world. Like much contemporary poetry, it is written in **free verse** (without regular lines or stanzas) and the language closely resembles everyday speech.

Carefully read through the poem and then answer the questions that follow.

The Lake

For years there have been no fish in the lake.
People hurrying through the park avoid it
like the plague. Birds steer clear
and the **sedge** of course has withered.
Trees lean away from it,
and at night it reflects, not the moon,
but the blackness of its own depths.
There are no fish in the lake.
But there is life there. There is life...

Underwater pigs glide between reefs of coral **debris**.
They love it here. They breed and multiply
in sties hollowed out of the mud
and lined with mattresses and bedsprings.
They live on dead fish and rotting things,
drowned pets, plastic and assorted **excreta**.
Rusty cans they like the best.
Holding them in web trotters
their teeth tear easily through the tin,
and poking in a snout, they noisily suck out
the putrid matter within.

There are no fish in the lake.
But there is life there. There is life...

For on certain evenings after dark
shoals of pigs surface
and look out at those houses near the park.
Where, in bathrooms,
Children feed stale bread to plastic ducks,
and in attics,
toy yachts have long since run aground.

Where, in living rooms,
anglers dangle their lines on patterned carpets,
and **bemoan** the fate of the ones that got away.

Down on the lake, piggy eyes glisten.
They have acquired a taste for flesh.
They are licking their lips. Listen...

ROGER McGOUGH
SEDGE: REEDS **DEBRIS:** RUBBISH **EXCRETA:** SEWAGE **BEMOAN:** COMPLAIN ABOUT

Answer **two** of the following questions. Each question is worth fifteen marks.

1 Do you think the poet is presenting a light-hearted fantasy about the future or a serious warning about pollution? Give reasons for your answer.

2 There are some effective images in the poem. Choose two you find interesting and explain why.

3 The last stanza has quite a menacing feel. What do you think it suggests about the future?

 SAMPLE ANSWERS (Q3)

(i) The last stanza is menacing because it I think it's acting like a warning against pollution. It's a hopeless future. People are aware of pollution and something should be done to stop it. 'The piggy eyes glisten.' This is a good sentence. It has become the done thing to pollute lakes. 'They have acquired a taste of flesh.' Pollution has become such a commonplace thing that people are finding it hard to stop.

This is a very basic grade D answer which lacks depth. There is little attempt to explain the sense of menace. To boost the grade, quotes should be accurately made and much better use could be made of the text, particularly the last line.

(ii) In the last stanza, the dark, cold mood conveys the theme in a menacing and graphic way. The powerful images 'piggy eyes glisten' and 'licking their lips' suggest worse is to come for our future world. The chilling language of the last stanza reinforces the atmosphere. Any reader would feel intimidated by the thought that pollution will eventually eat us all.

We are fearful for our future. Will we let pollution destroy us? The final word of the last stanza, 'listen', is dramatic and engages our attention. The poet is telling us that the threat is close, it is really happening. We wait to hear the underwater pigs 'licking their lips'. These are symbols of a polluted world out of control. Will these weird underwater creatures soon destroy the whole planet? We listen at the end and wonder if we have a future at all.

This is a thoughtful grade A answer that makes detailed and perceptive points. There is some unnecessary repetition, but all the comments are relevant and well supported by quotation. The use of questions adds variety and shows personal engagement.

Carefully read the following poem and then answer the questions that follow.

Stealing

The most unusual thing I ever stole? A snowman.
Midnight. He looked magnificent; a tall, white mute
beneath the winter moon. I wanted him, a mate
with a mind as cold as the slice of ice
within my own brain. I started with the head.

Better off dead than giving in, not taking
what you want. He weighed a ton; his torso,
frozen stiff, hugged to my chest, a fierce chill
piercing my gut. Part of the thrill was knowing
that children would cry in the morning. Life's tough.

Sometimes I steal things I don't need. I joy-ride cars
to nowhere, break into houses just to have a look.
I'm a mucky ghost, leave a mess, maybe pinch a camera.
I watch my gloved hand twisting the doorknob.
A stranger's bedroom. Mirrors. I sigh like this – *Aah.*

It took some time. Reassembled in the yard,
he didn't look the same. I took a run
and booted him. Again. Again. My breath ripped out
in rags. It seems daft now. Then I was standing
alone amongst lumps of snow, sick of the world.

Boredom. Mostly I'm so bored I could eat myself.
One time, I stole a guitar and thought I might
learn to play. I nicked a bust of Shakespeare once,
flogged it, but the snowman was strangest.
You don't understand a word I'm saying, do you?

CAROL ANN DUFFY

Answer **three** of the following questions. Each question is worth ten marks.

1 What do you find interesting about the person who is speaking in this poem?

2 Do you think the poet is sympathising with the speaker? Use evidence from the text to back up your answer.

3 Does the speaker ever see his life as glamorous and dramatic? What are your feelings towards the speaker at this stage?

4 Comment on the use of violent language in the poem.

 SAMPLE ANSWERS (Q1)

(i) The narrator is obviously insecure and lonely. His admission that he 'wanted him, a mate/With a mind as cold as the slice of ice/Within my own brain' is very moving. It is also interesting in that we usually associate close friendship with warmth. Although the speaker wants a companion, he admits that his own brain is too cold to understand real friendship.

The speaker appears to be full of contradictions. At times he seems to be a complete failure who steals things for no reason. He is vulnerable, even pathetic – 'Mostly I'm so bored I could eat myself'. But he is also vicious and destructive – 'Part of the thrill was knowing/that children would cry in the morning'.

My overall impression is of an unhappy character who is interesting because he is fully aware of his own unhappiness. I am left feeling that the speaker is leading a worthless life, 'sick of the world'. He has been pointlessly destroyed – just like the snowman – and ends up 'standing alone among lumps of snow'.

This answer made well-supported points of a high grade A standard. Very good use is made of short quotations to show interesting aspects of the speaker's complex character. The writer displays a close understanding of the whole poem. The ending is particularly impressive and the style is assured throughout.

> **(ii)** 'I'm a mucky ghost' is good because it's showing how the boy appeared to the victims, because a ghost isn't real, so here the boy is saying that he doesn't see himself as real. It makes him also a mystery. Also, the boy's bored and has nothing to interest him. I think he's just really bored. The boy steals because he hates people. That's what I find interesting about him.

This is an average grade D standard. The points need to be more clearly developed in a longer answer, and more use could be made of quotations. There is some needless repetition of 'bored' and the overall expression could also be improved.

The following poem by John Updike deals with an unlikely poetic subject. Updike is an American writer who is best known for his novels and short stories. In this poem, he treats the subject of rats in an unusual but very interesting way.

Carefully read through the poem and then answer the questions that follow.

Rats

A house has rotten places: cellar walls
where mud replaces mortar every rain,
the loosening board that begged for nails in vain,
the sawed-off stairs and smelly **nether** halls
the rare repairman never looks behind
and if he did would, disconcerted, find
long spaces, lathed, where dead air grows a scum
of fuzz, and rubble deepens crumb by crumb.

Here they live. Hear them on the **boulevards**
beneath the attic flooring tread their **shards**
of panes from long ago, and **Fiberglass**
fallen to dust, and droppings, and dry clues
to crimes no longer news. The villains pass
with **scrabbly** traffic-noise; their avenues
run parallel to chambers of our own
where we pretend we're clean and all alone.

JOHN UPDIKE
NETHER: CONCEALED   **BOULEVARDS:** FASHIONABLE ROADS   **SHARDS:** PIECES
FIBERGLASS: ROOF INSULATION (THE AMERICAN SPELLING IS USED IN THE POEM)
SCRABBLY: DISRUPTIVE

Answer **all** of the following questions. Each question is worth ten marks.

1 In your opinion, is the imagery in this poem realistic and convincing? Refer to at least two images when answering.

2 What do you think is the poet's attitude to human beings? Support your answer by appropriate reference.

3 Do you like or dislike the poem 'Rats'? Give reasons for your answer based on evidence from the poem.

 SAMPLE ANSWER (Q2)

John Updike likes to use detail to describe the house. He thinks about unusual things. He seems to have an active imagination because he talks about the unusual world of the rats up in the attic. He has a very good sense of humour since it turns out that the real rats are the humans who pollute everywhere and then pretend it's not their fault. He seems to be always complaining that people are every bit as bad at causing pollution as the rats.

An average grade C. This answer starts off with a number of undeveloped points about the poet, which could have been illustrated with key quotations and further comment. The final point about Updike's sense of humour is reasonably good, but some mention of the poet's ironic tone and how it mocks human behaviour would have improved the grade.

RHYME

Poetry has always been linked to rhyme (matching sounds) and some people still argue that a poem isn't 'proper poetry' unless it rhymes. Although this isn't true, rhyme can make an important contribution to a poem's overall impact.

While it is not so easy to explain exactly what rhyme contributes to a particular poem, these are some of the possible effects to look out for:

- The way rhyme draws attention to words and links them together.
- The emphasis and prominence given to rhymed (or half-rhymed) words.
- Rhyme can create a pattern to reinforce the theme.
- Rhymed sound effects can be musical and pleasant.
- They can also be the opposite, i.e. jarring and discordant.
- The repetition of sound can have a chanting, ritualistic effect.
- Rhyme can create a sense of finality at the end of stanzas.

Carefully read the following poem and then answer the questions that follow.

Piazza Piece

I am a gentleman in a dustcoat trying
To make you hear. Your ears are soft and small
And listen to an old man not at all,
They want the young man's whispering and sighing.
But see the roses on your trellis dying
And hear the spectral singing of the moon,
For I must have my lovely lady soon,
I am a gentleman in a dustcoat trying.

I am a lady young in beauty waiting
Until my true love comes and then we kiss.
But what grey man among the vines is this
Whose words are dry and faint as in a dream?
Back from my trellis, Sir, before I scream!
I am a lady young in beauty waiting.

JOHN CROWE RANSOM

Answer **three** of the following questions. Each question is worth ten marks.
1 What is the relationship between the gentleman and the lady?
2 In what ways is this sonnet dramatic?
3 How does rhyme add to your understanding of what is being described in this poem?
4 Who or what might the gentleman symbolise? Give reasons for your answer based on evidence from the poem.

SAMPLE ANSWERS (Q4)

(i) I think maybe the gentleman might be representing death, he seems like a ghost to everybody. The lady doesn't want to hear what he has to say, he has been pushed to the sidelines. His relationship with love is dead.

This very brief response starts off well but lacks development. Key quotations are needed to show how the gentleman is associated with death. For example, the 'dustcoat' and 'spectral singing of the moon' suggest a ghostly situation. The final sentence is unexplained and the answer ends abruptly. A basic grade D.

(ii) The 'gentleman in the dustcoat' might symbolise time. He is trying to woo the young lady but she isn't interested. She can only hear it as a faint cry at first, but the old man promises that she will eventually succumb to his charms: it is inevitable. The young woman does not want to grow old. She threatens to scream while trying to shun time. But the old man is sure that time will overshadow her temporary beauty. However, the delicate young lady will not listen, she is much too busy waiting for wonderful things to happen to hear the threatening whisper of time.

This is a clearly expressed and well-sustained answer. Although there is little direct quotation, the idea of the gentleman representing time is developed in some detail and supported by close reference to the poem. The last two sentences show a confident control of language. Grade A.

THE POET'S POINT OF VIEW

Sometimes you need to think very carefully about exactly what the poet is saying. Is he/she simply asking you to share a memory or some particular feeling, or **is the poet making a point** and trying to teach the reader some kind of lesson?

Poets often write about subjects that affect us all and their **themes may have universal significance**. You don't need to agree with the views expressed in a poem, such as 'Note to the Hurrying Man', but you might well be able to understand and relate to some of Brian Patten's sentiments. Most of us get annoyed over certain things, so it helps to hear other people letting off steam as well.

As you appreciate poetry more and **develop your own critical sense**, you will see that every poem is influenced by social and historical contexts. Brian Patten uses language that reflects our busy modern world, and his point of view and style of writing are both familiar to you.

Carefully read through the poem and then answer the questions that follow.

Note to the Hurrying Man

    All day I sit here doing nothing but
watching how at daybreak
birds fly out and return no fatter
when it's over. Yet hurrying about this room
you would have me do something similar;
would have me make myself a place
in that sad traffic you call a world.
    Don't hurry me into it; offer
no excuses, no apologies.
Until their brains snap open
I have no love for those who rush
about its mad business;
put their children on a starting line and push
into Christ knows what madness.

    You will not listen
'Work at life!' you scream,
and working I see you rush everywhere,
so fast most times you ignore
two quarters of your half a world.
    If all slow things are useless
and take no active part in nor justify your ignorance
that's fine; but why bother screaming after me?
Afraid perhaps to come to where I've stopped
in case you find
into some slow and glowing countryside
    yourself escaping.
Screams measure and keep up the distance between us;
    Be quieter –
I really do need to escape;
take the route you might take
if ever this hurrying is over.

BRIAN PATTEN

Answer **all** of the following questions. Each question is worth ten marks.

1 Which aspects of modern life is the poet most critical of in this poem? Use apt reference to support your answer.

2 Do you find yourself in sympathy with the poet's criticisms? Give reasons for your answer.

3 Using close reference to the poem, examine the poet's use of contrast in helping us understand his point of view.

 SAMPLE ANSWER (Q3)

The most obvious contrast in the poem is the contrast between the main speaker and the person he is arguing with, who seems to be his wife or maybe his partner. The tone is angry all the way through as if the two people involved are constantly arguing. He is constantly complaining about the rat race. In contrast, his wife is the complete opposite. '"Work at life!" you scream'.

Another important contrast is the difference between the busy town and the quiet countryside. The poet hates all the hurrying and madness. He would rather be like the birds – 'birds fly out and return no fatter'. Town life is mad, driving people insane. He wants to escape. He wants to escape with her 'into some glowing countryside'. From this, we can see that people have a choice in life.

This is a reasonably successful answer that would be given a high C grade. It makes two valid points. The expression is weak in places and there is unnecessary repetition. Apt references are used, though somewhat carelessly. A more carefully controlled use of language would improve the grade.

Carefully read the following poem and then answer the questions that follow.

On A Mountain Road

The first fall of snow has frozen
The earth white as a dead man's hand.
From where I stand on this lonely bog
They call the feather bed, to the
Curve in the road between the grotto
And the graveyard at quiet Glencree,
The sky is gone. So too the mountains
With their patchwork of hawthorns
That quilts the land into fields.
Rivers remain. Somewhere salmon leap
To catch the white flies before they
Melt on the river's wet back. Sheep die.
I have brought my small son out
To creature this white wilderness
With the memory of our footprints,
The dark shadow of our shades.
His small step steadies my step.
His eyes, slit like a hawk's, scan.
He tells me all he sees or thinks he sees:
A cloud is smoke drifting from the hostel
At Glencree; a bag caught on a fence,
Someone waving in the distance. He waves.
Awakening in me forgotten memories.
Kindling in my cold bones, a father's
Easily forgotten friendship for his son.

TONY CURTIS

Answer **all** of the following questions. Each question is worth ten marks.

1 What picture of the Irish landscape do you find in this poem?

2 There are some very effective comparisons used in the poem. Choose **two** that you find particularly interesting and explain why you like them.

3 In your view what is the most important theme in this poem? Give reasons for your answer.

SAMPLE ANSWER (Q3)

The poet starts off by describing the beauty and strangeness of the countryside in the winter. He uses many vivid images of the winter season when everything seems dead, e.g. 'the earth white as a dead man's hand.' However, I feel that the main theme is about human nature because most of the poem deals with the relationship between a father and his son.

We get to understand the closeness between the two of them when the poet says 'His small step steadies my step.' Perhaps the poet is also remembering the 'forgotten memories' between him and his own father. Maybe he was also taken to Glencree by his father when he was a young child. In conclusion, I think the single most important theme is the love between father and child, and the way this love keeps being repeated.

This is a good grade A answer that shows a clear understanding of the poem. Perceptive points are effectively made and supported. The central theme of the bond between father and child is very well developed at the end.

INSIGHTS

As you have already seen, poets often write about special experiences and special moments. They can find extraordinary meaning in ordinary things. Such golden moments are sometimes called **insights** or **epiphanies**. Poets understand life by seeing things clearly and with deep understanding, and sometimes they can help us appreciate the wonders of life a little better as well.

Carefully read the following poem and then answer the questions that follow.

Miracles

Why, who makes much of a miracle?
As to me, I know of nothing else but miracles,
Whether I walk the streets of Manhattan,
Or dart my sight over the roofs of houses toward the sky;
Or wade with naked feet along the beach just in the edge
  of the water,
Or stand under trees in the woods,

Or sit at table at dinner with the rest,
Or look at strangers opposite me riding in the car,
Or watch honey-bees busy around the hive of a summer
  forenoon,
Or animals feeding in the fields,
Or birds, or the wonderfulness of insects in the air,
Or the wonderfulness of the sundown, or of stars shining so
  quiet and bright,
Or the exquisite delicate thin curve of the new moon in
  spring;
These with the rest, one and all, are to me miracles,
The whole referring, yet each distinct and in its place.

To me every hour of the light and dark is a miracle,
Every cubic inch of space is a miracle,
Every square yard of the surface of the earth is spread with
  the same,
Every foot of the interior swarms with the same.

To me the sea is a continual miracle,
The fishes that swim – the rocks – the motion of the waves –
  the ships with men in them,
What stranger miracles are there?

WALT WHITMAN

Answer **all** the following questions. Each question is worth ten marks.

1 Which particular example of a miracle is the most dramatic and vivid? Briefly explain your choice.

2 How would you describe the tone of the poem? How is the tone established?

3 From your reading of the poem, what kind of man do you think Walt Whitman was?

 SAMPLE ANSWERS (Q2)

(i) *Everything is a miracle to the poet. His tone is excited and full of excited exaggeration. Unimportant things are miracles to him. He talks about all the things going on around him as if they are all wonderful. Walt gives many examples to show his tone. He is totally excited by such things as the streets and the trees. The sea is another miracle that he describes at the end.*

Grade D. This short answer only touches slightly on the poet's excited tone. It isn't common practice to refer to writers by their first names only. The use of key quotations to illustrate the enthusiastic tone of wonder would have improved the grade.

(ii) *The poem begins with an emphatic tone: 'I know of nothing else but miracles'. This is followed by a list of examples in which the poet praises some of the wonders of nature. The repetition of 'or' at the beginning of lines really adds to this tone of great excitement. The line 'Or wade with naked feet along the beach' makes the poet sound like a young child jumping for joy. The word 'wonderfulness' is also repeated to show how mysterious the world seems to the poet.*

In the final part of the poem, Whitman appears to be almost overcome by the sheer variety in nature and the beauty of the world: 'Every hour of the light and dark is a miracle'. He seems slightly annoyed that people are missing out on this beauty. The poet ends with a rhetorical question: 'What stranger miracles are there?' His tone has become almost impatient with anybody who cannot see the wonders of the world for themselves.

Grade A. This answer makes clear points about the changing tone in the poem. Relevant quotations are used throughout and the use of repetition is explored in some detail. Overall, this is a well-supported, focused response with fluent expression throughout.

RESPONDING TO SOUND QUESTIONS

- Read the poem 'aloud' in your head and note any words that have interesting or unusual sounds.

- Look out for any repetition or patterns of sound.
- Comment on the effects of sounds, explaining what they add to our understanding of what is being described.

Carefully read the following poem and then answer the questions that follow it.

London Snow

When men were all asleep the snow came flying,
In large white flakes falling on the city brown,
Stealthily and perpetually settling and loosely lying,
   Hushing the latest traffic of the drowsy town;
Deadening, muffling, stifling its murmurs failing;
Lazily and incessantly floating down and down:
   Silently sifting and veiling road, roof and railing;
Hiding difference, making unevenness even,
Into angles and crevices softly drifting and sailing.

   All night it fell, and when full inches seven
It lay in the depth of its uncompacted lightness,
The clouds blew off from a high and frosty heaven;
   And all woke earlier for the unaccustomed brightness
Of the winter dawning, the strange unheavenly glare:
The eye marvelled – marvelled at the dazzling whiteness;
   The ear **hearkened** to the stillness of the solemn air;
No sound of wheel rumbling nor of foot falling,
And the busy morning cries came thin and spare.

   Then boys I heard, as they went to school, calling,
They gathered up the crystal **manna** to freeze
Their tongues with tasting, their hands with snow-balling;

Or rioted in a drift, plunging up to the knees;
'O look at the trees!' they cried, 'O look at the trees!'
   With lessened load a few carts creak and blunder,
Following along the white deserted way,
A country **company** long **dispersed asunder:**
   When now already the sun, in pale display
Standing by **Paul's** high dome, spread forth below,
His sparkling beams, and awoke the stir of the day.

   For now doors open, and war is waged with the snow;
And **trains** of sombre men, past tale of number,
Tread long brown paths, as towards their **toil** they go;
   But even for them awhile no cares **encumber**
Their minds diverted; the daily word unspoken,
The daily thoughts of labour and sorrow slumber
At the sight of the beauty that greets them, for the charm
         they have broken.

ROBERT BRIDGES
HEARKENED: LISTENED **MANNA:** HEAVENLY FOOD
COMPANY: GROUP **DISPERSED ASUNDER:** SEPARATED **PAUL'S:** ST. PAUL'S CATHEDRAL
TRAINS: LINES **TOIL:** WORK **ENCUMBER:** BURDEN

Answer **all** of the following questions. Each question is worth ten marks.

1 The snowfall is a wonderful event that transforms the city. How does the poet suggest this?

2 In terms of sound, how does Robert Bridges depict the unexpected snowfall?

3 How does the poet show how the children's excitement about the snow differs from the adults' reactions?

The following is a suggestion for writing successfully about **sound effects** in 'London Snow'.

Robert Bridges chooses words very carefully to describe the sudden snowfall. The first nine lines of the poem are dominated by gentle sounds – especially the soft-sounding consonants 's' and 'l'. We can imagine the snow coming like a thief in the night, 'muffling, stifling its murmurs failing'.

The sibilance in such lines as 'Hushing the latest traffic of the drowsy town' as well as the adverbs ('loosely', 'lazily', etc.) emphasise this sense of quietness.

Bridges also uses assonance and alliteration to suggest the silence created by the snow. The effect of the slender vowels in 'marvelled at the dazzling whiteness' allows us to appreciate the brightness reflected in the landscape.

The repeated 'r' sound in the alliterative phrase 'road, roof and railing' helps us picture the way everything has been completely transformed overnight.

A new kind of aural image is heard when carts and people appear and 'war is waged with the snow'. The poet uses further alliteration ('trains', 'tale, 'tread', etc.) to stress the drudgery involved as men slowly tread 'towards their toil'.

The poem ends on a nostalgic note as the older people recall their own happy childhood games in the snow. There is a certain note of sadness about the passing of innocence, which is evoked by the recurring broad vowel sounds – 'the daily thoughts of labour and sorrow slumber'.

For the adults, however, the magical glimpse of playing in the snow is just a distant memory. The spell has been abruptly 'broken' and it is this harsh-sounding final word which leaves us with a poignant sense of deep disappointment.

RESPONDING TO IMAGERY QUESTIONS

Quite simply, an image is words used in such a way to create a picture in the reader's mind so as to convey ideas, feelings, description, etc. more clearly or vividly. (*Imagery* is the word we use for a series of images.)

On a simple level, an image can be used literally to describe something. For example, in the poem 'Slow Reader', the opening line 'He can make sculptures' helps us imagine the child playing and being inventive. This is just what the poet wants us to 'see'.

Other images are metaphorical, where a comparison is used to make the description more vivid to the reader. You will already have studied poems where **similes** and **metaphors** work in this way.

While **visual images** are the most common, some images are created through sound. These **aural images** may depend on **onomatopoeia** (where the actual sound of a word suggests its meaning). Other aural images involve repetition of the same sound, such as **alliteration** and **assonance** (see the glossary earlier in this unit).

In some poems there are images associated with the other senses – taste, touch and smell.

The important thing in the Poetry section is to explain the effects of key images in a poem. It's not enough just to pick out examples of particular images – you should try to comment on what these images contribute to the poem's overall effectiveness.

Carefully read the following poem and then answer the questions that follow.

Hawk Roosting

I sit in the top of the wood, my eyes closed.
Inaction, no falsifying dream
Between my hooked head and hooked feet:
Or in sleep rehearse perfect kills and eat.

The convenience of the high trees!
The air's **buoyancy** and the sun's ray
Are of advantage to me;
And the earth's face upward for my inspection.

My feet are locked upon the rough bark.
It took the whole of Creation
To produce my foot, my each feather:
Now I hold Creation in my foot

Or fly up, and revolve it all slowly –
I kill where I please because it is all mine.
There is no **sophistry** in my body:
My manners are tearing off heads –

The **allotment** of death.
For the one path of my flight is direct
Through the bones of the living.
No arguments **assert** my right:

The sun is behind me.
Nothing has changed since I began.
My eye has permitted no change.
I am going to keep things like this.

TED HUGHES
BUOYANCY: UPLIFT   **SOPHISTRY:** FALSENESS
ALLOTMENT: GARDEN   **ASSERT:** CLAIM

Answer **two** of the following questions. Each question is worth fifteen marks.

1 What do you think is the poet's attitude to the hawk (fear, disgust, admiration, etc.)? Use close reference to the text in your answer.

2 Are you impressed by Ted Hughes' imagery in this poem? Support your answer by close references or quotations.

3 Could this poem teach us something about power and violence in the world? What point do you think the poet might be making?

 SAMPLE ANSWER (Q2)

I think Ted Hughes uses very impressive images. First, he shows the hawk, which is proud and confident, sitting 'in the top of the wood'. The hawk is like a powerful, god-like creature. The repetition of 'hooked' seems sinister. This is because the hawk is violent and he plans his attacks – 'he rehearses perfect kills'.

The bird's power over everything is seen in the second stanza. It's as though all of nature is under his control – the trees, the air and sun are there for his benefit. I find the imagery very interesting, especially the unusual image of 'the earth's face upward for my inspection'. The surrounding land is compared to a very nervous soldier lined up to honour this great bird.

At the end of the poem, the images are even more impressive and dramatic – 'My manners are tearing off heads' and 'my flight is direct/Through the bones of the living'. These lines seem chilling. I get a picture of the hawk's great ferocity. Ted Hughes uses stark imagery throughout this poem and this leaves me with a clear feeling that the hawk is vicious and all powerful.

This is a very strong answer that shows a close understanding of a challenging poem. Quotations are well chosen and the comments about key images are insightful, reflecting a personal understanding of the poem. A good effort is made to vary the expression throughout, and the answer attains a grade A standard.

PERSONAL RESPONSE QUESTIONS

Examiners often look for your own response to a poem.

- Always give reasons for your reactions to poetry.
- Do not write a summary – instead, engage with the poem (relate to the poet's experience). Perhaps you have had similar feelings to those expressed in the poem.
- It is valid to explain why you dislike a poem (although it can be more difficult to write well about negative responses).
- Try to find the strengths and qualities in the writing.

Many poets have written about the tragedy of war. You have probably read some war poems already in class, perhaps by well-known World War One poets such as Wilfred Owen. The following poem by Brendan Kennelly is written about the Troubles in Northern Ireland.

Carefully read through the following poem and then answer the questions that follow.

Nails

The black van exploded
Fifty yards from the hotel entrance.
Two men, one black-haired, the other red,
Had parked it there as though for a few moments
While they walked around the corner
Not noticing, it seemed, the children
In single file behind their perky leader,
And certainly not seeing the van
Explode into the children's bodies.
Nails, nine inches long, lodged
In chest, ankle, thigh, buttock, shoulder, face.
The quickly-gathered crowd was outraged and shocked.
Some children were whole, others bits and pieces.
These blasted crucifixions are commonplace.

BRENDAN KENNELLY

Answer any **three** of the following questions. Each question is worth ten marks.

1 How does the poet highlight the differences between the two men and the schoolchildren?

2 Which image in the poem do you find most disturbing? Give reasons for your choice.

3 Is the poet's description of the explosion objective and factual, or does he exaggerate? Refer to the poem when commenting on the poet's style of writing.

4 What is your own personal response to this poem? Give reasons for your answer based on evidence from the text.

SAMPLE ANSWER (Q4)

This poem made me angry. The opening is dramatic and the children have no chance. This must be just like what happens in reality when an explosion happens. The poet uses the colour black to describe the van and the bomber's hair. I thought this was a good way of showing their evil. Also, black suggests sorrow.

The line 'In chest, ankle, thigh, buttock, shoulder, face' has a slow kind of rhythm which makes me think of all the wounds inflicted on these unfortunate children. They were innocent and this is why war is so tragic.

Also, I think it is important to protest against war just like Brendan Kennelly has. I liked the last line because it was a link with the nails hammered into Christ's hands. In my opinion, the poet is saying that evil still happens. People are not as Christian as they say.

This is a good personal response that makes a number of interesting points about both the message and style of the poem. There are some weaknesses in expression, e.g. beginning sentences with 'also'. However, the final paragraph is very perceptive and makes a strong point succinctly. Overall, a grade B answer.

COMPARING POEMS

You might be asked to compare two poems, probably on the same topic. This is more likely to happen in Question Two (studied poetry). Comparative questions will test your ability to analyse the two different approaches of the poets and explain what the poems say about **character** or **relationships** (if they are about people), **setting** (if they describe a place) and **themes** (the ideas and emotions expressed in the poems).

Strictly speaking, *compare* means examining similarities between poems while *contrast* refers to looking at differences. For Junior Cert English, however, no distinction is made. If you are asked to compare two poems, you can write about their similarities *and* differences.

Always remember that you are dealing with the links between the two poems. Try to say something about **both poems** in each paragraph you write. Point out how they are similar (or different) in ideas, language and structure. Quote evidence for each main point you make and explain how quotations support your views.

Areas for comparison/contrast are:
- How clearly themes are expressed.
- Literal and metaphorical language.
- The poets' descriptive powers.
- Use of imagery.
- Mood, atmosphere and tone.
- The attitudes of both poets.
- Your own reaction to each poem.

The following two poems both deal with aspects of school life. Carefully read through both and then answer the questions that follow.

Cloakroom

Anoraks hang limp and folded,
bats sleeping all day;

when steam rises from racked rows
they are kippers to be smoked.

These pipes are comfort from bullies,
hot and final sanctuary,

And the best place in hide-and-seek
is hanging crucified

across two pegs with knees drawn up
beneath a duffle-coat.

I hid once through assembly,
the piano mirage faint

and singing voices lapping
at some distant shore.

My teacher found me drowsed by rain forests
steaming under tropic sun.

She was kind and simply asked
why I was late.

I don't recall my answer, only that
my mind had drained

to rows of empty question-marks
turned upside down.

 BARRIE WADE

Maladjusted Boys

I have made ten minutes of silence.
I know they are afraid of silence
And the mind's pattern of order.
They gaze at me out of oblique faces
And try to fidget away the bleak thoughts
Simmering in the dark tangle of their minds.
I read their unfriendly eyes, cushion
The confused hatred, stand presumptuously
And pretend not to be afraid.
I keep at them with my eyes,
Will them to work, and ride
The storm in a roomful of cold attention.
Here and there faces cringe
And I read a future...the dark corner
Of a street hiding the cruel
Thud of a chain or boot.
I see a hunter mask glow on a face
And grimy nailbitten hands bend a ruler
To its limit...all this in a room
Yellow with June sun and music
Of birds from a private wood.

ROBERT MORGAN

Answer **either** question that follows. Each question is worth thirty marks.

1 In your opinion, is there anything positive about school life in these two poems, or do you find them entirely negative? Explain your response using appropriate reference.

2 Which of the two poems do you prefer? Give reasons for your answer.

 SAMPLE ANSWERS (Q1)

(i) Both these poems give a very negative picture of school. 'Cloakroom' is mainly about being bullied and hiding away from older boys bullying him which is one of the worst things that can happen to anyone at school. The pupil tries to block out the bullying by hiding in the cloakroom and daydreaming. The teacher seems kind hearted enough, which is one positive thing that happened. At least this is one part where the whole school isn't negative.

The title of 'Maladjusted Boys' shows that these lads have problems settling in and behaving. They all hate the class and can't wait to get away. This is where it's negative. The teacher says 'they are afraid of silence'. They also have 'unfriendly eyes'. He sees no future ahead for the boys. These boys will end up fighting in the streets. This is very negative altogether.

The teacher is also feeling down about the class. He can't be feeling too good if he is always looking at his watch. They are all negative. The only good thing is the sun shining because it's June. Both poems show no hope very much.

There are good points made in this short answer, but very little expansion of ideas. No quotations are used to discuss 'Cloakroom' and the expression could be more fluent. The points about 'Maladjusted Boys' are developed a little more successfully. Overall, language is not well controlled. Grade D standard.

(ii) 'Cloakroom' is a less negative poem than 'Maladjusted Boys'. However, the mood of the two poems is pessimistic and there are lots of sad images in both. The overall picture of the actual cloakroom is negative. 'The anoraks hang limp' suggests the young boy's mood as he looks for some comfort from the bullies. There is no comfort at all in 'Maladjusted Boys'. The images are very depressing, e.g. 'faces cringe' and 'the storm in a roomful of cold attention'.

In 'Cloakroom', the poet uses violent images to show pain, e.g. 'racked rows' and 'hanging crucified'. The boy thinks of faraway places and imagines himself in tropical rainforests. This is the only positive way out of his unhappy life at school. Unfortunately, the maladjusted boys cannot even drift away in their minds. The mood is even darker for them and there is tension in their silent classroom. The boys fidget as if they might suddenly lose their tempers. Their lives are empty. This is seen in such phrases as 'confused hatred', 'unfriendly eyes', 'cold attention', etc. The poet sees them as wild hunters who will spend their future in crime.

The boy in 'Cloakroom' seems to be younger and not as badly affected. The short stanzas help to break up his fear of the bullies, whereas 'Maladjusted Boys' is written in one long section. This adds to the feeling of being overpowered. Even at the end, when the poet describes the sun and the birds outside, this only adds to the feeling of being trapped indoors.

In general, both these poems are extremely negative. However, the boy in 'Cloakroom' seems smart enough to survive the bullies. The line 'I don't recall the answer' might mean that the bad school experiences happened a long time ago and he has moved on since then. The maladjusted boys are not looking back. There is great tension and tragedy in their lives and this is symbolised by the image of the ruler being bent. These boys have nothing positive to look forward to except violence.

The ideas in this answer are clearly expressed and the sentences are controlled. References and interesting quotations are also used effectively. Points are organised into paragraphs and the comparative approach is maintained at all times. Images in both poems are effectively linked to mood, and the second-last paragraph makes a strong point about the contrasting structures of the poems. With about twenty minutes to answer this thirty-mark question, answers need to be focused and wide ranging, as in this case. Grade A.

FIGURATIVE LANGUAGE

Poets frequently use figurative (metaphorical) language, such as metaphors, similes, personification and symbols, which makes their writing more vivid and interesting.

A **metaphor** is a direct comparison when something is said to be something else. In Seamus Heaney's poem 'Storm on the Island', the sound of the wind is described as 'a tragic chorus' and space is 'a salvo', an outburst similar to heavy gunfire.

A **simile** is an indirect comparison, saying that something is *like* (or *as*) something else, e.g. the sea-spray 'spits like a tame cat/turned savage'.

Personification gives life to things. Heaney describes the earth as 'wizened', suggesting the wrinkled skin of an elderly person. The image also makes us consider someone who has a long history and who has perhaps survived a great deal of trouble.

A **symbol** is another interesting type of image where an object represents something abstract, such as an idea or a feeling. The squat houses on the island might well be symbols of the strength and resilience of the local people.

Carefully read the following poem and then answer the questions that follow.

Storm on the Island

We are prepared: we build our houses squat,
Sink walls in rock and roof them with good slate.
This wizened earth has never troubled us
With hay, so, as you see, there are no stacks
Or **stooks** that can be lost. Nor are there trees
Which might prove company when it blows full
Blast: you know what I mean – leaves and branches
Can raise a tragic chorus in a gale
So that you listen to the thing you fear
Forgetting that it **pummels** your house too.
But there are no trees, no natural shelter.
You might think that the sea is company,
Exploding comfortably down on the cliffs
But no: when it begins, the flung spray hits
The very windows, spits like a tame cat
Turned savage. We just sit tight while wind dives
And **strafes** invisibly. Space is a **salvo,**
We are bombarded by the empty air.
Strange, it is a huge nothing that we fear.

SEAMUS HEANEY
STOOKS: SMALL HEAPS   **PUMMELS:** STRIKES
STRAFES: ATTACKS FROM ABOVE   **SALVO:** BURST OF GUNFIRE

Answer **two** of the following questions. Each question is worth fifteen marks.

1 From the many images in the poem, choose two that you think are particularly effective and explain what you like about them.

2 Heaney uses many sound effects in this poem. How do these emphasise what he is describing?

3 Most of the poem is taken up with the picture of a storm, yet the poem ends with 'it is a huge nothing that we fear'. How do you explain the ending?

SAMPLE ANSWER (Q2)

Sound is important in 'Storm on the Island', especially when the poet is trying to describe the rough noises heard during the gale. The onomatopoeia of dramatic words, such as 'blows full/Blast' and 'flung spray hits/The very windows' sees Heaney selecting harsh sounds. These echo the wild storm attacking the whole island.

The poet uses equally harsh-sounding verbs like 'spits' and 'hits' near the end of the poem.

There are also examples of alliteration, such as: 'we build our houses squat/Sink walls in rock and roof them with good slate.' This suggests the strong island houses – and even the hardy people who live in this remote place.

There are some contrasting quiet moments also, whenever Heaney is describing the isolation. At times, he uses broad vowels to get across this sense of loneliness. This use of assonance is seen in the line 'But there are no trees, no natural shelter'. This is a good example of how the repetition of vowels helps us to imagine how stranded the islanders are. Overall, sound effects play a very important part in describing the storm.

The answer here is of a very high standard and shows a clear understanding of how sound effects, such as alliteration and assonance, are used so effectively in the poem. Relevant points are strongly supported by key quotations and developed very well. The answer ranges through the whole poem and there is an overall assurance in the writing style. A high grade A.

FORM

Form (structure) usually refers to the way in which a poem is actually written down on the page. You will probably be familiar with some of these forms.

- **Lyric:** Usually a short poem expressing a feeling.
- **Ballad:** A longer traditional narrative poem in verse form.
- **Sonnet:** A more condensed form of fourteen lines.

The following poem by Seamus Heaney is a good example of a lyric based on a vivid memory from the poet's childhood.

Read through the poem and then answer the questions that follow.

Blackberry Picking

Late August, given heavy rain and sun
For a full week, the blackberries would ripen.
At first, just one, a glossy purple clot
Among others, red, green, hard as a knot.
You ate the first one and its flesh was sweet
Like thickened wine: summer's blood was in it
Leaving stains upon the tongue and lust for
Picking. Then red ones inked up and that hunger
Sent us out with milk-cans, pea-tins, jam-pots
Where briars scratched and wet grass bleached our boots.
Round hayfields, cornfields and potato drills
We trekked and picked until the cans were full,
Until the tinkling bottom had been covered
With green ones, and on top big dark blobs burned
Like a plate of eyes. Our hands were peppered
With thorn pricks, our palms sticky as **Bluebeard's.**

We hoarded the fresh berries in the **byre.**
But when the bath was filled we found a fur,
A rat-grey **fungus** glutting on our **cache**.
The juice was stinking too. Once off the bush
The fruit fermented, the sweet flesh would turn sour.
I always felt like crying. It wasn't fair
That all the lovely canfuls smelt of rot.
Each year I hoped they would keep, knew they would not.

SEAMUS HEANEY
BLUEBEARD: A PIRATE WHO KILLED MANY OF HIS WIVES BY CHOPPING OFF THEIR HEADS
BYRE: A COWSHED   **FUNGUS:** FURRY GROWTH   **CACHE:** HIDDEN TREASURE

Answer **two** of the following questions. Each question is worth fifteen marks.

1 Do you agree that the imagery used by the poet gives a vivid impression of ripeness? Give reasons for your response based on the evidence in the first stanza.

2 What common features can you find between 'Blackberry Picking' and 'Storm on the Island'?

3 Which of the two poems do you prefer? Give reasons for your answer.

 SAMPLE ANSWERS (Q2)

(i) The two poems by Seamus Heaney are about nature and the different sides to it. 'Blackberry Picking' is about the good side of nature, things growing and children enjoying picking their blackberries in August. This happens in the country. It is full of pleasure, like in another poem we read called 'This is just to say I've eaten some plums'. The fruit is just there to be enjoyed. The other poem is also about nature, but in 'Storm on the Island, the people are struggling more. We know this is true from the way the poet says they are bombarded and also comparing the sea to a cat spitting when it turns into a savage. The two poems are to do with nature.

This answer deals reasonably well with one point, the common nature theme, and there is some development based on reference. The answer is slight for a fifteen-mark question and there is nothing about the poet's style of writing in the two poems. The expression could also be improved. Grade D.

(ii) Even if his name was not on both poems, I think I would guess that they were written by the same person. They are personal and set in rural settings. Seamus Heaney is well known as Ireland's greatest nature poet and he uses very detailed descriptions in both poems.

The images are vivid in both, e.g. in 'Storm on the Island', Heaney shows us the strength of the houses – 'we build our houses squat'. The word 'squat' gives a feeling of something that is so strong it won't be easily knocked down. The poet also uses detailed comparisons when describing the spray of the sea 'exploding' on the cliffs. This is another key word that helps me imagine the power of the storm.

'Blackberry Picking' also uses metaphors and similes to show the colour and freshness of the actual blackberries. The berries are 'like thickened wine, summer's blood was in it'. These are very effective images. The poet also gives us details about the ways the black-berries were collected in 'milk-cans, pea-tins, jam-pots'.

Heaney's poetry is very personal. We see everything through the child's eyes and he even compares the colour of blood on his hands with the blood on Captain Bluebeard, a famous pirate he would have read stories about. 'Storm on the Island' also takes a personal subject that would worry the people there as they wait for the invisible wind storm in fear - 'It is a huge nothing that we fear.'

This is a very strong response that achieves a grade A standard. The main points focus clearly on comparing the two poems. They are thoughtful, well organised into paragraphs and effectively supported. The poet's use of vivid imagery is dealt with well and the final paragraph is particularly good. Quotations are fluently worked into the comments and observations.

STUDIED POETRY (QUESTION TWO)

When answering the second exam question (about poems you have studied in class) you will be expected to write a longer answer about poetry that has made an impression on you. While the questions tend to be general ones, they often require a personal response.

Typical questions include the following:

- A poem that dealt with a **particular theme**, e.g. friendship, conflict, nature, protest, childhood, sorrow, people, places, humour, love, choices, modern life, etc.
- A poem that **changed your attitudes** in some way.
- A poem in which a **particular mood** was created.
- A poem that **moved** you emotionally.
- A poem about an **unusual subject** or written in an **unusual style**.
- Comparing and contrasting **two poems**.

WRITING ABOUT STUDIED POETRY

- As with all questions, you will need to **study the wording** closely to find out what the examiners will be expecting in the answer.

- Underline or **highlight the key parts** of the question.
- **Write the title** of the poem you have studied in class **and the poet's name** clearly at the beginning of your answer.
- Spend some time planning your main points carefully, making sure that you **address the question** directly.
- **Support your points** with short relevant quotations and references.
- Always **comment on the quotation** and discuss its significance, explaining how it helps the reader's understanding of what is being described.
- Every paragraph should **relate directly to the question** you were given. Check that you are not just summarising the poem.
- Use all the skills you have learned in poetry classes to write an interesting **twenty-minute essay** based on three or four relevant points, well supported by references or quotations and organised in paragraphs.

SAMPLE ANSWER
(STUDIED POETRY)

From the poetry you have studied, choose a poem that dealt with the *theme of memories* and *discuss how that theme is treated* in the poem. (30 marks)

'Child with a Cause' by Moira Andrew

'Child with a Cause' is a lyric poem that deals with Moira Andrew's mixed feelings about her childhood. The poet gives us a revealing insight into the characters of her grandparents and the contrasting relationships she had with them. The poem centres around one particular memory of an incident when her grandfather lost his temper.

The mood at the beginning is relaxed and nostalgic. The poet remembers her grandmother as a motherly 'chicken-plump' figure who 'wore long earrings' and was full of surprises. But this fond memory is short-lived as she recalls her stern grandfather who kept everyone 'on a short rein'. For the rest of the poem, the theme of memories is linked to the poet's unhappy experiences. We soon understand that the cause mentioned in the title relates to the poet's resentment towards the grandfather she disliked so much.

The poet uses a gentle tone to describe her elderly grandmother and there is a sense of pride as she suggests their closeness in the simple statement 'I was her memory'. In contrast, the grandfather is remembered as an insensitive character who bullies others. When his tea isn't ready on time he becomes 'furious'. The poet's use of metaphors conveys the violent side of his nature. 'His shape vultured' compares him to a vicious bird of prey ready to attack anyone around him. She remembers her own reaction, 'picked clean' by feelings of anger.

In the last stanza, we are left with the impression of the poet's enduring rage over her grandfather's cruelty. It is clear that she has never really forgiven him for his rude manner. Her memories are anything but sentimental as she describes how he 'tore' into his stew. It is clear that the injustice of what happened affected her deeply and may well have been a turning point that was to shape her life. The poem ends on a defiant note as the poet remembers her final act of protest: 'I pushed my plate away'.

Aim to write good grade A answers like this one. Obviously, you must know your studied poetry very well before going into the exam. Keep reading your poems and revising your notes. Be sure to learn off key quotations. After all, the examiner will be expecting a high standard.

HOW EXAMINERS THINK

Forget any rumours you may have heard about examiners being out to get you. In fact, they love to see – and reward – good work, so try to think about your own written answers like examiners do. It depends on the actual question, of course, but these are the top ten thoughts going through the examiners' minds as they mark your work.

1 Was the question clearly understood?
2 Does the answer really address the question at all times?
3 Are points clearly made in paragraphs?
4 Is there comment and development?
5 Does the answer range over the whole poem?
6 Are themes and style dealt with?
7 Is there accurate textual support?
8 Is the expression lively, varied and fluent?
9 Does the answer represent twenty minutes' work?
10 Finally, what about spelling and grammar?

POETRY UNIT ROUND-UP

- Always read and **study the poem** (and questions) several times.
- **Consider key aspects** (theme, tone, imagery, sound effects, etc.).
- **Avoid summaries.** Very few questions ask for a mere line-by-line summary.
- **Respond directly** and relevantly to every question.
- Write every main point in a **paragraph**.
- Support all points with close **reference** or **quotation**.
- Refer to the effect of a **writer's style** and technique when answering.

CHECKLIST

Having worked through the Poetry unit, you should now feel more confident about the following:

- Knowing what to expect in the Junior Cert Poetry section.
- Recognising and using key critical terms such as theme, tone, imagery, etc.
- Reading and understanding new and unusual poems.
- The importance of imagery and comparisons in poetry.
- Comparing poems.
- Discussing poems you have already studied in class.
- Using relevant quotations and references effectively.
- Understanding poems from other cultures.
- Writing personal responses to poems.
- Being able to write successful answers of a high standard.

UNIT 7 Fiction

OVERVIEW

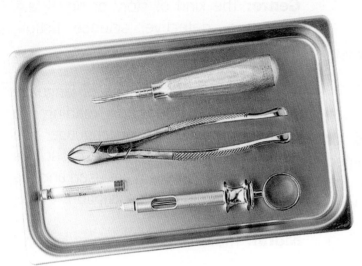

*Fiction is any writing that comes from the imagination rather than fact. It includes drama and poetry, but it more often refers to **novels** and **short stories**. Both narrative forms have much in common; however, short stories usually:*

- *Deal with one incident or experience.*

- *Have a small or limited number of characters.*

- *Go into less detail on background and description.*

AS WITH THE DRAMA and Poetry sections, the Junior Cert Fiction section consists of two questions. In Question One (unseen fiction) you will be asked to write about an extract from a short story or novel. Most questions relate to the key aspects of fiction that have already been mentioned in Unit 1, including **plot, setting, characters, relationships, themes** and **style of writing**.

When you are reading a fiction extract for the first time, ask yourself four basic questions:

- What is the story-line?
- Where is it set?
- Who are the main characters?
- What is their relationship?

For Question Two (studied fiction), you will be expected to show more detailed knowledge and understanding of the stories or novels you have worked on during English classes.

DISCUSSING FICTION

These are some of the **main terms** you will be using when responding to questions on fiction.

Atmosphere: This is the mood or general feeling in a story, often created by the background against which the story is set. For example, an author who emphasises the misery of a setting is likely to produce an atmosphere of hopelessness.

Caricatures: Stereotypical, one-dimensional characters who never change.

Characterisation: How the writer presents and develops characters. Are they credible and true to life? Do they have many sides to their personalities? Do they change over time?

Crisis: An important challenge for one or more characters, often a turning point in the character's development. We learn about characters when they are in trouble or facing difficult decisions.

Dialogue: Conversation between characters. It is always worth noting what characters say and what others say about them.

Empathy: Writers put themselves in the place of the characters they are writing about; a stronger sensation than sympathy.

Genre: The kind of story or novel, e.g. adventure, detective, science fiction, horror, comedy, love story, etc.

Language: Interesting use of language is often what keeps us reading. To comment on the use of language, you need to recognise how devices such as imagery and symbolism are used and the extent of the detailed description.

Moral: The writer's message or lesson.

Plot: The basic story-line. What happens? Why? How? In what order?

Relationships: How characters relate to one another. Relations can be friendly, loving, stormy, deep, shallow, good, bad, etc. The development of a relationship can often be the central element of the plot.

Setting: The where and when of the story. Writers can usually create a good sense of place. Settings can be the key to creating a particular atmosphere or reflecting a character's mood.

Structure: The way the story is constructed. Is the story told by one of the characters? Is it told in chronological order (as events happened), or are flashbacks used? Is it told partly through diaries or letters?

Subplot: A minor story-line that develops along with the main plot.

Theme: This refers to the main issue or idea in the story. Every part of a novel can express its theme. Titles and settings can point to what a story is about. Characters, events and endings also reflect the author's concerns and views.

NARRATION

The word used for storytelling is **narration**. A storyteller is a narrator. When you read a story (or extract), keep the following questions in mind:

- Is the story all told by one person?
- Is the narrator a character in the story?
- Is the narrator telling his or her own story?
- How does the narrator know about the story's events?
- Is the narrator remembering the past from a different viewpoint?

The type of narrator alters the way the story is told. **First person narratives** give an impression of closeness. The readers see everything from the narrator's point of view. **Third person narratives** allow authors to know about all the characters and present several points of view to the reader.

In *Great Expectations,* Pip is the narrator telling his own story. The same is true of Scout in *To Kill A Mocking Bird.* Both narrators are looking back on their young lives and this allows them to comment on their own behaviour. In Pip's case, he continually criticises his earlier selfishness.

In *Animal Farm,* however, the story is told by the **omniscient** (all-seeing) author, George Orwell. In this third person narrative, readers are not being told the story from one character's viewpoint. They are free to make up their own minds about the events as Orwell presents them.

Mildred D. Taylor was born in Mississippi in the American South. This area, the Deep South, has a history of black slavery and tension between black and white people. Her novel *Roll of Thunder, Hear My Cry* is set in the early 1930s. Cassie Logan and her brother, Stacey, along with their friend, T.J. Avery, are doing some shopping in the Barnett Store. Cassie narrates what happened next.

Carefully read the following extract and then answer the questions that follow.

The Barnett Store

We stood patiently waiting behind the people in front of us and when our turn came, T.J. handed his list to the man. 'Mr Barnett, sir,' he said, 'I got me this here list of things my mamma want.'

The storekeeper studied the list and without looking up asked, 'You one of Mr Granger's people?'

'Yessir,' answered T.J.

Mr Barnett walked to another counter and began filling the order, but before he finished a white woman called, 'Mr Barnett, you waiting on anybody just now?'

Mr Barnett turned around. 'Just them,' he said, indicating us with a wave of his hand. 'What can I do for you, Miz Emmaline?' The woman handed him a list twice as long as T.J.'s and the storekeeper, without a word of apology to us, proceeded to fill it.

'What's he doing?' I objected.

'Hush, Cassie,' said Stacey, looking very embarrassed and uncomfortable. T.J.'s face was totally bland, as if nothing at all had happened.

When the woman's order was finally filled, Mr Barnett again picked up T.J.'s list, but before he had gotten the next item his wife called, 'Jim Lee, these folks needing help over here and I got my hands full.' And as if we were not even there, he walked away.

'Where's he going?' I cried.

'He'll be back,' said T.J., wandering away.

After waiting several minutes for his return, Stacey said, 'Come on, Cassie, let's get out of here.' He started toward the door and I followed. But as we passed one of the counters, I spied Mr Barnett wrapping an order of pork chops for a white girl. Adults were one thing; I could almost understand that. They ruled things and there was nothing that could be done about them. But some kid who was no bigger than me was something else again. Certainly Mr Barnett had simply forgotten about T.J.'s order. I decided to remind him and, without saying anything to Stacey, I turned around and marched over to Mr Barnett.

'Um ... 'scuse me, Mr Barnett,' I said as politely as I could, waiting a moment for him to look up from his wrapping. 'I think you forgot, but you was waiting on us 'fore you was waiting on this girl here, and we been waiting a good while now for you to get back.'

The girl gazed at me strangely, but Mr Barnett did not look up. I assumed that he had not heard me. I was near the end of the counter so I merely went to the other side of it and tugged on his shirt sleeve to get his attention.

He recoiled as if I had struck him.

'Y-you was helping us,' I said, backing to the front of the counter again.

'Well, you just get your little black self back over there and wait some more,' he said in a low tight voice.

I was hot. I had been as nice as I could be to him and here he was talking like this. 'We been waiting on you for near an hour,' I hissed, 'while you 'round here waiting on everybody else. And it ain't fair. You got no right –'

'Whose little nigger is this!' bellowed Mr Barnett.

Everybody in the store turned and stared at me. 'I ain't nobody's little nigger!' I screamed, angry and humiliated. 'And you ought not be waiting on everybody 'fore you wait on us.'

'Hush up, child, hush up,' someone whispered behind me. I looked around. A woman who had occupied the wagon next to ours at the market looked down upon me. Mr Barnett, his face red and eyes bulging, immediately pounced on her.

'This gal yourn, Hazel?'

'No, suh,' answered the woman meekly, stepping hastily away to show she had nothing to do with me. As I watched her turn her back on me, Stacey emerged and took my hand.

'Come on, Cassie, let's get out of here.'

'Stacey!' I exclaimed, relieved to see him on my side. 'Tell him! You know he ain't fair making us wait –'

'She your sister, boy?' Mr Barnett spat across the counter.

Stacey bit his lower lip and gazed into Mr Barnett's eyes. 'Yessir.'

'Then you get her out of here,' he said with hateful force. 'And make sure she don't come back till yo' mammy teach her what she is.'

FROM *ROLL OF THUNDER*, HEAR MY CRY BY MILDRED D. TAYLOR

Answer **two** of the following questions. Each question is worth fifteen marks.
1 From your reading of the extract, what do you learn about Cassie's character?
2 What evidence can you find to show that Stacey is older and more mature than her?
3 Would you agree that the writer creates a very tense and uneasy mood in this short scene? Explain some of the ways by which she does this.

SAMPLE ANSWERS (Q3)

(i) I agree that the writer creates a tense and uneasy mood in this short scene. I agree with the way Cassie stands up for her rights. Mr Barnett has no respect. But he is the one who's the real low-life, not Cassie. This is a very tense place, especially when he walks away to serve the white people. When Cassie hits him on the shoulder, it's also very tense and uneasy. He is more than likely

to lose his temper and hit her back. Another tense time is when he picks on Hazel. He hopes he can bully Hazel over Cassie, but she isn't Cassie's mother and this just makes him worse. This is very tense. By this stage, he could really go ballistic and lose it completely. I agree that the writer, Mildred D. Taylor, creates a tense, uneasy mood in this short scene.

Less slang and some use of direct quotations would improve this response. There is poor control of language and too much pointless repetition. Apart from referring to two examples of uneasy moments, there is little to reward in this very short answer. A basic Grade D at best.

(ii) The uneasy atmosphere increases in this scene. At first, the children are relaxed, but the more Mr Barnett insults them, the more the tension slowly grows throughout this scene. It is a very dramatic situation with a lot of conflict between Cassie and the shop owner.

There is a great difference in the offhand way Mr Barnett treats the black children and the nice way he treats any white shoppers. This contrast tells me that it is making Cassie mad. Her anger builds up to a high point when she actually touches his shirt sleeve and 'He recoiled as if I had struck him'.

The way he speaks in 'a low tight voice' is where I can imagine his angry tone. At the end of the extract, he is so out of control that he even scares Stacey and the other shoppers. The writer lets the tension grow when Mr Barnett turns on Stacey – 'She your sister, boy?' The writer uses the word 'spat' to show the build-up of hatred in the shopkeeper. Other words like 'bellowed' and 'pounced' also bring out his hatred.

The scene is very dramatic and Cassie argues with this important white man. She seems to be out of control as well. Everyone else is watching and this adds to the conflict and to the tension. 'Everybody in the store turned and stared at me.' This puts all the attention on Cassie. I really admired her for doing what she did. I got the impression she was scared and brave at the same time – and this was a very uneasy situation.

Despite some awkward expression, this answer makes good use of quotations to examine the extract closely. There is a clear understanding of how a growing atmosphere of hostility is established by the author. Some strong points are made about contrast and drama within the scene. There is also an excellent reference to the way certain verbs emphasise Mr Barnett's angry tone of voice. Grade A.

SETTING AND CONTEXT

A story can be set anywhere – in an actual place, town or country, at sea, on another planet or even in a different time in history or the future. The imaginary world within which a story takes place is important for several reasons:

- It forms the **context** or circumstances for what happens in the story.
- It can help us to understand the **characters**.
- It might be a **symbol** of the writer's ideas.

An effective use of setting and background will enable the reader to experience the world of the narrative as the characters actually see it. Landscapes and surroundings are often used for this purpose. Descriptions of the weather can also help readers to understand a **character's state of mind**. For example, a violent storm could obviously reflect a confused or enraged personality. Setting can also be used as a **contrast to a character's mood**. A detailed description of a beautiful sunny day when a character is very upset can make readers have more sympathy for the character's feelings.

Always ask yourself:
- What is the setting?
- Why has the author created it in this way?

- How does the setting contribute to the story?
- How does the writer use language to create the setting?
- What is your response to this 'world'?

Good writers can bring words to life using well-chosen descriptive language. You have to use your own imagination to allow the words to work on you. One way of doing this is to use **your five senses**.

- **See** the colours that are mentioned. Do they contrast or harmonise? How do they help you understand what is happening?
- **Hear** the sounds. Are they loud and irritating or gentle and musical? How do they relate to the atmosphere?
- **Smell** the various aromas. Are these fresh or foul? How does the smell being described contribute to the story?
- **Touch** and feel the sensations described. Are they hot or cold, raw or invigorating?
- **Taste** flavours. Are they sweet, bitter, sharp, bland or tangy? How does this add to your understanding of what is being described?

Carefully read the following extract and then answer the questions that follow.

It is very early and time for Caithleen to get up. Through her eyes, we learn what life used to be like for a young Catholic girl growing up in Ireland. Downstairs a man called Hickey is already busy cooking breakfast.

The Country Girls

I rested for a moment on the edge of the bed, smoothing the green satin bedspread with my hand. We had forgotten to fold it the previous night, Mama and me. Slowly I slid on to the floor and the linoleum was cold on the soles of my feet. My toes curled up instinctively. I owned slippers but Mama made me save them for when I was visiting aunts and cousins; and we had rugs but they were rolled up and kept in drawers until visitors came in the summer-time from Dublin.

I put on my ankle socks.

There was a smell of frying bacon from the kitchen, but it didn't cheer me.

Then I went over to let up the blind. It shot up suddenly and the cord got twisted round it. It was lucky that Mama had gone downstairs, as she was always lecturing me how to let up blinds properly, gently.

The sun was not yet up, and the lawn was speckled with daisies that were fast asleep. There was dew everywhere. The grass below my window, the hedge around it, the rusty paling wire beyond that and the big outer field were each touched with a delicate, wandering mist, and the trees looked unreal, like trees in a dream. Around the forget-me-nots that sprouted out of the side of the hedge were haloes of water. Water that glistened like silver. It was quiet, it was perfectly still. There was smoke rising from the blue mountain in the distance. It would be a hot day.

Seeing me at the window, Bull's-Eye came out from under the hedge, shook himself free of water, and looked up lazily, sadly at me. He was our sheep-dog and I named him Bull's-Eye because his eyes were speckled black and white, like canned sweets. He usually slept in the turf-house, but last night he had stayed there to be on the watch-out when Dadda was away. I need not ask, my father had not come home.

Just then Hickey called from downstairs. I was lifting my nightdress over my head, so I couldn't hear him at first.

'What? What are you saying?' I asked, coming out on to the landing with the satin bedspread draped around me.

'Good God, I'm hoarse from saying it.' He beamed up at me, and asked, 'Do you want a white or a brown egg for your breakfast?'

'Ask me nicely, Hickey, and call me dotey.'

'Dotey. Ducky. Darling. Honeybunch, do you want a white or a brown egg for your breakfast?'

'A brown one, Hickey.'

'I have a gorgeous little pullet's egg here for you,' he said as he went back to the kitchen. He banged the door. Mama could never train him to close doors gently. He was our workman and I loved him. To prove it, I said so aloud to the Blessed Virgin who was looking at me icily from a gilt frame.

'I love Hickey,' I said. She said nothing. It surprised me that she didn't talk more often. Once she had spoken to me and what she said was very private. It happened when I got out of bed in the middle of the night to say an **aspiration.** I got out of bed six or seven times every night as an act of **penance.** I was afraid of hell.

'Yes, I love Hickey,' I thought; but of course what I really meant was that I was fond of him. When I was seven or eight I used to say I would marry him. I told everyone, including the **catechism examiner,** that we were going to live in the chicken-run and that we would get free eggs, free milk, and vegetables from Mama. Cabbage was the only vegetable they planted. But now I talked less of marriage. For one thing he never washed himself, except to splash rainwater when he stooped in over the barrel in the evenings.

I dressed quickly, and when I bent down to get my shoes, I saw fluff and dust and loose feathers under the bed. I was too miserable to mop the room, so I pulled the covers up on my bed and came out quickly.

> **The landing was dark as usual. An ugly stained-glass window gave it a mournful look as if someone had just died in the house.**
>
> **'This egg will be like a bullet,' Hickey called.**
>
> **'I'm coming,' I said.**

ADAPTED FROM *THE COUNTRY GIRLS* BY EDNA O'BRIEN

ASPIRATION: SHORT PRAYER   **PENANCE:** PUNISHMENT

CATECHISM EXAMINER: RELIGION INSPECTOR WHO VISITS SCHOOLS

Answer **two** of the following questions. Each question is worth fifteen marks.

1 How does the writer make Caithleen's home life seem happy and contented?

2 Throughout this extract, there is evidence that Caithleen is growing up and becoming more mature. How does the writer make us aware of this?

3 From your reading of the extract, would you agree that the writer is good at describing scenes? Support your answer by reference.

SAMPLE ANSWERS (Q3)

(i) Yes, the writer describes getting up and the rest of the story is about her thoughts. She goes into great detail. She remembers things from the night before. She remembers her mama lecturing her. The writer has a long conversation with Hickey about her breakfast. This is the main scene. She's imaginative. She talks to the holy picture. This is a good example of a descriptive scene. 'To prove so, I spoke aloud to the Blessed Virgin who was looking icily from a gilt frame.' I liked where she said she would marry Hickey and live off the mother and all the free stuff they could get for nothing. Like eggs and free milk. This was another detailed scene.

This answer makes a worthwhile point about the writer's use of detail, but the point could have been expanded more. The expression is disjointed in places and the one quotation used isn't altogether accurate. Overall, there is a need for a more focused and planned approach if the standard is to rise above a basic grade D.

(ii) In my opinion, Edna O'Brien is a very good writer who is skilled at detailed description. To me, her writing is very poetic and dramatic. There are a number of separate parts in the passage, e.g. the room where she wakes up, the scene outside her window and the description of the workman, Hickey.

Lots of delicate sounds are used, e.g. in the opening paragraph where the writer suggests the quiet start to her day with gentle phrases, such as 'smoothing the green satin bedspread' or 'slowly I slid onto the floor'. Even the sentences are slow-moving at the beginning. This adds to the sleepy morning atmosphere and the stillness being described by the writer.

The writer is very good at giving descriptions of water, e.g. the view across the lawn has many words to do with water. She describes the dampness as 'delicate wandering mist' and says it 'bathed' the leaves and trees. She also mentions 'haloes of water' and water 'that glistened like silver'. These are very poetic images. They are also giving the beautiful side of nature and this makes the scene seem attractive.

There are other shorter scenes in the passage and these are also very clear and easy to imagine, e.g. the description of the sheep dog and the dusty scene underneath the bed. Through the use of details, such as 'I saw fluff and dust and loose feathers', the writer makes it easy for me to picture her room.

After establishing that the passage contains a number of well-described scenes, this answer ambitiously tackles the writer's skill in using water imagery. The second and third paragraphs make excellent points about the use of sounds and the positive effect of water imagery. The answer ranges through the whole extract, with quotes being very well incorporated into the critical comments. A well-deserved grade A.

OPENINGS

The opening pages of a novel or short story are very important if the writer is to **capture the interest** of the readers so that they want to read on. Writers often begin by presenting important situations, characters or themes right from the start.

When you read the opening of a narrative, think about what the author is trying to do. You might find it useful to consider the following:

- Who the narrator is.
- What the characters are like.
- What setting or context is created.
- What you notice about the writer's style.
- Why you want to continue reading.

Carefully read the following extract and then answer the questions that follow. It is the opening of an American novel, *The Ballad of the Sad Café*, by Carson McCullers.

The town itself is dreary; not much is there except the cotton-mill, the two-room houses where the workers live, a few peach trees, a church with two coloured windows, and a miserable main street only a hundred yards long. On Saturdays the tenants from the near-by farms come in for a day of talk and trade. Otherwise the town is lonesome, sad, and like a place that is far off and estranged from all other places in the world. The nearest train stop is Society City and the Greyhound and White Bus Lines use the Forks Falls Road which is three miles away. The winters here are short and raw, the summers white with glare and fiery hot.

If you walk along the main street on an August afternoon there is nothing whatsoever to do. The largest building, in the very centre of town, is boarded up completely and leans so far to the right that it seems bound to collapse at any minute. The house is very old. There is about it a curious, cracked look that is very puzzling until you suddenly realize that at one time, and long ago, the right side of the front porch had been painted, and part of the wall – but the painting was left unfinished and one portion of the house is darker and dingier than the other. The building looks completely deserted. Nevertheless on the second floor there is one window which is not boarded; sometimes in the late afternoon when the heat is at its worst, a hand will slowly open the shutter and a face will look down on the town.

It is a face like the terrible dim faces known in dreams – sexless and white, with two grey crossed eyes which are turned inward so sharply that they seem to be exchanging with each other one long and secret gaze of grief. The face lingers at the window for an hour or so, then the shutters are closed once more, and as likely as not there will not be another soul to be seen along the main street. These August afternoons – when your shift is finished there is absolutely nothing to do; you might as well walk down to the Forks Falls Road and listen to the chain gang.

However, here in this very town there was once a café. And this old boarded-up house was unlike any other place for many miles around. There were tables with cloths and paper napkins, coloured streamers from the electric fans, great gatherings on Saturday nights. The owner of the place was Miss Amelia Evans. But the person most responsible for the success and gaiety of the place was a hunchback called Cousin Lymon. One other person had a part in the story of this café – he was the former husband of Miss Amelia, a terrible character who returned to the town after a long term in the **penitentiary,** caused ruin, and then went on his way again. The café has long since been closed, but it is still remembered.

FROM *THE BALLAD OF THE SAD CAFÉ* BY CARSON McCULLERS

PENITENTIARY: PRISON

Answer **two** of the following questions. Each question is worth fifteen marks.

1 How successfully has the author captured the atmosphere of a small, run-down American town? Support your answer by reference to the extract.

2 Some critics have described Carson McCullers as a poetic writer. What evidence of this do you find from reading the extract?

3 Do you agree that this is an effective opening to a novel? In your answer, you could consider the likely questions readers might ask after reading this opening section.

SAMPLE ANSWER (Q2)

Carson McCullers does write like a poet and uses repetition and short phrases which remind me of how poems are written with their own rhythm. A sentence like 'the town is lonesome, sad, and like a place that is far off' seems poetic to my way of thinking. Most good poems also have images which you remember. This writer uses very good, clear images, such as 'the summers white with glare and fiery hot.' This could easily be a line from a poem as the images show different colours.

Some poems are mysterious and can have many different meanings. I think this is the same with Carson McCullers, especially when describing the face of the person at the window. 'It is a face like the terrible dim faces known in dreams', which is another typical line of poetry. Some poems tell people's life stories and this is what is happening here. The writer is hinting at the secrets of the people who used to live in this small American town, not just the café owner but the hunchback and her husband.

Carson McCullers is a very poetic writer in capturing the atmosphere of the run-down town and the people in it. Some of the words are very gentle, e.g. 'the face lingers at the window' and everything sounds sad.

This is a reasonably strong answer to a fairly difficult question. It begins well and touches on some important aspects of the writer's poetic style, including repetition, imagery and sound. References are used but could have been explored more. A basic B grade.

CHARACTER STUDY

Just as with drama, many of the questions on fiction are about characters. Much of what was said in Unit 5 about characters in plays also applies to novels and short stories. It is worth remembering that **characters are creations**. The writer has complete control over everything the characters do, say and think, and all the circumstances in which characters find themselves. If we find the characters convincing, then it is the writer's skill that has made us feel like this.

Fiction writers use various methods of **presenting characters**.

Description: What the characters look like, e.g. physical appearance, dress, etc.

Actions: Their relationships with others and how characters behave and react, especially in a crisis, will affect how we see them.

Dialogue: What characters say (and what others say about them) is an important guide to our understanding of them.

Thoughts and feelings: The inner thoughts will reveal the truth about a character.

Imagery: Writers sometimes use comparisons or symbols to describe characters. For example, in *Wuthering Heights,* Heathcliff is often linked with the wild moors and with the colour black, symbols of his personality.

One of the questions that you might be asked to do in the Fiction section is to explore how characters are presented and how they change and develop during the course of the story. To answer successfully, you need to know the story well, particularly key scenes where the character is in conflict with others or is faced with a crisis of some sort.

Carefully read the following extract and then answer the questions that follow.

In this part of the story, a young boy named Kingshaw has gone for a walk in the fields and has a very frightening experience.

In the Cornfield

When he first saw the crow, he took no notice. There had been several crows. This one glided down into the corn on its enormous, ragged black wings. He began to be aware of it when it rose up suddenly, circled overhead, and then dived, to land not very far away from him. Kingshaw could see the feathers on its head, shining black in between the butter-coloured cornstalks. Then it rose, and circled, and came down again, this time not quite landing, but flapping about his head, beating its wings and making a sound like flat leather pieces being slapped together. It was the largest crow he had ever seen. As it came down for the third time, he looked up and noticed its beak, opening in a screech. The inside of its mouth was scarlet, it had small glinting eyes.

Kingshaw got up and flapped his arms. For a moment, the bird retreated a little way off, and higher up in the sky. He began to walk rather quickly back, through the path in the corn, looking ahead of him. Stupid to be scared of a rotten bird. What could a bird do? But he felt his own extreme isolation, high up in the cornfield.

For a moment, he could only hear the soft thudding of his own footsteps, and the silky sound of the corn, brushing against him. Then, there was a rush of air, as the great crow came beating down, and

wheeled about his head. The beak opened and the hoarse caw came out again and again, from inside the scarlet mouth.

Kingshaw began to run, not caring, now, if he trampled the corn, wanting to get away, down into the next field. He thought that the corn might be some kind of crow's food store, in which he was seen as an invader. Perhaps this was only the first of a whole battalion of crows that would rise up and swoop at him. Get on to the grass then, he thought, get on to the grass, that'll be safe, it'll go away. He wondered if it had mistaken him for some hostile animal, lurking down in the corn.

His progress was very slow, through the cornfield, the thick stalks bunched together and got in his way, and he had to shove them back with his arms. But he reached the gate and climbed it, and dropped on to the grass of the field on the other side. Sweat was running down his forehead and into his eyes. He looked up. The crow kept on coming. He ran.

But it wasn't easy to run down this field, either, because of the tractor ruts. He began to leap wildly from side to side of them, his legs stretched as wide as they could go, and for a short time, it seemed that he did go faster. The crow dived again, and, as it rose, Kingshaw felt the tip of its black wing beating against his face. He gave a sudden, dry sob. Then, his left foot caught in one of the ruts and he keeled over, going down straight forwards.

He lay with his face in the coarse grass, panting and sobbing by turns, with the sound of his own blood pumping through his ears. He felt the sun on the back of his neck, and his ankle was wrenched. But he would be able to get up. He raised his head and wiped two fingers across his face. A streak of blood came off, from where a thistle had scratched him. He got unsteadily to his feet, taking in deep, desperate breaths of the close air. He could not see the crow.

But when he began to walk forwards again, it rose from the grass a little way off, and began to circle and swoop. Kingshaw broke into a run, sobbing and wiping the damp mess of tears and sweat off his face with one hand. There was a blister on his ankle, rubbed raw by the sandal strap. The crow was still quite high, soaring easily, to keep pace with him. Now, he had scrambled over the third gate, and he was in the field next to the one that belonged to Warings. He could see the back of the house. He began to run much faster.

This time, he fell and lay completely winded. Through the runnels of sweat and the sticky tufts of his own hair, he could see a figure looking down at him from one of the top windows of the house. Then, there was a single screech and the terrible beating of wings, and the crow swooped down and landed in the middle of his back.

Kingshaw thought that, in the end, it must have been his screaming that frightened it off, for he dared not move. He lay and closed his eyes and felt the claws of the bird, digging into his skin, through the thin shirt, and began to scream in a queer, gasping sort of way. After a moment or two, the bird rose. He had expected it to begin pecking at him with its beak, remembering terrible stories about vultures that went for living people's eyes. He could not believe in his own escape.

 FROM *I'M THE KING OF THE CASTLE* BY SUSAN HILL

Answer **two** of the following questions. Each question is worth fifteen marks.

1 From your reading of the extract, what did you learn about Kingshaw's character?

2 How important is the setting in this story? Support your answer by reference to the extract.

3 The crow's strength and power is emphasised throughout this extract. How does the writer achieve this effect?

SAMPLE ANSWER (Q3)

Although the story is written through the boy's point of view, I think the crow is the main character. There is a strong image of the crow in the very first paragraph. We are given a picture of 'its enormous black wings'. It stands out from the butter-coloured corn like a black symbol of evil. There are all these action words to show the speed of the crow circling and swooping around the boy. Colours are a very important part of how the crow is described. I think the description 'the inside of its mouth was scarlet' gives the most frightening image of all. Red is always a sign of danger, blood and violence.

I think what happens is the crow becomes the hunter and the boy becomes the victim who is being hunted. So the crow is obviously powerful. The crow is described in paragraph three as 'the great crow' and this again adds to his power. At the end of the extract, the crow attacks – 'there was a single screech and a terrible beating of wings'. This is another good example of how strong and powerful the crow is. The boy felt the claws digging into his skin.

A solid response that addresses the question competently. There are a number of interesting observations about the use of imagery and strong verbs and some good use of supporting reference, particularly in the first paragraph. Had the expression been better, the answer would have reached a higher grade than an average B standard.

RELATIONSHIPS

In your response to fiction texts, you will often be dealing with two or more characters and you will probably be asked to comment on their relationship. To be believable, fictional characters must **develop relationships** within a text. Such a development can be central to the plot.

When trying to understand how one character relates to another, ask yourself:

- Is the relationship friendly, or is it hostile?
- Are the characters afraid of each other, or afraid of what is happening around them?

There may be a great deal of conflict that causes tension in a relationship. Always think about **how the writer is presenting the relationship** and how this affects the reader. Look at the things the characters say and think about each other, how they act and react to each other and whether their thoughts and attitudes to each other change. Relationships in stories can be traced in the same way as individual characters.

Carefully read the following extract and then answer the questions that follow.

This extract is taken from *A Family Likeness* by Mary Lavin. The story concerns an extended family. Ada is Laura's mother. She has come to live with Laura, her husband Richard and their young daughter, Daff (Daphne). Laura is finding motherhood difficult and Ada has suggested a walk in the woods where Daff can pick flowers.

A Family Likeness

Laura turned aside. 'Well, Daff? What do you think of the primroses?' The primroses were unbelievably plentiful.

'Can I pick them?' Daff asked in awe.

'Of course, darling.'

'This is how we do it, Daff.' Ada forgot the cattle. Burrowing, with fingers still nimble, down between the thick leaves of a large clump that bore twenty flowers or more, she grubbed close to the roots and pinched off a primrose with a long stem, cool and green, its base softly flushed with pink.

'We don't want to pull off their poor heads, do we?' she said gaily. 'And we'll only take one from each clump, so there'll be some left for other people to enjoy.' It was such a pleasure to guide the young mind. She was glad to see that Daff was watching intently. There ought to be no need of a scolding next time she beheaded a flower in the garden.

'For goodness sake, Mother! They're only wild flowers. Let her enjoy them!'

'She could hardly be enjoying them more,' Ada said as Daff proudly held up a primrose with a stem as long as a beanstalk. 'It's precisely because these are wild that we can teach her how to pick flowers properly.'

She guided Daff's hands into the moist depths of another clump. Then, seeing that Daff had got the hang of things, she began to pick a bunch herself to bring back for her room, taking care to pick a few leaves to make a collarette for them. But when Laura, disregarding the fact that she was crushing several clumps, lowered herself down on the bank and lay back to bask in the sun, she was instinctively impelled to caution her. 'It's too early in the season for that, Laura.'

Laura sat up at once, but only the better to deliver an angry retort. 'I don't care if I get pneumonia. You haven't the faintest notion how exhausted I am, Mother. When I was Daff's age, you had servants to wait on you hand and foot.'

Taken off her feet by this outburst, Ada abruptly sat down. 'You are greatly mistaken, Laura. The only help I ever had was an incompetent local girl who came in for a few hours to do a bit of cleaning. I never let her into the nursery.'

'More fool you!' Laura let her head flop back on the grass. Ada stared. What had precipitated this attack?

'Your father, of course, was wonderful,' she said. 'If you woke at night it was him, not me, who walked the floor with you.'

Again, Laura sat bolt upright. 'Are you insinuating that Richard does not pull his weight? You forget he provides for us. The child is my concern.'

'No one is disputing that. Don't think, dear, I haven't noticed how tired you've been looking lately. It's not easy for me to see you so white and drawn.'

Laura, who lay with her beautiful face framed in flowers, made a move as if to sit up for the third time, but instead she turned her head and fixed on Ada a stare that went through her, not like a needle this time, but a pitchfork.

'Just exactly what are you trying to do to me, Mother? Bad enough to feel like Hell, without being told I look like Hell.'

'Did I say that?' Ada stared miserably at the bunch of wild flowers in her hand. 'Here, Daff, you can have mine,' she said. Daff shook her head; her interest in primroses was waning. The few she'd picked were scattered about on the grass. Ada left her own bunch down beside them, where it fell apart, the stems now looking more pink than green.

Answer **two** of the following questions. Each question is worth fifteen marks.

1 How would you describe the relationship between Laura and Ada? Support your answer by reference to the extract.

2 To which of the characters, Ada and Laura, does the writer show more sympathy? Give reasons for your answer.

3 Do you think that the conflict between Ada and Laura is true to life? In your opinion, is there any way to avoid such conflict?

SAMPLE ANSWER (Q2)

I thought the writer first had more sympathy for Laura, even though she is in a bad mood mostly. The grandmother is always interfering and telling the child what to do. I thought the worst part was where she said 'there ought to be no need of a scolding next time she beheaded a flower in the garden.' To me, this is the writer's way of showing that the grandmother is often giving out to the child and bossing Laura. So, at first it looks like more sympathy is shown for Laura mainly.

My opinion changed a little bit at the end of the extract, especially after Laura got angry with Ada for saying she wasn't looking so well. It seems as if Ada is also feeling very hurt when the writer tells us 'Ada stared miserably'. Then the worst thing of all happens when the child won't take the primroses. The writer makes the ending very symbolic when the bunch of flowers fell apart. It's a real symbol or sign of the whole family falling apart at that point.

In a way, it seems as if the writer is sorry for the two of them. Laura and Ada both seem to be stressed out and ready to fight with their nerves. The chemistry between them is explosive. Like mother, like daughter, as the old saying goes.

Overall, a good response that attempts to keep the focus on the writer's intentions. The choice of reference and supporting quotation is also effective. The expression could be more fluent, but the answer is well rounded and deserves a grade B.

EXPLORING THEMES

Novels and short stories often explore particular themes and issues, and writers present their own views on these. A **theme is the central idea** that lies behind the story as a whole and which the writer is interested in developing through the story. Narratives usually have several main ideas or themes and it is worth noting these as you read.

Some exam questions, particularly on studied fiction, will test whether you understand what the book is about. Such questions relate directly to the theme. Every author has an outlook on life that the story expresses. In some cases, the author's own 'voice' can be clearly heard. At other times, ideas may be aired through a particular character's thoughts. Of course, it is only when you have finished reading the story that you can really say what it is about.

Carefully read the following extract (in edited form) and then answer the questions that follow.

George Orwell published *Animal Farm* in 1945. In this fable (a moral tale with animal characters), Orwell tells the story of what happens when a group of animals rebel against Mr Jones and try to run their farm themselves. Immediately after the revolution, the animals are overjoyed at their new freedom and can hardly believe what has happened. The pigs are the cleverest animals and three of them, Napoleon, Squealer and Snowball, soon begin to organise everything.

Animal Farm

But they woke at dawn as usual, and suddenly remembering the glorious thing that had happened they all raced out into the pasture together. A little way down the pasture there was a **knoll** that commanded a view of most of the farm. The animals rushed to the top of it and gazed round them in the clear morning light. Yes, it was theirs – everything that they could see was theirs! In the ecstasy of that thought they **gambolled** round and round, they hurled themselves into the air in great leaps of excitement. They rolled in the dew, they cropped mouthfuls of the sweet summer grass, they kicked up clods of the black earth and snuffed its rich scent. Then they made a tour of inspection of the whole farm and surveyed with speechless admiration the ploughland, the hayfield, the orchard, the pool, the **spinney**. It was as though they had never seen these things before, and even now they could hardly believe that it was all their own.

The animals had their breakfast, and then Snowball and Napoleon called them together again.

'Comrades,' said Snowball, 'it is half-past six and we have a long day before us. Today we begin the hay harvest. But there is another matter that must be attended to first.'

The pigs now revealed that during the past three months they had taught themselves to read and write from an old spelling book which had belonged to Mr Jones' children and which had been thrown on the rubbish heap. Napoleon sent for pots of black and white paint and led the way down to the five-barred gate that gave on the main road. Then Snowball (for it was Snowball who was best at writing) took a brush between the two knuckles of his trotter, painted out MANOR FARM from the top bar of the gate and in its place painted ANIMAL FARM. This was to be the name of the farm from now onwards. After this they went back to the farm buildings, where Snowball and Napoleon sent for a ladder which they caused to be set against the end wall of the big barn. They explained that by their studies of the past three months the pigs had succeeded in reducing the principles of Animalism to seven commandments. These seven commandments would now be inscribed on the wall; they would form an unalterable law by which all the animals on Animal Farm must live for ever after. With some difficulty (for it is not easy for a pig to balance himself on a ladder) Snowball climbed up and set to work, with Squealer a few rungs below him holding the paint-pot. The commandments were written on the tarred wall in great white letters that could be read thirty yards away. They ran thus:

THE SEVEN COMMANDMENTS
1. Whatever goes upon two legs is an enemy.
2. Whatever goes upon four legs, or has wings, is a friend.
3. No animal shall wear clothes.
4. No animal shall sleep in a bed.
5. No animal shall drink alcohol.
6. No animal shall kill any other animal.
7. All animals are equal.

It was very neatly written, and except that 'friend' was written 'freind' and one of the S's was the wrong way round, the spelling was correct all the way through. Snowball read it aloud for the benefit of the others. All the animals nodded in complete agreement, and the cleverer ones at once began to learn the commandments by heart.

'Now, comrades,' cried Snowball, throwing down the paint-brush, 'to the hayfield! Let us make it a point of honour to get in the harvest more quickly than Jones and his men could do.'

But at this moment the three cows, who had seemed uneasy for some time past, set up a loud lowing. They had not been milked for twenty-four hours, and their udders were almost bursting. After a little thought the pigs sent for buckets and milked the cows fairly successfully, their trotters being well adapted to this task. Soon there were five buckets of frothing creamy milk at which many of the animals looked with considerable interest.

'What is going to happen to all that milk?' said someone.

'Jones used sometimes to mix some of it in our mash,' said one of the hens.

'Never mind the milk, comrades!' cried Napoleon, placing himself in front of the buckets. 'That will be attended to. The harvest is more important. Comrade Snowball will lead the way. I shall follow in a few minutes. Forward, comrades! The hay is waiting.'

So the animals trooped down to the hayfield to begin the harvest, and when they came back in the evening it was noticed that the milk had disappeared.

 FROM *ANIMAL FARM* BY GEORGE ORWELL

KNOLL: LOW HILL   **GAMBOLLED:** RAN   **SPINNEY:** SMALL WOOD

Answer **two** of the following questions. Each question is worth fifteen marks.

1 How does the author capture the animals' happy mood? Support your answer by close reference to the extract.

2 From the animals' point of view, who will make the better leader, Napoleon or Snowball? Give reasons for your answer.

3 Fables explore themes and teach us lessons about life. From your reading of the extract, what themes do you think Orwell is exploring in *Animal Farm?* Support your answer by reference to the text.

SAMPLE ANSWER (Q1)

The first paragraph captures their excitement. The animals can't believe they are free. They're really up for celebrating. They are running about like little children after school. They can't believe life can be so good. It says, 'It was as though they had never seen these things before, and even now they could hardly believe that it was all their own.' There is a lot of description showing them rushing around mad for all they are worth. It says that what happened to them was a glorious thing and this is why they are so happy. It says, 'They rolled in the dew, they cropped mouthfuls of the sweet summer grass, they kicked up clods of the black earth and snuffed its rich scent.' This shows the happy mood they're in. They feel so good that they all behave like young animals racing for joy.

While this answer is on the right track, the expression could be much better. In addition to the slang and the clumsy use of 'it says', the answer relies too much on overlong quotes. It would have been more effective to focus on the key verbs and the repetition of 'theirs'. An average C grade.

Carefully read the following extract and then answer the questions that follow.

Francie Brady is a troubled young teenager who runs away from home and his dysfunctional family. Francie is the narrator of the story and this edited extract is written (and punctuated) in a way that reflects his thoughts.

The Butcher Boy

Every day I walked until it got dark. I slept under bushes and once in a tyre. I didn't know what day it was when I reached the city. I was exhausted so I leaned against the big sign. It read: WELCOME TO DUBLIN.

The buses were green as gooseberries and a stone pillar cut the sky. This is Dublin I says to a fellow yeah it's Dublin where do you think it is for the love of Jaysus. I liked the way he said that and I tried to say it myself. Jay-zuss. Who's that over there I says to this woman and she looks at me with her mouth open. A big grey statue mouthing about something in the middle of the street. I thought it was the president but she told me it was Daniel O'Connell. I didn't know anything about him except he was something to do with the English and all that.

The way they were going across the bridge you'd think someone had said: I'm sorry but we're going to let off an atomic bomb any minute now. Bicycles going by in dozens, tick tick tick. Where were they all going? If they were all going to work there was a lot of jobs in Dublin. It was eight o'clock in the morning. There was picture houses and everything. Over I

went. The Corinthian Cinema written in unlit lights. What's going on here I said. The creatures were coming to take over the planet earth because their own was finished there was nothing left on it. The shaky writing said they came from beyond the stars bringing death and destruction. I'd have to go and see them aliens when it opened up.

I went into a chip shop. There was a woman with bags and half a beard muttering to herself and spilling tea on the saucer. She said she hoped the communists won she said they're no worse than the rest of them and told me she had two sons. And neither of them were any good she said.

I wasn't listening to her. I was thinking about how I was going to get money to see the aliens. The girl says to me what would you like. I says chips. What have you been up to she says you look like you've been dragged backwards through a ditch. Oh just walking I says. You'll need a few extra chips so she says and gives me a big heap. I could see her counting money in behind the counter. Then off she'd go into the kitchen with the door swinging behind her I could hear her going on about dances. I wished the old woman would hurry up and get out, her and her sons and her bags. Soon as she waddled off I waited for the girl to go back into the kitchen.

I was in behind the counter like a bullet and I stuffed any notes I could into my pocket. Then I ran. All the way down the street I kept thinking: Hunted from town to town for a crime he didn't commit – Francie Brady – The Fugitive!

Except for one thing – I did commit it. The first thing I did was I went into a sweetshop with bullseyes and the whole lot. There was a woman there with a chain on her glasses. What did she think – someone was going to try and steal the glasses off her face? Thirty Flash Bars I said. I put them all into my pockets and ate as many of them as I could.

There was a smell of stout and a big ship pulling into the dock. I wondered was it time for the aliens yet. How would it be? I went into the Gresham Hotel and ordered a slap-up feed. Who's going to pay for this? Says the waiter licking his pencil hmm hmm. I am my man I said, Mr Algernon Carruthers. I seen that in one of Philip's comics. Algernon Carruthers always on these ships going around the world and eating big dinners. Certainly Master Carruthers he says. I knew what he thought that I was one of these boy millionaires. There was a woman smiling at me. Good day madam!

 FROM *THE BUTCHER BOY* BY PATRICK McCABE

Answer **two** of the following questions. Each question is worth fifteen marks.

1 Do you think Francie is a carefree character with a lively imagination, or is he a disturbed character? Or is he a bit of both? Support your answer with reference from the extract.

2 Based on your reading of the extract, how would you describe the atmosphere in Dublin?

3 In your view, is this extract an example of comic writing? Give reasons for your answer.

 SAMPLE ANSWER (Q2)

I think the atmosphere is very busy and there is a lively picture painted of the traffic and the people he meets in the city who are going off to work across the bridge and on buses. There are a lot of so-called unusual characters around the city, such as the woman with the bags and half a beard muttering to herself and spilling tea on the saucer. Also, the waiter licking his pencil and the other woman in the sweetshop who had glasses on a chain. He seems to bump into a lot of strange people whenever he goes anywhere and the city seems full of these characters.

Francie seems to be pretty excited by the atmosphere. The city centre seems to have a lot of noise and there was picture houses and everything. Most of the people are friendly. If they were all going to work there was a lot of jobs in Dublin. Dublin seems to have a very friendly atmosphere. They all take an interest in Francie, such as the woman smiling at him in the hotel at the end.

One or two worthwhile points are raised about the activity of the city and its characters. References could have been properly quoted instead of copied without quotation marks. The sentences tend to ramble on as well. Some comment about the old-fashioned world of bicycles and bullseyes would have improved the grade from a basic C standard.

Carefully read the following extract and then answer the questions that follow.

Every Man for Himself

Butt and he left at half-past eleven. I knew that because Butt took out his watch and expressed surprise at the lateness of the hour, I guess he was desperate to get to his bed. They had been gone no more than ten minutes – Ginsberg had ordered a whisky and Charlie and I had just won three tricks in succession – when suddenly the room juddered; the lights flickered and Ginsberg's cigarette case, which sat at his elbow, jolted to the floor. It was the sound accompanying the juddering that startled us, a long drawn-out tearing, like a vast length of calico slowly ripping apart. Melchett said, 'We're in collision with another ship,' and with that we threw down our cards, ran to the doors, sprinted through the Palm Court and out on to the deck.

A voice called, 'We've bumped an iceberg – there it goes,' but though I peered into the darkness, I could see nothing. From somewhere forward we heard laughter, voices excitedly shouting. Coming to the starboard rail I looked down on to the well of the third class recreation area; there were chunks of ice spilling and sliding in every direction, all shapes and sizes, glittering under the light of the foremast. Steerage passengers, most in their ragged nightclothes, were chucking it at each other as though playing snowballs.

Hopper raced off to go down there and join in the fun. Charlie and I found it too cold to linger and hurried back indoors. A dozen or so men had poured out of the smoke-room and were milling about in the foyer, pestering the stewards for information. Astor was there, still dressed but without his tie, leaning down to shout into the ear of Seefax who had been woken from sleep in the library and now sat on the staircase with his stick raised like a weapon. Everyone had a different explanation for whatever it was that had jarred the ship; Ginsberg swore we had lost a propeller, but what did he know?

We couldn't resume our game until Hopper returned, which he did quite soon, triumphantly carrying a lump of ice in his handkerchief. He thrust it under my nose and it smelt rank, a bit like a sliver of rotten mackerel. He dropped it into Ginsberg's whisky when the poor devil wasn't looking.

We must have played for another ten minutes, by which time Hopper said he'd had enough. Remembering Andrews' injunction that I should read while others slept, I decided to spend an hour in the library. I was crossing the foyer when the man himself swept past on his way to the stairs. I didn't think he'd seen me but he said quite distinctly, 'Follow me. You may be needed.'

He led me up to the navigating bridge. Captain Smith was evidently expecting him because as we approached the wheelhouse, the quarter-master flung open the door. I would have followed on Andrews' heels but he shouted over his shoulders that I was to wait outside. Through the glass panels I could see Smith and his first and second officers clustering about him. Ismay was there too, dressed in a fur coat and wearing carpet slippers. He seemed to be excluded, roaming up and down, hands in pockets.

I was glad I wasn't outdoors, for even in the comparative warmth of the bridge house, I found myself shivering. The silence wrapped me like a cloak and it was only then that I realised the ship no longer moved. When I pressed my face to the window to look down at the sea, there was nothing but darkness; when I tilted my head, the blackness was fiery with stars.

 FROM *EVERY MAN FOR HIMSELF* BY BERYL BAINBRIDGE

Answer **two** of the three questions that follow. Each question is worth fifteen marks.

1 Does this extract give you a strong impression of the actual collision? Support your answer by reference to the passage.

2 In your opinion, does the author succeed in gaining – and then holding – your attention throughout the passage? Give reasons for your answer.

3 What features in this extract would make it very suitable as the basis for a scene in a film? Explain the points you make by referring to the extract.

 SAMPLE ANSWER (Q3)

I think this is a very good scene for a film, a very action-packed scene. There have already been films made about the Titanic, so the accident itself is obviously interesting. It was one of the greatest news items of all time, like the 9-11 attacks on the Twin Towers. The story has loads of cool action and this is what people go for these days. You could see how they do when the ice gets into the ship later on. Look at any list of movies and it's the same thing. It's all action packed. There's loads of characters in this. It would be good to see how they all do when the ship is sinking. Will one of them be a hero?

This is like a movie script because it goes into a whole load of directions about where people go. The actors wouldn't need to think about what they were to do. It's all done for them. The bit at the end is cool where the captain, who is called

Captain Smith, is having emergency talks with his crew. I can imagine this being a good scene and with loads of close-ups of their faces. It would get the audience into the mood.

This answer has the potential to make much better use of points that are raised. The ideas could be phrased more effectively and slang ('loads of' and 'cool') is a distraction. However, the use of a rhetorical question varies the writing and makes a relevant point at the same time. A basic grade C.

DIALOGUE

Dialogue is speech between characters. In fiction this is more than mere communication because dialogue makes characters seem more vivid and lifelike. An author can create characters by letting readers judge them from **what they say**.

In novels and short stories, dialogue shows what characters think about other characters. This also helps readers to make up their minds about them and understand how they relate to the main **themes, messages** and **ideas** in the narrative.

Sometimes it's what is *not* actually spoken that tells you about a character's mood, manner or motives. **Hesitation** is a sign of doubt and uncertainty, no matter what is being said. Always ask yourself: *why is the speaker hesitating?* You can then find a motive to explain the character's behaviour.

Carefully read the following extract and answer the questions that follow.

The aeroplane carrying a group of English schoolboys has crashed on a tropical island. No adults have survived and the boys are left to fend for themselves. Two of the boys, Ralph and Piggy, find a shell (a conch) which they use as a trumpet to try to round up any other children who might be alive after the crash.

The Sound of the Shell

Within the diamond haze of the beach something dark was fumbling along. Ralph saw it first, and watched till the intentness of his gaze drew all eyes that way. Then the creature stepped from mirage on to clear sand, and they saw that the darkness was not all shadow but mostly clothing. The creature was a party of boys, marching approximately in step in two parallel lines and dressed in strangely eccentric clothing. Shorts, shirts, and different garments they carried in their hands: but each boy wore a square black cap with a silver badge on it. Their bodies, from throat to ankle, were hidden by black cloaks which bore a long silver cross on the left breast and each neck was finished off with a hambone frill. The heat of the tropics, the descent, the search for food, and now this sweaty march along the blazing beach had given them the complexions of newly washed plums. The boy who controlled them was dressed in the same way though his cap badge was golden. When his party was about ten yards from the platform he shouted an order and they halted, gasping, sweating, swaying in the fierce light. The boy himself came forward, vaulted on to the platform with his cloak flying, and peered into what to him was almost complete darkness.

'Where's the man with the trumpet?'

Ralph, sensing his sun-blindness, answered him,

'There's no man with a trumpet. Only me.'

The boy came closer and peered down at Ralph, screwing up his face as he did so. What he saw of the fair-haired boy with the creamy shell on his knees did not seem to satisfy him. He turned quickly, his black cloak circling.

'Isn't there a ship, then?'

Inside the floating cloak he was tall, thin, and bony: and his hair was red beneath the black cap. His face was crumpled and freckled, and ugly without silliness. Out of his face stared two light blue eyes, frustrated now, and turning, or ready to turn, to anger.

'Isn't there a man here?'

Ralph spoke to his back.

'No we're having a meeting. Come and join in.'

The group of cloaked boys began to scatter from close line. The tall boy shouted at them.

'Choir! Stand still!'

Wearily obedient, the choir huddled into line and stood there swaying in the sun. None the less, some began to protest faintly.

'But, Merridew. Please, Merridew…can't we?'

Then one of the boys flopped on his face in the sand and the line broke up. They heaved the fallen boy to the platform and let him lie. Merridew, his eyes staring, made the best of a bad job.

'All right then. Sit down. Let him alone.'

'But Merridew.'

'He's always throwing a faint,' said Merridew. 'He did in **Gib**; and **Addis**; and at **matins** over the **precentor**.'

This last piece of **shop** brought sniggers from the choir, who perched like black birds on the criss-cross trunks and examined Ralph with interest. Piggy asked no names. He was intimidated by this uniformed superiority and the offhand authority in Merridew's voice. He shrank to the other side of Ralph and busied himself with his glasses.

Merridew turned to Ralph.

'Aren't there any grown-ups?'

'No.'

Merridew sat down on a trunk and looked round the circle.

'Then we'll have to look after ourselves.'

FROM *LORD OF THE FLIES* BY WILLIAM GOLDING
GIB: GIBRALTAR   **ADDIS:** ADDIS ABABA (CAPITAL OF ETHIOPIA)
MATINS: MORNING PRAYER   **PRECENTOR:** CHOIR-MASTER
SHOP: GOSSIP

Answer **two** of the following questions. Each question is worth fifteen marks.

1 What is revealed about Merridew through the dialogue? Support your answer by close reference to the extract.

2 How does the author succeed in creating a hot tropical island atmosphere? Refer to the extract in support of your answer.

3 'Then we'll have to look after ourselves.' From the evidence of the extract, what do you think will happen to the boys? Support your answer by reference to the text.

SAMPLE ANSWER (Q1)

Merridew is very abrupt when he speaks. Most of the time he asks questions, such as, 'Isn't there a man here?' and 'Aren't there any grown-ups?' It's very interesting that he is thinking so much about adults. To me, this says he wants to be in control himself. Every time he speaks, he seems to want to show off his authority.

The other thing I noticed about Merridew was the way he kept ordering the choir about all the time. In fact, he shouts at them and seems to rule by fear, for instance, 'Choir! Stand still!' Even the exclamation marks are a sign of his angry tone of voice.

The way the other children in the choir speak to Merridew is also a clue to how he bullies them and always keeps them under his rule. One boy is afraid to openly ask to be allowed to sit down and rest. He says, 'But Merridew. Please Merridew…can't we?' It suggests to me that Merridew has bullied the choir in the past for complaining. In fact, another boy faints rather than dare to say a word. Nobody else in the choir seems to have any say at all in what happens. Merridew likes to be in total control and this comes through in every word he says.

A very well-supported answer that keeps the focus firmly on how dialogue reveals character. In addition to dealing with what Merridew himself says – and how he speaks – there is an important point about the members of the choir who dare to speak up. Overall, a good, clear response, well organised and perceptive. Grade A.

Imagine what you would think if you suddenly woke up one morning and found that your human body had been replaced by something completely different. How would you feel as you slowly realised that you were not having a terrible nightmare? This is exactly what happens to the main character in Franz Kafka's famous story *Metamorphosis,* written in 1912.

Read the following extract (in edited form), which is taken from the opening part of the story, and then answer the questions that follow.

The Transformation

When Gregor Samsa awoke one morning from uneasy dreams he found himself transformed in his bed into a gigantic insect. He was lying on his hard shell-like back and by lifting his head a little he could see his curved brown belly divided by stiff arching ribs, on top of which the bed-quilt could hardly keep in position and was about to slide off completely. His numerous legs, which were pitifully thin compared to the rest of his bulk, danced helplessly before his eyes.

What has happened to me? He thought. It was no dream. His room, an ordinary human bedroom, if somewhat too small, lay peacefully between the four familiar walls. Above the table, on which an assortment of cloth samples had been unpacked and spread out – Samsa was a commercial traveller – there hung the picture which he had recently cut out of a glossy magazine and put in a pretty gilt frame.

Gregor's eyes turned next to the window, and the dull weather – raindrops could be heard beating on the metal window-ledge – made him quite **melancholy**. 'Suppose I went back to sleep for a little and forgot all this nonsense,' he thought, but it could not be done, for he was accustomed to sleep on his right side and in his present condition he could not turn himself over. However violently he forced himself towards his right side, he always rolled onto his back again. He tried it at least a hundred times, shutting his eyes to keep from seeing his struggling legs, and only left off when he began to feel a faint dull ache in his side which was entirely new to him.

'O God,' he thought, 'what an exhausting job I've chosen! On the move day in, day out. The business worries are far worse than they are on the actual premises at home, and on top of that I'm saddled with the strain of all this travelling, the anxiety about train connections, the bad and irregular meals, the constant stream of changing faces with no chance of any warmer, lasting companionship.'

* * *

Disposing of the bed-quilt was quite simple; he only had to inflate himself a little and it fell off automatically. But after that things became difficult, especially since he was so uncommonly broad. He would have needed arms and hands to raise himself to a sitting position; but instead he only had these numerous legs, which were constantly executing the most varied movements and which moreover he was unable to control. Whenever he tried to bend one of them, that was the first to straighten itself; and if he finally succeeded in getting this leg to do what he wanted, in the meantime all the others began working away, as if set free, in the highest state of painful **agitation**. 'It's simply no use lying idle in bed,' said Gregor to himself.

First of all he tried to get the lower part of his body out of bed, but this lower part, which in fact he had not seen yet, proved too **cumbersome**; he made such slow progress; and when at last, becoming almost frantic, he summoned up all his strength and thrust himself recklessly forward, he found he had misjudged the direction and bumped hard against the bottom end of the bed; and the **searing** pain he felt informed him that it was precisely this lower part of his body that was perhaps the most sensitive at present.

METAMORPHOSIS: TRANSFORMATION **MELANCHOLY:** SAD **AGITATION:** DISORDER
CUMBERSOME: AWKWARD **SEARING:** INTENSE

Answer **two** of the following questions. Each question is worth fifteen marks.

1 This is the opening of a short story. What do you think will happen when Gregor's mother comes to wake him? (He can still speak and communicate with his family.)

2 Although Gregor changes physically, his inner character remains human. From the evidence of the extract, what kind of character is he?

3 How would you like to see this story end? Will his family still care for him, or will they reject him?

 SAMPLE ANSWER (Q2)

Gregor has 'uneasy dreams' which might suggest that he is a man who is stressed out. Perhaps he is having a nervous breakdown and is imagining everything. It's clear that he hates his work and is very lonely. He keeps a picture of a beautiful model by his bedside and he admits that he would like to be in a relationship with someone. He seems to be a very sad man who longs for a 'lasting companionship'.

He also seems to be a serious or strong-willed type who forces himself to keep calm, even though he is in a living nightmare. Perhaps he is in a state of shock. However, he is extremely determined to get out of bed. In the third paragraph, we can see that 'he tried it at least a hundred times'. The last paragraph of the extract also shows how he struggles to move his body as he 'summoned up all his strength and thrust himself recklessly forward'.

To some extent, Gregor is a pathetic character. He is trapped in a job he dislikes and has nothing much in his life. When he wakes up transformed into a gigantic insect, he seems to just accept this. Most people would scream in horror, but he just tries to get on with life as if what has happened is normal. This seems very weird to me. It looks as though he really is mad.

This is a very good response to a challenging piece of fiction. There are a number of penetrating points clearly focused on Gregor's character as it is revealed in the extract. All of these are thoughtfully developed and supported by useful reference. The quotations are very naturally worked into the critical discussion and there is a high grade A standard throughout.

STUDIED FICTION (QUESTION TWO)

As with the Drama and Poetry sections, the second Fiction question is worth thirty marks. You will be expected to write in greater detail about a novel or short story already studied in class.

Always write the correct title of the novel or story and the author's name. It is usually helpful to let the examiner know you have a clear overview of the plot, so begin your answer with a brief background summary of the story. This should usually not be more than two or three sentences.

Knowing key scenes and significant moments in the story will be essential if you are to answer questions successfully.

QUESTION TIME

The following questions are typical of what can be expected in Question Two of the Fiction section. Each question is worth thirty marks and you should spend about twenty minutes writing your answer.

1 Select a novel or short story you have studied that is based on a close relationship between two very different types of characters. Describe both characters and outline how their relationship developed during the course of the story.

2 You have been asked to select an episode from a novel or short story that could be dramatised for a youth theatre festival performance. Give a detailed description of the scene you

would choose and explain its dramatic qualities.

3 Of all the fiction you have studied, which character made the greatest impression on you? Describe the character's qualities (or faults) and explain why this character made such an impact on you.

4 From a novel or short story you have studied that dealt with a disturbing issue:
   (a) Show how the issue was dealt with in the story.
   (b) Explain what you learned about the issue from the way it was treated by the author.

5 Select a novel **or** short story you have studied that dealt with **one** of the following themes:
   (a) Injustice.
   (b) Conflict.
   (c) Change.

   Explain how the author presented the theme and how it was dealt with at the end of the story.

6 Choose a novel or short story you have studied where a particularly memorable atmosphere or mood is created. Describe the atmosphere or mood and explain how it was created and sustained throughout the narrative.

7 Basing your answer on a novel or short story you've studied, would you say that the central character was powerful or weak, or a combination of both? Support the points you make by detailed and relevant reference.

8 If you had to recommend just one novel **or** one short story to be read by Junior Cert students, which one would it be? Explain your choice.

9 Choose a novel **or** short story where the setting was very different from your own time and place. It may be set in a different country or a different time in history. Explain what you learned from the story and the world in which it was set.

10 From the novels and short stories you have studied, choose one where the opening **or** ending was particularly impressive. Explain your choice using close reference to the text.

The best way to learn about short stories is to read lots of them. You have probably studied a variety of stories and novels already in class. The following short story by the Liverpool writer, Roger McGough, is about two young boys who go off to sea for a day.

The Stowaways

When I lived in Liverpool, my best friend was a boy called Midge. Kevin Midgeley was his real name, but we called him Midge for short. And he was short, only about three cornflake packets high (empty ones at that). No three ways about it. Midge was my best friend and we had lots of things in common. Things we enjoyed doing like...climbing trees, playing footy, going to the pictures, hitting each other really hard. And there were things we didn't enjoy doing like...sums, washing behind our ears, eating cabbage.

But there was one thing that really bound us together, one thing we had in common – love of the sea.

In the old days (but not so long ago) the river Mersey was far busier than it is today. Those were the days of the great passenger liners and cargo boats. Large ships sailed out of Liverpool for Canada, the United States, South Africa, the West Indies, all over the world. My father had been to sea and so had all my uncles, and my grandfather. Six foot six, muscles rippling in the wind, huge hands grappling with the helm, rum-soaked and fierce as a wounded shark (and that was only my grand-mother!). By the time they were twenty, most young men in this city had visited parts of the globe I can't even spell.

In my bedroom each night, I used to lie in bed (best place to lie really), I used to lie there, especially in winter, and listen to the foghorns being sounded all down the river. I could picture the ship nosing its way out of the docks into the channel and out into the Irish Sea. It was exciting. All those exotic places. All those exciting adventures.

Midge and I knew what we wanted to do when we left school...become sailors. A captain, an admiral, perhaps one day even a steward. Of course we were only about seven or eight at the time so we thought we'd have a long time to wait. But oddly enough, the call of the sea came sooner than we'd expected.

It was a Wednesday if I remember rightly. I never liked Wednesdays for some reason. I could never spell it for a start and it always seemed to be raining, and there were still two days to go before the weekend. Anyway, Midge and I got into trouble at school. I don't remember what for (something trivial I suppose like chewing gum in class, forgetting how to read, setting fire to the music teacher), I forget now. But we were picked on, nagged, told off and all those boring things that grown-ups get up to sometimes.

And, of course, to make matters worse, my mum and dad were in a right mood when I got home. Nothing to do with me, of course, because as you have no doubt gathered by now, I was the perfect child: clean, well-mannered, obedient...soft in the head. But for some reason I was clipped round the ear and sent to bed early for being childish. Childish! I ask you. I *was* a child. A child acts his age, what does he get? Wallop!

So that night in bed I decided...Yes, you've guessed it. I could hear the big ships calling out to each other as they sidled out of the Mersey into the oceans beyond. The tugs leading the way like proud little guide dogs. That's it. We'd run away to sea, Midge and I. I'd tell him the good news in the morning.

The next two days just couldn't pass quickly enough for us. We had decided to begin our amazing around-the-world voyage on Saturday morning so that in case we didn't like it we would be back in time for school on Monday. As you can imagine there was a lot to think about – what clothes to take, how much food and drink. We decided on two sweaters each and wellies in case we ran into storms around Cape Horn. I read somewhere that sailors lived off rum and dry biscuits, so I poured some of my dad's into an empty pop bottle, and borrowed a handful of half-coated chocolate digestives. I also packed my lonestar cap gun and Midge settled on a magnifying glass.

On Friday night we met round at his house to make the final plans. He lived with his granny and his sister, so there were no nosy parents to discover what we were up to. We hid all the stuff in the shed in the yard and arranged to meet outside his back door next morning at the crack of dawn, or sunrise – whichever came first.

Sure enough, Saturday morning, when the big finger was on twelve and the little one was on six, Midge and I met with our little bundles under our arms and ran up the street as fast as our tiptoes could carry us.

Hardly anyone was about, and the streets were so quiet and deserted except for a few pigeons straddling home after all-night parties. It was a very strange feeling, as if we were the only people alive and the city belonged entirely to us. And soon the world would be ours as well – once we'd stowed away on a ship bound for somewhere far off and exciting.

By the time we'd got down to the Pier Head, though, a lot more people were up and about, including a policeman who eyed us suspiciously. 'Ello, Ello, Ello,' he said, 'and where are you two going so early in the morning?'

'Fishing,' I said.

'Train spotting,' said Midge and we looked at each other.

'Just so long as you're not running away to sea.'

'Oh no,' we chorused. 'Just as if.'

He winked at us. 'Off you go then, and remember to look both ways before crossing your eyes.'

We ran off and straight down on to the landing-stage where a lot of ships were tied up. There was no time to lose because already quite a few were putting out to sea, their sirens blowing, the hundreds of seagulls squeaking excitedly, all tossed into the air like giant handfuls of confetti.

Then I noticed a small ship just to the left where the crew were getting ready to cast off. They were so busy doing their work that it was easy for Midge and me to slip on board unnoticed. Up the gang-plank we went and straight up on to the top deck where there was nobody around. The sailors were all busy down below, hauling in the heavy ropes and revving up the engine that turned the great propellers.

We looked around for somewhere to hide. 'I know, let's climb down the funnel,' said Midge.

'Great idea,' I said, taking the mickey. 'Or, better still, let's disguise ourselves as a pair of seagulls and perch up there on the mast.'

Then I spotted them. The lifeboats. 'Quick, let's climb into one of those, they'll never look in there – not unless we run into icebergs anyway.' So in we climbed, and no sooner had we covered ourselves with the tarpaulin than there was a great shuddering and the whole ship seemed to turn round on itself. We were off! Soon we'd be digging for diamonds in the Brazilian jungle or building sandcastles on a tropical island. But we had to be patient, we knew that. Those places are a long way away, it could take days, even months.

So we were patient. Very patient. Until after what seemed like hours and hours we decided to eat our rations, which I divided up equally. I gave Midge all the rum and I had all the biscuits. Looking back on it now, that probably wasn't a good idea, especially for Midge.

What with the rolling of the ship and not having had any breakfast, and the excitement, and the couple of swigs of rum – well, you can guess what happened – woooorrppp! All over the place. We pulled back the sheet and decided to give ourselves up. We were too far away at sea now for the captain to turn back. The worst he could do was to clap us in irons or shiver our timbers.

We climbed down on to the deck and as Midge staggered to the nearest rail to feed the fishes, I looked out to sea hoping to catch sight of a whale, a shoal of dolphins, perhaps see the coast of America coming in to view. And what did I see? The Liver Buildings.

Anyone can make a mistake, can't they? I mean, we weren't to know we'd stowed away on a ferryboat.

One that goes from Liverpool to Birkenhead and back again, toing and froing across the Mersey. We'd done four trips hidden in the lifeboat and ended up back in Liverpool. And we'd only been away for about an hour and a half. 'Ah well, so much for running away to sea,' we thought as we disembarked (although disembowelled might be a better word as far as Midge was concerned). Rum? Yuck.

We got the bus home. My mum and dad were having their breakfast. 'Aye, aye,' said my dad, 'here comes the early bird. And what have you been up to then?'

'I ran away to sea,' I said.

'Mm, that's nice,' said my mum, shaking out the cornflakes. 'That's nice.'

Answer **one** of the following questions. Each question is worth thirty marks.

1 Write the diary entry that Midge would make after recovering from his adventure at sea.

2 Do you think this story is particularly true to life? Explain your response using close reference to the text.

3 A good story holds your attention all the way through. To what extent is this true of *The Stowaways*? In your answer, you might wish to consider the plot, setting, characters and the style of writing.

4 Did you enjoy this story? Give reasons for your answer.

SAMPLE ANSWER (Q2)

I thought the whole story, The Stowaways, *was very true to life and this is one reason why I liked it. It's just a typical situation that little boys do, running away from home for an adventure. Even the way Roger's friend has a nickname, Midge, is typical. It's also true to life the way the boys are only away from home for two hours. When you are a child, two hours could seem like two days. It's all typical. The parents are also true to life.*

The way the characters speak is laid back, real Liverpool. This is also convincing and very realistic, e.g. 'playing footy' or the way the police officer tells them to look both ways before crossing their eyes. Liverpool is well known for a sense of humour and this makes the whole story true to life. Roger himself is very funny. He makes jokes about his grandmother and setting fire to the music teacher, which he says is trivial.

Both Roger and Midge love adventures. This is the same for most boys who dream of going into space or fighting in wars. This is the whole basis of the story. It's very convincing the way he shows us how children have great vivid imaginations. They're really innocent the way they pack rum and biscuits. I think this must have really happened to Roger McGough because it's exactly how imaginative children would act.

The thing I felt was most true to life was the way the writer was able to tell the story from a seven-year-old child's eyes. This was what I noticed from the opening. He says things like, 'No three ways about it.' Children always go on like this, trying to be funny. Later on, Roger has a plan to become an important officer on the ship. First he wants to be a captain or admiral. Then he admits that his biggest dream would be to become a steward. I think only a child would think that serving drinks would be better than being in charge of the actual ship. This is very realistic from the child's point of view.

We have done poems in school by Seamus Heaney and these were the same. It was as if he was writing about childhood as a child but also as an adult. I think it's the same with Roger McGough. He has two voices in the story. It's mainly the voice of the child, but he makes smart remarks at times, which seem to me to be the voice of the older writer just remembering what it was like. Roger admits this at one point in the story when he says, 'I was a child.'

The story is from a good while ago and this comes across very well. Everything is old-fashioned. It's obvious that Roger knows Liverpool and the docks very well. This is what makes the story convincing and true to life.

This is a good solid response to the question and makes a number of relevant, well-supported points. The expression could be improved in some places, e.g. the first paragraph, but the main points are reasonably well organised after the disjointed opening. The answer is also the right length, considering that roughly twenty minutes is suggested for this thirty-mark question in the exam. Grade B.

The following short story by O Henry (1862–1910) is set in New York. Sue and Joanna are two artists who have their studio at the top of an apartment block. Below them lives old Behrman, another artist, who for all his life has been planning to start working on a great masterpiece.

The Last Leaf

In November a cold, unseen stranger, Pneumonia, stalked about the district, touching one here and one there with his icy finger. He smote Joanna. She lay, scarcely moving, looking through the small window-panes at the blank wall of the next house.

One morning the busy doctor invited Sue into the hallway.

'She has one chance in – let us say, ten,' he said, as he shook the thermometer. 'And that chance is for her to want to live. She has made up her mind that she's not going to get well. Has she anything on her mind?'

'She wanted to paint the Bay of Naples some day,' said Sue.

'Paint? – bosh! Has she anything on her mind worth thinking about?'

'No, doctor, not that I know about,' Sue replied.

After the doctor had gone, Sue went into the workroom and cried.

Joanna lay with her face turned towards the window. Sue stopped whistling, thinking she was asleep, and began a pen-and-ink drawing to illustrate a magazine story. But Joanna's eyes were wide open. She was looking out of the window and counting – counting backwards.

'Twelve,' she said, and a little later, 'eleven,' and then 'ten, nine, eight,' then 'seven.'

Sue looked anxiously out of the window. What was there to count? There was only the blank wall and an old ivy vine, gnarled and decayed at the roots, climbing half-way up it.

'What is it, Joanna?' asked Sue.

'Six,' said Joanna, in almost a whisper. 'They're falling faster now. Three days ago there were almost a hundred. There goes another one. There are only five left now.'

'Five what, Joanna? Tell me.'

'Leaves. When the last one falls, I shall die.'

'Oh, I never heard such nonsense,' complained Sue. 'What have old ivy leaves to do with your getting well?'

'There goes another. That leaves just four. I want to see the last one fall before it gets dark. Then I'll go too.'

'Joanna,' said Sue, bending over her, 'will you promise me to keep your eyes closed and not look out of the window until I am done working? I must hand these drawings in tomorrow and I need the daylight. Try to sleep. I'll just go and see Behrman to ask him to be my model for the old miner. I'll not be gone a minute.'

In one corner of Behrman's room was a blank canvas on an easel that had been waiting there for twenty-five years to receive the first line of the masterpiece. Sue told him of Joanna's words about the leaves.

'What!' he cried. 'Are there people in the world with the foolishness to die because leaves drop off an ivy vine? I have never heard of such a thing!'

Joanna was sleeping when they went upstairs. Sue pulled the blind down to the window-sill, and motioned Behrman into the other room. In there they peered out of the window fearfully at the ivy. Then they looked at each other for a moment without speaking. A persistent, cold rain was falling, mingled with snow. Behrman in his old blue shirt took his seat as the miner.

When awoken from an hour's sleep the next morning, Sue found Joanna, with dull, wide-open eyes staring at the drawn green blind.

'Pull it up; I want to see,' she ordered in a whisper.

Wearily Sue obeyed.

But lo! after the beating rain and fierce gusts of wind that had endured through the livelong night, there yet stood out against the brick wall one ivy leaf. It was the last on the vine. Still dark green near its stem, but with its serrated edges tinted with the yellow of decay, it hung bravely from a branch some twenty feet above the ground.

'It is the last one,' said Joanna. 'I thought it would fall during the night. I heard the wind. It will fall today, and I shall die at the same time.'

The day wore away, and even through the twilight they could see the lone ivy leaf clinging to its stem against the wall. And then, with the coming of the night, the north wind was again loosed, while the rain still beat against the window.

The next day, the leaf was still there. Joanna lay for a long time looking at it. And then she called to Sue.

'I've been a bad girl, Sue,' said Joanna. 'Something has made that leaf stay there to show me how wicked I was. It is a sin to want to die. You may bring me a little broth now and I'll sit up.'

An hour later she said: 'Sue, some day I hope to paint the Bay of Naples.'

The doctor came in the afternoon, and Sue had an excuse to go into the hallway as he left.

'Even chances,' said the doctor, taking Sue's thin, shaking hand in his. 'With good nursing you'll win. And now I must see another case downstairs. Behrman his name is – some kind of artist, I believe. Pneumonia, too. He is an old, weak man, and the attack is acute. There is no hope for him; but he goes to the hospital today to be made more comfortable.'

Next day the doctor said to Sue: 'She's out of danger. You've won.

Nutrition and care now – that's all.'

And that afternoon Sue came to the bed where Joanna lay.

'I have something to tell you,' she said. 'Mr Behrman died of pneumonia today in the hospital. He was ill only two days. The janitor found him on the morning of the first day in his room downstairs helpless with pain. His shoes and clothing were wet through and icy cold. They couldn't imagine where he had been on such a dreadful night. And then they found a lantern, still lighted, and a ladder that had been dragged from its place and some scattered brushes, and a palette with green and yellow colours mixed on it, and – look out of the window, dear, at the last ivy on the wall. Didn't you wonder why it never fluttered or moved when the wind blew? Ah, it's Behrman's masterpiece – he painted it there the night the last leaf fell.'

ADAPTED FROM *THE LAST LEAF* BY O HENRY

Answer **one** of the following questions. Each question is worth thirty marks.

1 In your opinion, who is the main character in this story, or are the characters equally important? Give reasons for your answer.

2 What main theme or issue does this story deal with? Describe how the writer deals with this issue.

3 The writer of this short story manages to make the ending unexpected. How does he do this?

4 Did you like this story? Give reasons for your answer.

SAMPLE ANSWER (Q3)

I would agree that the end of the story is a little unexpected, even though I had a slight feeling that there was something strange going on with the last leaf. The ending is a good example of irony. The person who actually dies is the old man and I didn't expect him to die. It is ironic that the girl I was sure would die is alive because of what the old artist did for her. He gave his life for Joanna.

Most of the first part of the story is about Joanna's sickness. To be honest, I thought it was just going to be another sad story of a young girl who would die. I was expecting tragedy and her friend to put the last leaf in Joanna's coffin or else keep it in memory of her. Also, the fact that Joanna dreamed of painting the Bay of Naples made me think that she might even go there on a holiday just before her death. I suppose it takes a good writer to keep you guessing about different endings.

The middle part of the story is mostly about Sue worrying about her dying friend. This just adds to the story that there is no hope for Joanna. I might have known that when Sue and Behrman were together that something was being planned - 'Then they looked at each other for a moment without speaking.' That must have been the time he decided to paint the leaf on the tree to keep her alive.

A lot of the story is given over to the actual leaves and this also led me to think they were a symbol of Joanna slowly dying. The writer keeps us counting them. This builds up a kind of suspense. They are like a calendar or the hands of a clock – 'There goes another one. That leaves just four.' Everybody knows that all the leaves will fall sooner or later, so I was fully prepared for Joanna's death.

The ending is very clever. It's not drawn out or anything. The writer quickly explains what Behrman did to give Joanna some hope. I knew he had to play some part in the

story, especially since he had his dream of painting a great master-piece one day. I suppose I should have guessed what was coming.

The answer starts off by making a key point about the way the ending is foreshadowed. While the expression could be much better, there is a clear understanding of irony. Points are ordered into separate paragraphs and good use is made of reference. The personal approach shows an engagement with the story and there are some interesting ideas, such as comparing the ivy leaves to a clock. A solid grade B standard.

FICTION UNIT ROUND-UP

- Ask yourself: **who narrates the text?** Whose thoughts and feelings are you invited to share?
- Which of the characters do you **sympathise** with?
- Think about the **style of writing**. Was the language simple or complex? Did the author use much **description** or **dialogue** to help narrate the events?
- Address questions directly and develop the main points you make by using **relevant reference**.
- Read as many stories and novels as you can. There is no shortage of **interesting fiction** in libraries and bookshops.

CHECKLIST

Having worked through the Fiction unit, you should now feel more confident about the following:

- Appreciating a range of literature by writers from Ireland and elsewhere.
- Being prepared for a variety of exam questions in the Fiction section.
- Knowing and using critical terms, such as plot, dialogue and point of view.
- Understanding an author's aims and intentions in a piece of writing.
- The importance of setting and mood in stories.
- Understanding characters and relationships.
- Being able to explore themes and issues in fiction.
- Discussing important features of an author's style and use of language.
- Giving a personal response based on the text.
- Knowing how to write relevant and well-organised answers of a high standard.

UNIT 8 **Revision**

OVERVIEW

*There are many ways to revise for examinations and you will find that some work better than others. It makes sense to **do what works best for you**. It's important, however, to plan your revision with a **timetable**.*

*Revising for your Junior Cert English examination involves many activities, including rereading key literary texts, studying notes and corrected homework assignments, and practising timed questions. You won't have time to go over all your work, so **select carefully** to make sure that you are familiar with your poems, play, novel or short stories.*

TRY TO FIND SOMEWHERE where you won't be disturbed and make sure you have all the books and materials you need on your desk. Plan revision sessions of between forty to sixty minutes each, and don't forget to take **a short break every half hour or so**. Aim to have something to look forward to at the end, for example, some music or a little television.

Remember the old saying: *A healthy mind in a healthy body.* Drink plenty of water, rest properly, get some fresh air and ease up on the social life – there'll be lots of time for that after the exams!

EFFECTIVE NOTE-TAKING

Some students find it useful to jot down key points while they are doing revision. Writing out notes can be very helpful in refreshing your memory and re-enforcing important information that will be needed on the day of the exam.

Obviously, it is important to develop effective note-taking skills in the early years of secondary school. It is impossible to remember everything you read

R E V I S I O N 🔹 **317**

or hear, so to be able to write up a set of well-organised notes that make sense when read later is of immense value to any student.

Note-taking may be needed when:
- Planning essays.
- Revising for exams.
- Reading for information.
- Preparing for giving a talk.
- When a topic is being explained in class.

COMPILING NOTES

Whether it's during English class or doing revision at home, effective note-taking is a skill that develops with practice and it will soon become obvious which notes are useful to you and which are not.

Some suggestions for note-taking include the following:
- Don't try to write down everything. Try to condense main points in your own words.
- If taking notes from a book, skim the relevant section first in order to make sense of the whole piece. Make sure you understand what you have read before you begin to summarise.
- Do not write in sentences – key words or phrases are enough to trigger your memory later.
- Read over your notes when you have finished. If they don't make sense now, they never will.
- Ensure that you have included all the important points and details.
- Emphasise all key points by underlining or highlighting.

SPELLING

Difficulty with spelling does not mean that you are going to fail your exam. However, it may prevent you from achieving the grade you could get if your spelling was better. Most people have some problems with spelling and there is plenty you can do to improve it.

Here are some suggestions for ways to improve your spelling:
- Read as much as possible – seeing words in print can help you to visualise them as you write.
- Make a list of words that you have difficulty with and learn them.
- Look up problem words in the dictionary when writing essays.
- Check your spelling before handing up a piece of work.

Look at this list of common words. All of them are spelled incorrectly. See if you can rewrite them correctly in your notebook. (Use a dictionary if you are unsure of the right spelling.)

Incorrect Spellings

addres

autum

acomadation

argueing

awkard

beleive

begining

beutiful

buisness

comittee

concious

concience

decieve

definitaly

dissapear

envoirment

existance

Febuary

fourty

imagion

imediately

Incorrect Spellings

independant

intresting

knowlege

libary

neccesary

peotry

priveledge

que

recieve

reccommend

restaurent

repitition

rythm

ryhme

seperate

similer

sincerly

truely

tradgedy

untill

Wedensday

AMERICAN SPELLINGS

Americans tend to spell words as they are pronounced and to drop unnecessary letters in their words. They also use *z* in some words where we use *s*.

Standard English	U.S.A.
colour	*color*
centre	*center*
cheque	*check*
criticise	*criticize*
grey	*gray*
humour	*humor*
honour	*honor*
jewellery	*jewelry*
judgement	*judgment*
labour	*labor*
licence	*license*
organisation	*organization*
programme	*program*
realise	*realize*
theatre	*theater*

Remember to use Standard English and always try to proofread your work to correct any errors.

PUNCTUATION

Punctuation has not been invented by warped English teachers simply to make life even more difficult for students. It exists to make communication in writing easier. When we speak, we pause between words. We alter our tone of voice and even the expression on our face or our body language can change to help the listener understand our meaning. All these things can help to shape our speech.

When words are written down, they also need shaping. The first thing we do is to leave a space between words but this is not always enough to make the writing clear. Punctuation helps to make meaning clearer still.

Capital Letters
The misuse of capital letters is very common. It is probably also one of the easiest mistakes for you to correct for yourself. Capital letters should be used to start the names of:
- People and titles.
- Places.
- Days of the week, months, holidays, special days.
- Countries, nations, languages, religions.
- Books and films (first and main words only).

Capital letters should also be used to start the first word of a new sentence and when referring to yourself in terms of *I*.

Sometimes not using a capital letter can give a very different meaning. For example:

- Yesterday a girl was suspended by her head for dyeing her hair red.
- Yesterday a girl was suspended by her Head for dyeing her hair red.

Full Stops

Full stops and capital letters are closely linked, because just as sentences begin with a capital letter, they usually end with a full stop. Each completed statement requires a full stop at the end.

How you divide your writing into sentences, though, depends to some extent on the effects that you want your writing to achieve.

Rewrite each of these sentences as two short statements and punctuate them correctly.

- Although I stay up late, I am still always up early.
- I'd arrange for you to change groups, as you seem to dislike this one.
- Sara thoroughly enjoyed the few days that she spent in Athlone.

Commas

Commas are used to separate parts of a sentence and help us to understand it better. Specifically they are used for the following:

- To separate parts of a sentence.
- To separate explanations.
- To separate items in a list.
- To indicate a brief pause in the sentence.
- To separate names of people being spoken to.
- To separate words such as *no, yes* and *thank you.*

Question Marks

Most students are quite clear about where to use question marks – a question mark should be put at the end of every sentence that asks a direct question. The biggest problem is remembering to put them in!

However, other difficulties do occur, often relating to whether or not a question mark is needed at the end of a particular request. This is not always clear. Remember:

- Do not write a full stop and a question mark together.
- Do not use a question mark in a sentence that is an indirect question.
  - (a) Have you finished with the ketchup? (**direct**)
  - (b) Amy asked me if I had finished with the ketchup. (**indirect**)

Exclamation Marks

An exclamation mark should be used after a word or group of words to show strong feelings, such as anger, surprise, happiness, fear, etc.

Inverted Commas (Speech Marks or Quotation Marks)

Inverted commas are used for three main purposes:

- To indicate **direct speech**.
- To indicate the use of a **direct quotation**.
- To indicate the **titles** of books, TV shows, films, etc.

Speech Punctuation

Direct speech is writing down what somebody said using the exact words they used. Here are some simple rules to follow when using speech marks:

- Speech marks enclose everything that is actually said.
- The first speech mark goes at the beginning of the first word spoken and the second speech mark goes after the punctuation at the end of the words spoken, as in this simple sentence:
  The weather forecaster said, 'It is not very windy today.'

However, not all direct speech follows this sentence pattern. In fact, there are several sentence patterns that direct speech can follow. These are as follows:

- The narrative (or part that tells you who is speaking) followed by the part actually spoken.
  Example: The superintendent said, 'Stop writing and put your pens down.'
- The spoken part first, followed by the narrative.
  Example: 'Close your textbooks and listen carefully,' she told us.
- One or more sentences of speech interrupted by narrative.
  Example: 'Get out your maps and search for the nearest roadway,' said our leader. 'As soon as you have found it, work out how long it will take us to get there.'

Titles and Quotations

The use of inverted commas for titles and quotations is quite straightforward. However, the main problem is forgetting to put them in.

Remember to use inverted commas around the titles of books, magazines, newspapers, films, television programmes, etc. For example:

- I bought a copy of 'The Irish Star' and 'The Irish Independent' to compare their stories.
- We are studying 'Macbeth' for our English course.

Use inverted commas around quotations. Their use in this respect is similar to the way they are used in speech punctuation. For example:

- One of my favourite speeches from 'Hamlet' begins, 'To be, or not to be.' But another well-known one begins, 'Alas, poor Yorick! I knew him, Horatio.'

Inverted commas can also be used when you want to stress or emphasise a particular word or phrase. For example:

- How do you spell 'onomatopoeia'?
- 'Civilised' is not the first word I would use to describe him.

Apostrophes

In written English, apostrophes are used for one of two purposes:

- They can be used for shortening words (contractions).
- They can be used to indicate possession.

Contractions

This use of the apostrophe is quite straightforward and most students do not have a problem with it. An apostrophe shows that one or more letters have been missed out. For example:

- I **can't** stand being alone.
- **I'll** try to visit you.

An apostrophe is also used to indicate the missing out of numbers, as in 23 August '05.

Apostrophes can also be used where simply adding an *s* would be confusing, such as 'Mind your p's and q's.'

The Possessive Apostrophe

The use of an apostrophe shows that someone owns something and it is probably the most misused of all the punctuation marks. However, the correct way to use it is quite straightforward if the following rules are remembered:

- If something is owned by **one person**, use 's.

   Example: Barry's bike was quite new.
   Evanna's new hairstyle was cool.

- If something is owned by **more than one person**, then the apostrophe should come after the *s* (s').

   Example: The girls' house is near the town.
   The cows' field was very muddy.

- Some words have **special plurals** that do not end in *s*, such as men, women, mice and children. With these words, when an *s* is added, then an apostrophe always comes before the s ('s).

   Example: The women's changing room was flooded.
   The children's swimming lesson was cancelled.

Colons

Many students are unsure how to use colons correctly. While they are found less in written English than they used to be, they still perform a special function.

Colons can be used for the following:

- To introduce lists.

   Example: You will need to bring the following items: a tent, a sleeping bag, a change of clothes, some food, a rucksack and walking boots.

- To punctuate dialogue in a play.

   Example: DETECTIVE: Don't stammer and yammer at me, man!

- As an alternative to a comma in direct speech.

   Example: My friend kept shouting: 'Keep going!'

PRESENTATION

Good, legible handwriting is an asset both in school and in later life. If your handwriting is difficult to read, now is the time to do something about it. There are various styles of handwriting, but they all have several points in common.

- They are legible.
- The letters are even (*a, e, o, r,* for example, are all the same height).
- If the words slant, they slant in the same direction.

Apart from taking care with handwriting, you should try to make the overall appearance of a page attractive. Leave a clear margin on the left-hand side and avoid cramming a word in at the end of a line.

When using a computer to present work, choose different font sizes and types to make headings stand out.

Finally, proofread work to ensure it is presented in the best way possible.

PARAGRAPHS

- A paragraph is a group of sentences linked to the same topic. In other words, each paragraph carries one main idea.
- Paragraphs help you to organise your work.
- In handwriting, indicate paragraphs by starting a new line and indenting by about 2 cm.

Paragraphs give readers a rest and help them to follow the writer's meaning. Start a new paragraph to indicate a new idea or a change of some kind, e.g. a change of scene, time, mood, etc. A new paragraph is also needed for every change of speaker.

This extract from the novel *Tobacco Road* by Erskine Caldwell shows the organisation of paragraphs.

> **Dude waited outside the garage and looked at the new automobile on display in the shop window. Bessie had gone inside. Dude had said he would stay on the street and look through the window for a while.**
>
> **Bessie waited in the middle of the floor several minutes before anyone came out of the back room to ask what she wanted. Presently a salesman walked over to her and asked her if she wanted anything. He noticed that there was something unusual about her nose the moment he first saw her.**
>
> **'I came to buy a new Ford,' she said.**

You can skilfully link paragraphs together by using **connecting words**, as shown in the following list.

similarly

nevertheless

however

compared with

to turn to

on the other hand

equally

still

despite this

on the contrary

likewise

although

alternatively

of course

in the same way

EXAM TECHNIQUE AND GENERAL ADVICE

When you write exam answers, keep the following points in mind:

- Number questions clearly. Don't waste time rewriting the actual question. Avoid long introductions to answers. Get straight into your answer with only a brief introduction, remembering to use Standard English, that is, make sure your writing is formal. Avoid abbreviations and slang.

- Time management is very important if you are to answer all the questions you are supposed to. You need a watch in front of you during practice questions and especially during the actual examination. Work out the time you will spend on each section before the exam. It's likely that your teacher will have spoken to you about this on many occasions.

- Brainstorm and plan before answering. Show your understanding of texts by reading between the lines and by putting information in your own words. Remember to use brief quotations as evidence for your points and work these into your own sentences. Constantly refer back to the question and use the key words from the question.

- Focus on your purpose (what you want the reader to know). Write fluently, expressing yourself with flair. It's essential to stop your sentences from rambling – examiners can always spot when writing is getting out of control. By varying the length of sentences, you will hold the reader's attention and keep the writing interesting. Always make sure that what you write is relevant.

- Add points to your plan while writing in case you forget them. Your brain is remarkable because you can think of two things at once. Do not lose track of fresh ideas as you write your answers. Simply break off from your answer and add the necessary points to your plan.

- Divide your time sensibly according to the marks at stake for each question. Do not get bogged down looking for an extra one or two marks when there is a fresh question with several marks at stake. You must spread your effort and aim for an overall mark in your answers. This is a successful technique.

- Your aim is to build up marks in each answer and to share your effort efficiently. A paragraph or so is fine for a ten-mark question but you should be writing much more for a twenty-mark question. Do not spend too much time on questions worth low marks.

UNDERSTANDING KEY TERMS

- **Explain** means to show knowledge and understanding by giving a detailed account of something.
- **Describe** means to set forth the characteristics or details of something.
- **Argue** means to maintain a standpoint through logic, as you would in a persuasive essay.
- **Inform** means to show an understanding of something by giving a clear account of it to someone else.
- **Advise** means to teach someone or a particular audience something as clearly as possible.

READING EXAM QUESTIONS

- **Use of language** means word choices, emotive words and phrases to affect the audience, description, persuasive phrases, imagery, alliteration, etc. Avoid saying that the language is 'very good', which suggest you do not know what to say.
- The **attitude to the reader** is the tone of voice adopted by the author. Is it formal, sarcastic, ironic, comic, etc.?
- **Convey** means to get across. For example, 'How does the writer convey a sense of…?'

- **Compare and contrast** means asking what is similar and what is different between two pieces of writing, characters, etc.

PREPARING FOR THE ENGLISH EXAM

In the Weeks Before the Examination
- Read over your main texts. Revise poems you have studied during the year and carefully read key scenes in your play and novel. Look over all your notes.
- Ask your teacher (nicely) to go over any topics you are worried about.
- Make sure that you know how the exam papers are organised.
- Practise writing examination answers within the permitted time.

The Night Before
- Do a last-minute check on any notes you have made.
- Check your equipment – take two pens that are both the same type.
- Go to bed at a reasonable time and get a good night's sleep.

On the Day
- Read through all of the paper, identi-fying what you have to do. If something about the instructions is unclear, ask the exam supervisor for help.
- Don't rush – read the whole thing through – twice if you need to – before you start work on the task. Decide roughly how long to spend on each task or part of a task. Leave time to check and correct your work. Make sure you stick to this schedule during the examination. An incomplete paper where questions have not been attempted is much more likely to lower your grade than the odd piece of unfinished work.
- Start your answer with a plan and make sure that this plan is legible. Allow a few minutes at the end to check your work. You will be rewarded for good organisation and careful answers. Always make clear, neat corrections.
- Finally, remember to be positive! Exam success will make your future brighter. If you have studied and worked reasonably hard over the past year, then you are likely to do well in your Junior Cert Higher Level English exam!
Good luck!

ACKNOWLEDGMENTS

The author would like to thank Hubert Mahony, Tess Tattersall, Graham Thew and the staff of Gill & Macmillan. Thanks also to Declan Honan, Frances Rocks, Oliver Short, Maria Hamill, Laura McAvoy, helpful colleagues and students at St. Vincent's School, Dundalk. And, finally, thanks to my family, for their continuing support.

For permission to reproduce published material, grateful acknowledgment is made to the following:

Extracts from *Mysterious Stranger* by David Blaine, *Holidays in Hell* by P.J. O'Rourke and *The Butcher Boy* by Patrick McCabe, courtesy of Macmillan Publishers Ltd, London, UK.

Extracts from *The Lost Continent* © Bill Bryson, published by Black Swan, a division of Transworld Publishers. All rights reserved.

Mae Leonard for 'Holding Court' article.

Extracts from *Down and Out in Paris and London* by George Orwell (Copyright © George Orwell, 1933) and *Animal Farm* by George Orwell (Copyright © George Orwell 1945) by permission of Bill Hamilton as the Literary Executor of the Estate of the Late Sonia Brownell and Secker & Warburg Ltd.

Extracts from *The Happy Isles of Oceania* by Paul Theroux, *Fast Food Nation*, by Eric Schlosser and *Roll of Thunder, Hear My Cry* by Mildred D. Taylor (Victor Gollancz/Hamish Hamilton, 1977) Copyright © Mildred D. Taylor, 1976, courtesy of Penguin Books Ltd.

Extract from *Death of a President* by William Manchester. Reprinted by permission of Don Congdon Associates, Inc. © 1967, renewed 1995 by William Manchester.

Extract from *Talking Gaelic* by Patrick Kielty, courtesy of Blackwater Press.

'Diary Victoria Beckham' by Craig Brown. Copyright Pressdram Limited 200[2]. Reproduced by permission.

Extract from *Bury My Heart at Wounded Knee* reprinted by permission of PFD on behalf of Alexander Dee Brown © 1971, Alexander Dee Brown.

'The Life of Brian' article adapted from *Best of Times, Worst of Times*, © Caroline Scott, *The Sunday Times Magazine*, London.

Extracts from *Dr Fegg's Encyclopaedia of All World Knowledge* by Terry Jones and Michael Palin, *Educating Rita* by Willy Russell and *Teechers* by John Godber, courtesy of Methuen Publishing Ltd.

'Salad Days for Winning Gardener' © Sarah Marriott.

'Artist milks art exhibition for all its worth' by Siobhan Gaffney © Ireland on Sunday (1 June 2003).

'Close shave as shearers go into action' by Sean McConnell © *The Irish Times* (2 June 2003).

'Sinead Quits Shock' © *The Phoenix* (9 May 2003).

'O'Connor Quits' © AFP Newsagency.

Contents page of *Sports Digest* © *Sports Digest* (2 May 2003).

Extracts from *The Caretaker* by Harold Pinter; *Waiting for Godot* by Samuel Beckett; 'Cataract Operation' by Simon Armitage, from *Book of Matches*; 'Hawk Roosting' by Ted Hughes, from *Lupercal*; 'Storm on the Island' and 'Blackberry Picking' by Seamus Heaney, from *Death of a Naturalist*; courtesy of Faber & Faber Ltd.

Extract from *Tragically I Was An Only Twin* by Peter Cook, published by Century, courtesy of David Higham Associates.

Extract from *The Long and the Short and the Tall* by Willis Hall. Reprinted by permission of Harcourt Education.

Extract from *Our Town* by Thornton Wilder © Thornton Wilder, 1962, courtesy of Penguin Books Limited, 1962.

'Family' by Vona Groarke, from *Flight* (2002). By kind permission of the author and The Gallery Press, Loughcrew, Oldcastle, County Meath, Ireland.

'Fable' from *János Pilinszky: The Desert of Love* translated by János Csokits and Ted Hughes. Published by Anvil Press Poetry in 1989.

'Woman Work' by Maya Angelou, from *And Still I Rise*, courtesy of Virago Press.

'Half Caste' by John Agard, from *Get Back Pimple*, by kind permission of John Agard c/o Caroline Sheldon Literary Agency, published by Viking (1996).

'The Lake' by Roger McGough from *Holiday on Death Row*. Reprinted by permission of PFD on behalf of Roger McGough © 1979, Roger McGough.

'Stealing' from *Selling Manhattan* by Carol Ann Duffy, published by Anvil Press Poetry in 1987.

'Piazza Piece' by John Crowe Ransom from *Selected Poems*, published by Carcanet Press Ltd.

'Note to the Hurrying Man' from *Notes to the Hurrying Man* © Brian Patten (1980) and extract from *Every Man For Himself* © Beryl Bainbridge (1997), reprinted by permission of HarperCollins Publishers Ltd.

'On a Mountain Road' © Tony Curtis.

'Nails' by Brendan Kennelly, from *Cromwell*, Bloodaxe Books, 1987.

Extract from *The Country Girls* by Edna O'Brien, reproduced by kind permission of the author, Edna O'Brien.

Extract from *The Ballad of the Sad Café* by Carson McCullers, Random House. Reprinted by permission of Pollinger Limited.

Extract from *I'm the King of the Castle* © Susan Hill 1970, published by Longman Imprint Books.

Extract from *The Stowaways* by Roger McGough. Reprinted by permission of PFD on behalf of Roger McGough © 1986, Roger McGough.

PICTURE CREDITS

For permission to reproduce photographs and other material, the author and publisher gratefully acknowledge the following:

PHOTOS
ALAMY IMAGES: 5, 246 © Alamy Images
ARDEA: 227 © Pat Morris
BRITISH FILM INSTITUTE: 67 © BFI Stills
BUBBLES: 97 © Angela Hampton; 247 © Jennie Woodcock; 327 © Pauline Cutler
CAMERA PRESS IRELAND: 104 © Camera Press Ireland
CORBIS: 16, 66 © Hulton-Deutsch Collection; 20 © Anders Ryman; 25, 179, 229, 273 © Bettmann; 29 © Baldev/Corbis Sygma; 44, 234 © Corbis; 52 © Alan Lewis/Corbis Sygma; 101 © Michael St. Maur Sheil; 191 © Robbie Jack; 205 © David Hall; 210 © H. Armstrong Roberts; 214 © Tom Brakefield; 221 © Chinch Gryniewicz/Ecoscene; 225 © Joseph Sohm/ChromoSohm Inc.; 238 © E.O. Hoppe; 240 © James A. Sugar; 243 © Leif Skoogfors; 251 © Jon Sparks; 253 © Patrick Johns; 264 © Joel Katz; 288 © Corbis Sygma; 299 © Maurizio Lanini; 309 © David H. Wells
EDUCATION PHOTOS: 61, 62, 106 © educationphotos.co.uk/Walmsley
GREENHILL PHOTO LIBRARY: 325 © Richard Greenhill
IMAGEFILE IRELAND: 301 © Imagefile Ireland
INPHO: 32 © Inpho
IRISH IMAGE COLLECTION: 233 © Irish Image Collection
IRISH PICTURE LIBRARY: 269 © Evans Collection; 303 © Fr. Browne S.J. Collection
IRISH TIMES: 124 © Matt Kavanagh; 145 right © Brenda Fitzsimons; 145 left Fran Veale; 146 top left © Valerie O'Sullivan; 146 bottom left and right © Alan Betson
THE KOBAL COLLECTION: 13 © Paramount/Universal/David Appleby; 90 © Columbia/Suzanne Tenner; 156 © Fine Line/Renaissance; 163 © Castlerock/Dakota Films/Rolf Konow; 167 © Acorn Pictures Ltd; 175 © Caretaker Films; 277 © Universal; 281 © Annie Griffiths Belt; 291 © 20th Century Fox/Paramount/Merie W. Wallace; 296 © Two Arts/CD
MAGNUM PHOTOS: 48 © David Hurn
PANOS: 10 © Jeremy Horner
PA PHOTOS: 118 © Matthew Fearn
PHOTOCALL IRELAND: 109, 123, 128, 212, 231 © Photocall Ireland
REUTERS: 37 © Mike Segar; 120 © Yves Heerman HRM; 146 top right © Guang Niu
REX FEATURES: 41 © Nils Jorgensen; 102 © Modica/Canitano; 216 © GXJ; 218 © Julian Makey;

CARTOONS
148 left, 148 right © Graeme Keyes; 149 top © Martyn Turner; 149 middle © Kerber/Private Eye, 149 bottom © Declan Considine

OTHER MATERIAL
96 courtesy of Methuen Publishing Ltd; 129 courtesy of 2FM; 130 courtesy of Sports Digest; 133 courtesy of J17; 135 © courtesy of BUAV; 137 courtesy of DULUX Paints Ireland Limited © ICI 2003; 139 top courtesy of VHI; 139 bottom courtesy of Executive Nannies; 143 top and bottom courtesy of Amnesty International

The author and publishers have made every effort to trace all copyright holders, but if any has been inadvertently overlooked we would be pleased to make the necessary arrangements at the first opportunity.

INDEX